Wayward Girls in Victorian and Edwardian England

History of Crime, Deviance and Punishment

Series Editor: Anne-Marie Kilday, Vice Chancellor and Professor of
Criminal History, University of Northampton, UK

Editorial Board: Neil Davie, University of Lyon II, France
Johannes Dillinger, University of Maine, Germany
Wilbur Miller, State University of New York, USA
Marianna Muravyeva, University of Helsinki, Finland
David Nash, Oxford Brookes University, UK
Judith Rowbotham, Nottingham Trent University, UK

Academic interest in the history of crime and punishment has never been
greater and the *History of Crime, Deviance and Punishment* series provides
a home for the wealth of new research being produced. Individual volumes
within the series cover topics related to the history of crime and punishment,
from the later medieval to modern period and in both Europe and North
America, and seek to demonstrate the importance of this subject in furthering
understanding of the way in which various societies and cultures operate.
When taken together, the works in the series will show the evolution of the
nature of illegality and attitudes towards its perpetration over time and will
offer their readers a rounded and coherent history of crime and punishment
through the centuries. The series' broad chronological and geographical
coverage encourages comparative historical analysis of crime history
between countries and cultures.

Published:
Policing the Factory, Barry Godfrey
Crime and Poverty in 19th-Century England, Adrian Ager
Print Culture, Crime and Justice in Eighteenth-Century London, Richard Ward
Rehabilitation and Probation in England and Wales, 1900–1950, Raymond Gard
The Policing of Belfast 1870–1914, Mark Radford
Crime, Regulation and Control during the Blitz,
Peter Adey, David J. Cox and Barry Godfrey
The Italian Prison in the Age of Positivism, 1861–1914, Mary Gibson
Life Courses of Young Convicts Transported to Van Diemen's Land,
Emma D. Watkins
Fair and Unfair Trials in the British Isles, 1800–1940,
eds. David Nash and Anne-Marie Kilday

Wayward Girls in Victorian and Edwardian England

Pathways In and Out of Juvenile Institutions, 1854–1920

Tahaney Alghrani

BLOOMSBURY ACADEMIC
LONDON · NEW YORK · OXFORD · NEW DELHI · SYDNEY

BLOOMSBURY ACADEMIC
Bloomsbury Publishing Plc
50 Bedford Square, London, WC1B 3DP, UK
1385 Broadway, New York, NY 10018, USA
29 Earlsfort Terrace, Dublin 2, Ireland

BLOOMSBURY, BLOOMSBURY ACADEMIC and the Diana logo are
trademarks of Bloomsbury Publishing Plc

First published in Great Britain 2024

A catalogue record for this book is available from the British Library.

A catalog record for this book is available from the Library of Congress.

ISBN: HB: 978-1-3504-0711-4
        ePDF: 978-1-3504-0712-1
        eBook: 978-1-3504-0713-8

Series: History of Crime, Deviance, and Punishment

Typeset by Integra Software Services Pvt. Ltd.

To find out more about our authors and books visit www.bloomsbury.com
and sign up for our newsletters.

Contents

Tables

Images

Figures

Abbreviations

BRO   Bristol Record Office

LRO   Liverpool Record Office

MRO   Manchester Record Office

MEPO   Metropolitan Police

Acknowledgements

I owe a huge debt of thanks to the many people who assisted me, in one way or another, in conducting and completing this book. First, huge thanks go to my family, my sister and my children, who have provided me with endless love, limitless patience and lots of chocolate. Second, I wish to thank my fellow researchers: Dr Alison Pedley, Dr Emma Watkins, and Dr Susie Casson. Third, thanks go to my former colleagues, particularly Samantha and Deinice, who enthusiastically listened to me discussing the many case studies in the book during our breaks. Last but not least, I would like to thank Dr Diane Frost and Dr Zoe Alker for their helpful guidance and support when I was a PhD student under their wings. Although my PhD is now completed, I feel like my research in this area has only just begun and constantly recalled their helpful feedback while undertaking this project. Special thanks go to other academics who have both inspired and helped me during my academic journey, namely Professor Anne-Marie Kilday, Professor Barry Goldson, Professor Helen Johnston and Professor Pamela Cox, for their invaluable comments and feedback.

I am also very grateful to the archivists, particularly those at Bristol Archive and Manchester Archive. Special thanks go to Dr Jessamy Carlson, who not only provided me with expertise on archives, but was also always on hand to assist me with locating sources and databases. I would also like to thank the librarians at the University of Liverpool, particularly Catherine McManamon whose assistance was invaluable in locating sources in the early stages of the research. Finally, I would like to acknowledge the girls who feature in this study, whose histories have been marginalized up until now. I hope in this study to give them a voice.

Prologue

'She had carried out these miserable acts to dress beyond her station'

In 1886, Beatrice Meylor, aged eleven, was charged with obtaining two pairs of boots under false pretences, for which she was sentenced to ten days in prison and five years at Red Lodge Reformatory. Beatrice completed her sentence on 23 October 1891. The records reveal she attempted to work as a domestic servant but left after a month and returned to live with her grandmother in Newport. In 1893, she returned to visit the matron of the Lodge. Shortly afterwards, on 31 January 1894, a policeman arrived to report that Beatrice had committed extensive fraud, using the alias surname Williams. Beatrice was charged with obtaining clothes belonging to various tradesmen under false pretences. When asked where the articles were located, she replied, 'I would rather die than tell you where the other things are'. An old tin box was found near the railway station where she was arrested, containing twenty pawn tickets, and three additional pawn tickets were subsequently found in her room. Beatrice had carved out a lucrative criminal career for herself. She would take a train to various localities, discover who the local customers were and obtain goods (clothes) under false pretences. She wore some of the clothes and others she pawned. On 5 February 1894, Beatrice appeared in court charged with obtaining under false pretences. Miss Langabeer, the matron of Red Lodge, informed the judge that 'the only thing that I could imagine that induced her to act as she had done was a love of dress'. The judge declared that 'she had carried out these miserable acts to dress beyond her station' and that he would give Beatrice one more chance, as it would be extremely difficult for her to obtain decent employment if she was sent to prison. His advice to her was 'not to associate with people better than herself or to dress beyond her station in life' (Bristol Police Court, *Western Daily*

Press, 5 February 1894). Beatrice then went to work in London as a laundry maid for two years. The matron had maintained contact with Beatrice, and it was recorded that letters and postcards were sent to Red Lodge. There are no further records of any crimes and the discharge book reported, that in January 1897 Beatrice 'married a most respectable young man in Bristol'. In 1914, some twenty-eight years after Beatrice was first admitted to Red Lodge, the final entry in the discharge book stated: 'Beatrice was Head of the women's department store at Bristol Hippodrome, receiving a good salary and does not live with her husband anymore and has not in years' (Miss Sullivan's Discharge Reports, 5137/1:73–4, BRO).

Beatrice's pathway into the reformatory was theft and stealing two pairs of boots, for which she received a five-year sentence in Red Lodge Reformatory. On her release, during her licence period, she did not settle in domestic service but returned to criminality within two years. However, fortunately for Beatrice, she was not re-admitted to prison, but the magistrate decided to give her 'one more chance' (Bristol Police Court, *Western Daily Press*, 5 February 1894). Beatrice entered domestic service, married and later went on to live independently in stable employment, even achieving a modest degree of social mobility (Miss Sullivan's Discharge Reports, 5137/1:73–4, BRO).

The case study reveals the factors that motivated her law-breaking as well as those that promoted her stability. Although Beatrice's case is unique, it provides us with a working-class female experience of entering and leaving a juvenile institution to uncover these marginalized histories (Gallagher et al., 2013).

This book examines historical documentation through digital and archival records of three specific juvenile institutions; namely, Red Lodge Reformatory, Carlton Industrial School and Manchester Sale. The aim is to first examine the pathways into these female reformatories and industrial schools by exploring gendered ideologies around the construction of female deviance and 'at risk' girls. It is important to note that the girls entering the institutions were, on average, aged 11–15 years old and left the institutions when they were 16–18 years old when they went out on licence for three years. Thus, the focus of this book is on juvenile girls and exploring how girlhood was experienced by working-class girls during this period, I examine the nature of juvenile female crime and delinquency and what sort of actions and behaviour led to their placement in the female reformatories and industrial schools.

Second, I investigate gendered regulation and reform within the institutions. What strategies the institutions used to regulate and reform the girls and whether the girls they complied or resist this reform.

Third, the book explores the immediate destinations of the girls beyond the reformatory and industrial schools. How, for example, they navigated society following their discharge. Through examining the impact that the interventions had on their pathways during their licence period and beyond, we can explore how they transitioned back into society post discharge from the institutions.

This book provides a snapshot of the local application of the institutional policies and regimes and how juvenile girls responded to these. The admission records tell us about the lived experiences of working-class girls' pre-adulthood and the licences expose how they navigated their early adulthood, thus providing an important contribution to the scholarship on juvenile delinquency and crime history literature.

Theoretically, I adopt a feminist criminological framework, proposed by Chesney-Lind (1997); Chesney-Lind and Sheldon (2014) and other feminist criminologists who have criticized the lack of attention that the field of criminology has paid to assessing female offenders and questioning whether male pathways into and out of penal institutions can also account for females' experiences. Rather, they argue, there is a need to develop a feminist model of female delinquency by examining the available evidence on girls' offending (Chesney-Lind, 1989; Worrall, 1990; Batchelor, 2005; Belknap and Holsinger, 2006; Gelsthorpe and Sharpe, 2006; Sharpe, 2011, 2015; Goodfellow, 2019). My contribution to utilizing this framework is that I undertake historical case studies to advance our understanding of female delinquency and how the gendered ideologies and modes of discipline within the female institutions became ingrained within the present carceral estate for juvenile girls. It is important to examine the past in order to understand how gender and gendered social constructions of femininity are central to not only conditioning the criminal justice responses but also understanding the modes of social control over females in both the past and the present (Heidensohn, 1985; Cain, 1989; Smart, 1992). My approach is interdisciplinary in nature, working across the boundaries of knowledge within a Feminist Criminology framework and within Historical Criminology to add fresh perspectives and approaches to research (Churchill, Yeomans and Channing, 2022).

This book foregrounds the dynamics and intersection of both class and gender, interrogating how the dominant hegemonic discourses of respectability, domesticity and motherhood, underpinned by the medical and religious discourses, were used to regulate female behaviour within juvenile institutions. The ideals of 'respectable femininity' were deeply integrated and embedded in the day-to-day running and operation of the institutions, reflecting the wider societal ideas around gender and class. The girls were expected to undertake feminized industrial labour and were primed to fulfil the traditional gendered roles of servant, wife or mother. I examine the historical evidence to analyse how these gendered discourses played a central role in regulating the working-class girls, both while they were within the institutions and after they had left.

This book argues that the female institutions played a critical role in both the criminalization and re-socialization of working-class girls along the bourgeois ideals of feminine codes of behaviour. The expected gendered pathways into domestic service and then, eventually marriage, not only defined the girls' gendered roles but also sought to place them in marginal, dependent positions, ensuring a continuum of surveillance and social control beyond the walls of the institutions (Heidensohn, 1985, 1996; Smart, 1992; Barr, 2019). The case studies illustrate, however, not all the girls discharged from the institutions adhered to the 'expected' pathways.

1

Introduction

During the nineteenth century, philanthropists, reformers, politicians and members of the clergy turned their attention towards the urban poor in large cities such as London, Bristol, Liverpool and Manchester, arguing that the uncontrollable growth in the number of young 'criminals' was threatening the social order. 'Juvenile offending became an emblem for social breakdown and domestic instability' (Shore, 2002a: 1). Radzinowicz and Hood argue that the concept of a 'juvenile offender' is a Victorian creation. They maintain that there was no sudden rise in criminal behaviour but, instead, it was simply the result of the criminalization of traditional youthful activities. They argue that, at the end of the 1840s and in the early 1850s, 'a deluge of "speech and pamphlet philanthropy" swept the country' (Radzinowicz and Hood, 1990: 172). However, Shore (2002a) locates the changes towards juveniles as occurring three decades earlier, in the 1810s, as the official surveys, such as the 1816 report on the *Alarming Increase of Juvenile Delinquency in the Metropolis*, painted an alarming picture of juvenile delinquency.

> Juvenile Delinquency existed in the Metropolis to a very alarming extent that a system was in action, by which these unfortunate lads were organised into gangs; that they regularly conspired together in public houses, where they planned their enterprises and afterwards divided the produce of their plunder.
>
> (1816: 5)

The quote taken from the report reveals the first instance of the use of the phrase 'juvenile delinquency'. The survey, undertaken by a Whig Politician and several Quaker social reformers, concluded that the main factors associated with 'juvenile delinquency' were: parental neglect, a lack of education, a want of employment, illicit practices including gambling, the violation of the Sabbath and the existing prison regime, based on the belief that incarcerating children alongside hardened criminals exacerbated the criminal associations and behaviour of the youths (Report 1816 cited in Shore, 2002a: 20). The term 'juvenile delinquency' has been much debated within the literature (May 1973; Magarey, 1978; Radzinowicz and Hood, 1990; Griffiths, 1996; King, 1998; Shore, 2002). However, Shore (2002a) argues that 'whilst it would be untenable to argue that the juvenile offender was "invented" in the nineteenth century that elite constructions of delinquent youth are matched by legislative enactment' (2002: 14).

Legislative reform regarding the administration of juveniles, argues King (1998), may have contributed to the increase in the number of young 'criminals'; namely, the gradual lifting of capital sentences for theft (King, 1998: 159). Magarey (1978) argues that the criminalizing of petty behaviour, previously ignored by the courts, legislated juvenile delinquency into existence. The Juvenile Offenders Act 1847 stipulated that anyone under the age of fourteen years should be tried at the petty sessions, ruling that the treatment, trial and punishment of juvenile offenders were adopted (May, 1973: 7). This Act set a maximum penalty of three months' imprisonment upon conviction, although this could include hard labour or whipping. This statute was followed by the Juvenile Offenders Act 1850, which increased the age limit to sixteen years.

The enactment of these statutes and changes in the law towards juveniles also need to be contextualized within the judicial changes made regarding disciplining of the poor in urban environments. Emsley (1991) argues that the street life of the poor and public behaviour that had been previously tolerated was now subject to an 'unprecedented degree of scrutiny and control' (1991: 59–60). The approach of the police was to assert public order on the streets, asserting control over those deemed 'social deviants'. The Peel's Metropolitan Police Act 1829 represented a revolution in terms of the traditional methods of law enforcement and granted police officers the power to arrest 'all loose, idle, disorderly persons whom he shall find disturbing the public peace, or whom he should suspect of any evil designs' (Lyman, 1964: 141). Further statutes, such as the Contagious Disease Act 1864, sought to remove from the streets women who posed a threat to the health of the nation.

This legislation allowed the police to arrest women suspected of being 'prostitutes', to forcibly test them for infections and, if the women were found to be infected, place them in a lock hospital for up to three months. To begin with, the Contagious Disease Act 1864 was a sanitary measure, initially passed in naval ports and army towns with the goal of preventing sexual diseases occurring within the armed forces. However, the additional amendment acts of 1866 and 1869 extended this to the North of England and the civilian population, bringing into sharp focus the sexual 'morality', prostitution and the brothels in the large cities (Walkowitz, 1980). Hartley (1986) argues that 'the early nineteenth century response to social deviants, whether they were paupers, vagrants, criminals or mentally ill was manifested in the development of institutions which were designed to be mechanisms of both treatment and control' (1986: 1). According to Shore, 'the institutional experience underpinned the Victorian system' (2011: 12). The number of penal welfare institutions, such as workhouses, prisons, asylums and penitentiaries, steadily increased over the nineteenth century, initially housing men, women and children together. The reformers voiced their concern that placing children with adults in workhouses and prisons would result in the corruption of the children, thereby contributing to the moral and religious appeals for the need to separate children from adults. Goldson (1997) maintains that the concepts of 'immorality, irreligion, corruption and contagion combined with constructs of dangerousness, sedition and political subversion were applied in analyses of crime in general, and juvenile crime in particular' (1997: 5).

However, Hendrick maintains that the social and economic changes that occurred during the nineteenth century are significant in understanding the increase in the number of juveniles in the urban locations. In the first half of the nineteenth century, reformers voiced concerns about the human cost of the industrial revolution, particularly child labour. The 1833 Factories Act limited the conditions regarding the employment of children in factories, which was deemed dangerous and exploitative. The introduction of the Factories Act, along with the long-term decline in the number of apprenticeships, reduced the employment opportunities for children, leading to a swelling number of unemployed, unsupervised juveniles roaming the streets, who turned to petty larceny and offending in order to survive the harsh life during the nineteenth century. Hendrick (1990) posits that, effectively, the 'factory child' was replaced by the 'delinquent child'.

During these changes in the employment of children, Hendrick maintains that what also begins to emerge within the Victorian discourse and reform literature is a new construction of childhood: 'the wage-earning child was no longer considered to be the norm. Instead, childhood was now seen as a distinct set of characteristics requiring protection and a fostering through school education' (1997: 38). This distinction marked a critical turning point in the constructions of childhood that had been emerging since the eighteenth century (May 1973; Pinchbeck and Hewitt, 1973; Plumb, 1975; Cunningham, 1995). At the core of the reconstruction, which is so important in the history of childhood, lay the successfully advanced belief of reformer Mary Carpenter that 'a child is to be treated as a child' (Manton, 1976 cited in Hendrick, 1997: 42). These ideals set in motion the idea that children, now a distinct category, needed to be separated from hardened adult offenders.

The placing of children within adult prisons alongside hardened criminals, which became regarded as 'nurseries of vice', now spurred on reformers regarding the need to separate juveniles, resulting in legislative changes. The Gaol Act 1823 required the separation within prisons of men, women, boys and girls (Stack, 1979; Johnston, 2015). The 1835 Select Committee on Gaols and Houses of Correction recommended the establishment of a separate juvenile prison. Separate institutions for juvenile offenders were discussed and debated – although these institutions were not new – and various philanthropic schools were established, such as the Stretton Colony in Warwickshire in 1818 and Elizabeth Fry's reform school in Chelsea, known as the 'school of discipline', in 1825. Johnston maintains, however, that these were voluntary institutions and developed on an *ad hoc* basis (Johnston, 2015: 141). Nevertheless, Godfrey et al., (2017) argue that this philanthropic voluntary sector, these 'child-saving' charities and agencies, contributed to the emergent youth justice system (Godfrey et al., 2017: 23). The emergence of the 'child-saving' rhetoric was based around the changing attitudes towards childhood and adolescence in the nineteenth century, argues Hendrick (1997).

The first government experiment with a juvenile prison was Parkhurst Prison on the Isle of Wight in 1838, designed to instruct offenders before they were transported to the colonies. During their detention, the boys were trained in trades, such as shoemaking, brick-making and blacksmithing, providing skills and training to facilitate their rehabilitation upon release and enable them to find paid employment. However, the prison regime was a strongly disciplined environment, in which the inmates were treated harshly; they were shackled with iron manacles, under strict surveillance, fed a minimal diet and forced to remain silent (Stack, 1979; McConville, 1981). Parkhurst attracted much criticism, including from Carpenter who influenced by her religious Unitarian background and her moral principles, argued sending children to prison was injurious to the child 'physically and mentally' (Carpenter, 1851: 273–6). Carpenter maintained that the reformation of the child should be based on love for the child, ideally in a suitable environment in which corporal punishment should be kept at a minimum. Carpenter stated:

> It is utterly vain to look for any reformation where the heart is not touched, and where the inner springs of action are not called into healthful exercise; this cannot possibly be done for children under the mechanical and military discipline of Parkhurst.

(Carpenter, 1851: 322)

Parkhurst received much criticism and was deemed a failure by contemporaries such as Carpenter and Matthew Davenport Hill, the Recorder of Birmingham. However, Parkhurst had succeeded in establishing a precedent in Britain for treating young juvenile offenders distinctly from adults (Watkins and Godfrey, 2018: 39). Public and political sentiment rejected retribution and deterrence in favour of reform (Carlebach, 1970), based on the idea that children should be reformed rather than imprisoned under harsh disciplinary regimes, from which the reformatory schools originated. Reformatories were thus created as an alternative to prison for juveniles.

The establishment of the reformatory and industrial schools

Following the unsuccessful youth detention experiment at Parkhurst (which continued to operate until 1864), the reformatory school movement gained considerable support and momentum. In 1846, a parliamentary Bill to establish a national system of reformatory schools was presented by Lord Houghton. Although the Bill did not find its way onto the statute books, it sparked interest from the Philanthropic Society, who, in 1849, visited the agricultural colony for delinquent boys in Mettray, France. The Philanthropic Society established a pioneering farm colony for boys in Redhill, Surrey, based on the Mettray model (Higginbotham, 2017: 13). The Mettray colony in France was a reformatory establishment which, as Driver claims, exerted an 'extraordinary influence' outside France (Driver, 1990: 272). Carpenter was greatly influenced by both the Pestalozzian experiments being carried out on the continent and Joseph Tuckerman, who founded the first state-supported institution for boys in America, the Massachusetts' State Reform School. She argued that the state had a role to play in addressing juvenile crime which she attributed to neglectful parents, a lack of moral education, socialization and poverty (Manton, 1976). Carpenter's treatise, *Reformatory Schools for the Children of the Perishing and Dangerous Classes and for Juvenile Offenders* (1851, digitally reprinted 2013), laid out a three-point plan regarding which institutions were needed: Reformatory Schools, Industrial Schools and Free Day Schools. She distinguished between what she called the children of the perishing classes and those of the dangerous classes, echoing the rhetoric of the provision of 'deserving' and 'undeserving' poor. Carpenter stated:

> Those who have not fallen into actual crime, but who are almost certain from ignorance, destitution and the circumstances in which they are growing up,

to do so … and those who have already received the prison brand … who are notoriously living by plunder.

(Carpenter, 2013: 2)

Carpenter's writings and evidence were presented to the 1852 parliamentary enquiry that was appointed to examine the treatment of criminal and destitute children. Stack (1986), in 'Interests and Ideas in nineteenth Century Social Policy', examined the attitudes of the people involved in the reformatory school movement. He concluded that they fell into two main groups: the 'realists' and the 'humanitarians'. The humanitarians included Matthew Davenport Hill, a staunch ally of Carpenter, who had extensive experience as a criminal judge and the 'realists' Sydney Turner (who established Red Hill farm, also soon to be the first Home Office inspector for Reformatory and Industrial schools), T. B. Lloyd-Baker (a Gloucestershire Magistrate) and Jelinger Symons (a barrister, school inspector). Reformatory schools were debated before parliament with regard to many issues, but the most contentious issue was whether imprisonment should be imposed prior to entry. The 'realists' Turner, Lloyd Baker and Symons deemed that punishment should be imposed prior to entry. However, Carpenter and Davenport opposed imprisonment, arguing that prisons were a place for punishment, rather than reform of the child.

In 1854, parliament enacted the Youthful Offenders (Reformatory Schools) Act, which enabled the establishment of reformatory schools to reclaim juveniles from a 'criminal career', designed to house children under sixteen years of age who had been convicted of a crime, for a period of between two and five years, after they had served an initial fourteen days in a local prison. The 1854 legislation was followed by the Industrial Schools Act 1857, which established industrial schools to prevent 'at risk' children from slipping into criminality. Both statutes established separate institutions for children and were central to the treatment of juveniles in the nineteenth century. The juvenile reform movement and establishment of reformatory and industrial schools in the second half of the nineteenth century marked a watershed in the history of delinquent children and the penal system's response to their criminal behaviour. Never before had state-run juvenile institutions been set up on such a scale across England. Approximately 4,000 young offenders were housed in 48 reformatories by 1860 and, by 1900, over 30,000 young people were being held in over 200 state reformatories or industrial schools (Godfrey and Lawrence, 2005: 136). The institutions were segregated by gender; boys and girls were reformed, trained and regulated in gender-specific ways.

However, revisionist historians have questioned the motives and objectives of the Victorian benevolent institutional regimes. Revisionist history and critical criminology seek to research 'from the bottom up', drawing upon the social control and links between the penal laws and the labour market (Rusche and Kirsheimer, 1938; Platt, 1969; Clarke, 1975; Rush, 1992). The enactment and changes in the law regarding juveniles also need to be contextualized within the judicial changes made regarding disciplining the poor in an expanding industrial environment. Clark (1975) argues that the reformers' commentaries on children have a 'double thrust – at both the moral condition of children and the leisure habits of the labouring classes, which provide sources of moral corruption and unnatural knowledge' (Clark, 1975, cited in Muncie et al., 2002: 126). However, the social control of working-class girls and the role of the reformatory and industrial schools in the disciplining and regulation of gendered roles have not been fully explored. Naffine maintains that, even within the field of critical criminology, men are still regarded as 'the natural heartland' of the discipline (Naffine, 1997: 2 cited in Menis, 2020: 22).

Juvenile girls and delinquency

The debate on the invention of 'juvenile delinquency', however, offered no substantial gendered analysis of the role of juvenile females during this period. Most of the literature written on crime during this period reflected the contemporary discourses, which focused on male criminality. Zedner's (1991b) argues that 'criminal men were, indeed, the primary target of the development of formal policing and the proliferation of prisons – and the histories have reflected this' (1991b : 312). Certainly, no one would deny that more men were involved in criminality, but the absence of literature and contemporary discussion on female criminality does not mean that it did not exist. Rather, females were not regarded as active agents, initiating crime, but merely as associates. Shore maintains that the preoccupation was with male criminality and 'when girls were considered it was from the confines of narrow descriptive categories, which stereotyped them as either prostitutes or flash girls' (an early nineteenth-century equivalent of a gangster's moll) (2002b: 164). Cale, in the opening pages of her thesis entitled 'Saved from a Life of Vice and Crime', states that 'historians interested in juvenile delinquency have overlooked girls because to discover the Victorian attitude toward the female juvenile delinquent it is necessary to turn to the literature on prostitution instead of that on juvenile delinquency' (Cale, 1993: i).

Within the reform discourse, influenced mainly by philanthropists and social purity groups, juvenile girls were presented as, 'on the one hand, a victim, on the other, a "sexualised demon", and a danger not just to herself but to the wider society' (Pasko, 2010: 1102). Feminist criminologist Pasko (2010) argues that a critical interrogation is needed of how gender constructions (femininities/ masculinities) related to girls' delinquency and systematic control in the juvenile justice system. King argues that the moral panic around 'juvenile delinquency' represented the boys as thieves and the girls as prostitutes (King, 2006: 90). This concern was highly gendered; with boys, there was concern about thieving whereas, for girls, the concern focused on sexual immorality and promiscuity (Lammasniemi, 2020: 242). 'Wayward' and 'immoral' females in the public space stood in direct opposition to the conventional, respectable, feminine domestic ideal, which was reinforced by the paternalistic, patriarchal state, courts, police, church and philanthropists like Carpenter, who was instrumental in the reformatory movement and the establishment of juvenile institutions for girls. The Victorian reform discourse to generate support for the institutions drew widely on images of 'excessive sexuality'. Thus, from the outset sexuality became a key marker of female delinquency (Mahood, 1995). However, Heidensohn argues that 'it is clearly not true that girl delinquents are or mainly sexually delinquent' (1985: 137). Cox (2013) points out that 'a problem with this genre is that it can overemphasise girls' sexuality while underplaying their involvement in other kinds of crime' (2013: 9).

However, Davies' research 'These Viragoes are no less Cruel than the lads' (1999) marked a shift in the literature and is particularly notable for the suggestion that girls participated in gangs and violence in Manchester in the 1830s. Female 'Scuttlers' tended to fight with clogs and boots rather than with the knives and belts favoured by male gang members. Davies argues that 'in the case of the scuttling gangs of the late nineteenth-century Manchester and Salford, the label "moll" is highly misleading if it is used to signify a passive female role as the ornamental property of a violent male' (Davies, 1999: 74). Davies maintains that 'female Scuttlers' tended to be young, working-class, and single, in their mid-to-late teens. Davies argues that the 'magisterial concern with the moral welfare of young women was manifested in a determination to remove female gang members from the corrupting environment of the streets' (1999: 74). As well as the presence of girls in the gangs of Manchester, there is evidence to suggest their presence in gangs in other urban cities (Macilwee, 2007, 2011).

Investigating urban cities and female presence ultimately highlights that girl gang membership is not a modern phenomenon (Miller, 2001). However, trying to determine the number of girls involved in gangs during this period would prove difficult if using records alone. Shore argues that, despite the fact that almost half of the admissions to the London Bridewell were females in 1835, these tended to be seen as 'Molls'. Shore explains that 'while juvenile girls had also been corrupted at some stage, they tended to be treated as part of the threat to boys, rather than assessed as offenders in their own right' (2002b: 168). We see glimpses of this within the popular literature produced at the time. Notably, the character of 'Nancy' in *Oliver Twist* was situated at the periphery of crime, in the context of the sexual threat she posed to the boys and the fact that she consorted with thieves. Emsley points out that, even for the offence of being drunk, arresting policemen catalogued females as 'prostitutes' (1996: 122).

The contemporary view of females as 'molls' meant that they were largely ignored, or not taken seriously by magistrates; nor were they included in criminal investigations. Shore argues that the 1816 *'Report of the Committee for Investigating the Causes of Delinquency in the Metropolis'* interviewed and considered several hundred boys in Middlesex prisons and houses of correction. No female juvenile offenders were interviewed and 'typically girls were referred to only in the context of prostitution' (Shore, 2002b: 168). Reports, commissions and texts of the period predominately focused on male criminality and the majority of those entering the criminal justice system were males. Even the legislation used male nouns and pronouns to describe offenders. Emsley argues that this may have 'contributed to the overall perception of crime as a masculine behaviour' (Emsley, 2005: 92). Thus, the contemporary agenda, investigations and references were centred on males, which may have led earlier historians of this contemporary material to gain the impression that crimes were wholly committed by males. Cox maintains that, in many of the distinguished works of recent decades on the history of crime, 'from street Arabs, garrotters, hooligans, motor-bandits, bag-snatchers, to teds, mods and rockers – have been overwhelmingly male' (2013: 8). Feminist Historians maintain that examination of the archival sources and data is needed, with a critical eye, often reading between the lines to examine the omission of females or the situating of them at the periphery of crime (Cox, 2013; Williams, 2016). This book seeks to readdress the absence of juvenile girls within the literature, by examining their pathways into the reformatories and industrial schools and placing their experiences centrally within the book.

The institutions and locations examined in this book

The three institutions examined (Red Lodge Reformatory, Carlton Industrial School and Manchester Sale) were based in two geographical locations (Bristol and Manchester) over a 66-year period (1854–1920). This timeframe was chosen principally because it coincided with the enactment of the Youth Offenders Act (1854) and the opening of the first female reformatory in England, Red Lodge Reformatory. The end date of 1920 was dictated by data protection restrictions, whereby the archival documents of the institutions become unavailable due to the 100-year rule. The decision to focus on these three institutions in these two locations was based on two factors: the first was the fact that source materials on individual admissions and discharges from the archives of these institutions were available; and the second was the fact that the analysis of these three institutions in these two locations provides insight into the localized pattern of incarceration and aftercare provisions in two contrasting geographical locations in a South-West port city and a North-West industrial town to foreground the particular characteristics of the various regional and institutional practices related to juvenile delinquency and reform. It aims to identify the socio-economic similarities and differences in these two locations as well as local concerns around working-class urban family life and how this impacted on the pathways of the girls in and out of the institutions in these two locations.

Both Manchester and Bristol were undergoing significant economic and social changes during this period. Bristol, a port city, was considered the second largest city in the eighteenth century. The port had played a central role in the Transatlantic slave trade, accumulating significant wealth which underpinned Bristol's urban development (Dresser, 2016). However, during the early nineteenth century, the abolishment of the slave trade in 1807, together with the limitation on shipping imposed by the Avon Gorge and the rise of the Lancashire cotton industry, meant that a loss of trade occurred to competitor ports, such as Glasgow and Liverpool. The economic and social effects of the declining port had a significant impact on the city in the nineteenth century. The old houses, once occupied by wealthy merchants and ship-owners in the eighteenth century, became let out as tenements and lodging houses inhabited by the drifting populations, sailors, prostitutes, beggars and gangs of children who lived by scavenging (Manton, 1976: 72). The desolate area stretching from the docks to Lewin's Mead was 'notorious as being among the worst slums in Britain' (Manton, 1976: 72).

In contrast to Bristol, Manchester was an industrial town that, according to Kidd, 'entered the second half of the nineteenth century as one of the world's greatest cities. An economic marvel in an age of great cities' (Kidd, 1993: 36). With the boom in cotton manufacturing, Manchester became an important urban centre worldwide. However, Kidd maintains that 'the massive urban growth brought enormous problems of organisation, provision of amenities and amenities of public order' (Kidd, 1993: 36). Despite the industrial boom, there was moral anxiety about the crime, vice and drunkenness beleaguering the city (Davies, 1999; Stafford, 2018). In particular, juvenile crime and concerns about the prospect of a 'criminal class' destabilizing the social order turned the focus towards neglectful parents, particularly neglectful mothers.

Work in Manchester was dominated by the cotton mills and factories which employed numerous women and believed to turn homes and marriages 'upside down', as married women primarily went 'out' to work (Gomersall, 1997; Holmes, 2017). Indeed, women formed a significant majority of the cotton workforce. By 1841, there were 11,427 women working in Manchester's cotton mills and workshops (Kidd, 1993: 25). Female independence, their increasing presence in the public sphere and working in mills and factories were seen as threatening the gendered social order. Gomersall maintains that, for Evangelical Christians, the factory work of women signalled the moral degeneracy that was the root cause of social disorder (1997: 28). Goodman maintains that 'fears of the Manchester mill girls' independence, lack of chastity and subversion of sexual difference, formed long-standing tropes of prostitution' (Goodman, 2003: 77).

> The factory girls are strangers to modesty … their language is gross and often obscene; and when they do not marry early, they form illicit connections which degrade them still more than premature marriage.
>
> (Leon Faucher cited in Goodman, 2003: 77)

Local anxiety around female 'immorality' and a 'lack of chastity' was also a concern in Bristol. The influx of sailors, merchant traders and migrant workers meant that the port locations became associated with brothels and prostitution. Archer (2011) argues that the majority of seaports, such as Liverpool, Bristol and London, had an extended sex industry, where brothels were active and tolerated. The limited employment opportunities for females in a port city meant that there was constant supply and demand for prostitution, with a large number of brothels operating in the port cities. The introduction of the Contagious Diseases Act 1864 in naval ports and army towns, as well as the additional amendment acts of 1866 and 1869 heightened the anxiety around prostitution in other towns and cities. The prostitute became associated with venereal disease, which was viewed as a pollutant in society that needed to be removed (Joyce, 2008).

Anxiety about prostitution and the breakdown of the family in Victorian urban spaces, such as Manchester and Bristol, were underpinned by religious discourses that drew on medical and scientific ideologies, such as social Darwinism (Goodman, 2003). Indeed, during the nineteenth century, we see an upsurge in the number of reports on the health of the nation, such as Edwin Chadwick's sanitation and public health. Poovey, *In Making a Social Body*, analysed this period and maintains that: 'The "diseased" (unproductive, criminal, plague-ridden) members, the poor were considered inimical to the health of the body politic' (1995: 7). Both the lodging house/brothel and the prostitute who resided in it were frequently represented as the carriers of disease, dirt and death (Goodman, 2003: 79). Sexual excess stressed that the subversion of Christian marital principles would lead to national degeneracy. Goodman maintains that 'In such rhetoric, the brothel was the antithesis of the middle-class view of home at the heart of national identities, health and regeneration' (Goodman, 2003: 80). Rose, in *Limited Livelihoods: Gender and Class in Nineteenth-century England* (1993), argues that notions of working-class domesticity spread from the mid-century and made women's activities outside the private sphere suspect and undesirable (Rose, 1993: 138).

As well as the concerns around prostitution, research by Davies (1999, 2008) and Stafford (2018) highlights that there were concerns around the increasing levels of violence and drunkenness in Manchester. Stafford (2018) examines female drunkenness during the Victorian period, when there was intense concern about drunkenness in general and female drunkenness in particular. He maintains that 'the county of Lancashire had developed a reputation, particularly amongst the London press, as being a singularly drunken and violent place' (Stafford, 2018: 115). Stafford argues that working-class women were targeted by the police and that the personal views of policemen and magistrates were instrumental in their drive against drunkenness. It was feared that neglectful mothers, not fathers, would lead their children into a life of crime (Stafford, 2018). Zedner (1991a) maintains that Victorians were particularly concerned about mothers who were deemed criminal and that the children of criminal mothers would become criminal themselves, due to the influence of their home life (Zedner, 1991: 156–7). Working-class mothers, deemed 'immoral', 'drunken' or as leaving their children to fend for themselves, were often mentioned in the admission records, suggesting that juveniles, particularly girls, who came from these backgrounds were 'at risk'. Furthermore, the introduction of the Industrial Amendment Act (1880) stipulated that children could be removed from homes deemed brothels or lodgings associated with prostitutes.

Thus, it is important to explore how the social and economic background of these two urban locations may have impacted on working-class girls' pathways into juvenile institutions and also their re-integration after leaving them. Research has tended to focus on these locations, without referencing working-class females and the interplay between class, gender and deviance (Briggs, 1963; Messinger, 1985; Kidd, 1993). D'Cruze and Jackson commented, in their study of women and crime from the early modern period to the present day, that the experiences of female offenders should be considered within the 'gender and class disadvantages that brought women into prison in the first place' (2009: 134). Rose also maintains that 'in the nineteenth century, working-class women, as a group, were more disadvantaged than working-class men, as a group. They earned less money and faced more difficult circumstances in their jobs in addition to the trying conditions under which they fulfilled their family responsibilities' (1993: 190). Influential studies by Clark (1995), Roberts (1984), Ross (1993), Tebbutt (1983) and Griffiths (2020) have shed light on the previously neglected experiences of working-class women in Victorian and Edwardian Britain. However, research on juvenile girls in urban spaces in the nineteenth century, particularly around the second half of the nineteenth century, has not been mapped within the literature.

Both Bristol and Manchester's urban environments, although one was a port city and the other an industrial town, facing contrasting economic conditions, shared the same anxiety about crime and disorder. The authorities in both cities were concerned about Victorian 'immorality' related to drunkenness, prostitution and crime, particularly among working-class females and the breakdown of social order (Davies, 1999; Goodman, 2003; Stafford, 2018). During the second half of the nineteenth century, Croll maintains that there was a 'civic project' which consisted of a collection of strategies developed to 'order, civilize and rationalize the urban experience' (2000: 3). Victorian environmentalism deemed urban towns and cities 'immoral' sites of vice and degradation. Prostitution was seen as a symptom of urbanization. Contemporary commentators, such as William Acton, in *Prostitution Considered in Its Moral, Social and Sanitary Aspects* (1857), emphasized the link between prostitution and the urban environment, thus creating moral boundaries between pure and fallen women, that became reflected in the private/public spheres (Kerber, 1988). Godfrey maintains that 'gender intersected with class to produce women vulnerable to police attention, mostly working-class women who occupied public spaces' (2014: 161–2). The surveillance and criminalization of working-class juveniles was high on the national agenda. This study will foreground the particularities of the institutions and networks established in the two urban locations of Manchester and Bristol.

Previous research on youth by Jackson (2000) examines the rescue and reform of children in Leeds, a 'new urban environment' in the Victorian Period, and finds that there was a proliferation of children's homes and welfare organizations (2000: 135). Jackson maintains that an examination of the implementation of policy at a regional level and the locations where the juvenile institutions were established is essential. Godfrey et al., (2017), in *Young Criminal Lives*, highlighted the local delivery of youth justice for boys in the Northwest of England, examining the local networks. They examine the contribution of the local voluntary sector, businessmen and reformers, arguing that the emergent youth justice system was 'developed by local interests to suit local needs' (2017: 41). This research, exploring the emerging youth reform for girls, will enhance our understanding of what was happening at the local level. Examining Bristol and Manchester, two major Victorian cities, will facilitate micro-research regarding what was happening on a macro-scale in terms of the socialization and social control of young juvenile girls as well as the role of the reformatory and industrial schools during the nineteenth century.

Sources and methods

The research utilizes hitherto untapped primary historical sources to examine three female institutions (namely, Red Lodge Reformatory, Carlton Industrial School and Manchester Sale Industrial School) by considering the pathways of girls in two specific urban locations: Manchester and Bristol. I examined both the institutions themselves and the girls who were incarcerated within them. I created a dedicated database of the girls who entered the institutions. The dataset for each admission contained details of the factors that brought the girls into the institutions, personal details pertaining to their age, the charge on which they were committed, their home and family background, and the occupation and characters of their parents. The discharges contained the work life of the girls on licence, where they were relocated, whether or not they married, whether or not they had children and any criminal offences committed during their licence period. The qualitative comments in the records were added to the database, which included descriptions on the girls when admitted, their educational ability and additional comments made by policemen or school board officers.

Utilizing record linkage, the dataset examines the pathways and immediate discharge period for a core sample of 465 girls who entered the institutions in the period 1854–1900. I additionally examined a larger sample of discharge records covering the period up to 1920 to analyse the experience for the girls during the licence period after they left the institutions. The principal source was the admission and discharge records of the girls who were placed in the three juvenile institutions, as well as institutional records, such as annual report books, minute books, letters, medical books, visitor books and the private diary of the superintendent of Red Lodge, Mary Carpenter. There sources provide untapped records of the girls and the institutions. However, these must be used with a critical eye to avoid institutional bias, acknowledging the social and cultural contexts in which they were recorded. I also cross-checked the institutions and the girls who entered them within the historical newspapers and census records using *Find My Past* and *Ancestry*. The study also utilizes digitized historical records, such as Home Office Reports on the institutions within the *UK Parliamentary Papers* database.

Leading research within the crime history of youth and crime by Watkins (2020) and Godfrey et al., (2017), in *Young Criminal Lives*, used both archival and digital sources to examine the lives of juveniles in the nineteenth century and trace their destinations after release utilizing the life course methodology. *Young Criminal Lives* (2017) focused on juvenile institutions in the North West of England, tracing 500 boys who entered the institutions in order to investigate the extent to which these interventions 'worked' in terms of assessing their life course and whether they went on to commit further crime or had reformed. Williams, in her unpublished PhD, *'At Large': Women's Lives and Offending in Victorian Liverpool and London* (2014), examined the lives of offending women but acknowledged that she was compelled to work with the sources available, which did not in every instance provide the 'cradle to grave' information that was needed to apply a life course methodology. Attempting to trace young females throughout their life course is made virtually impossible mainly due to the fact that the girls changed their names on marriage. Cox et al., (2019) maintain that the similarities between the names and ages amongst the female cohort in a reform institution mean that identifying specific girls is difficult. The difficulties associated with name changes in terms of locating sources of information with reference to specific girls have undermined attempts to capture the female experience within crime history and resulted in its marginalization.

This study will utilize the admission records, to examine the girls' pathways into the institutions and the discharge records to examine their immediate destinations and experiences during their three-year licence period. In some instances, information on the girls was available for a longer period, offering crucial micro-histories of the experiences of the girls who passed through the juvenile institutions in the nineteenth century. This methodology has recently been adopted by Rogers, in her research on juvenile offenders in Yarmouth Gaol, who argues that micro-histories 'lend' themselves to crime history, as studies of criminal records and court reports give a voice to people who did not leave a first-person testimony (2017: 287).

Building on research which utilizes historical data within criminological studies (Bosworth, 2001; Cox, 2013; Turner and Johnston, 2015; Godfrey et al., 2017; Williams and Walklate, 2020), this research explores untapped sources to shine a spotlight on juvenile girls who entered the juvenile institutions during this period. These sources are critical in that they highlight female pathways in and out of juvenile institutions and contribute in some way to ensuring that their histories and experiences are recorded. Utilizing the sources in this way provides a cogent historical comparator to criminology debates on offending and sentencing (Lawrence, 2019). As Goldson posits, the purpose of 'longitudinal excavation and analysis of youth justice reform not only enables us to situate and to understand the present but – if those with power care to take heed – it might even serve as a basis for crafting policy into the future' (2020: 317).

The major challenge to historical research is the nature of locating the historical sources, particularly those pertaining to females. In the case of female history, the challenge is to piece together a jigsaw with pieces missing. At the outset of this research, a lot of time was spent going down avenues in search of archives only to come up with material with little or no use. It proved challenging, at the early stages of the research, to unearth what existed in the archives. However, this also highlights the importance of doing this research to investigate marginalized voices, in particular those of working-class females, who come into contact with the criminal justice system. The inconsistent, fragmentary nature of the sources for female records means that the sources that do exist must be woven together.

Analysing the archival process itself, Ogborn argues that 'what is created and what survives is a social and political process that can tell us much about the conditions under which information of different sorts is produced, used and evaluated' (Ogborn, 2010: 92). Hakim states that a dependence on archival data alone will produce a methodological problem; namely, that only an 'official' picture of the histories of these institutions can be presented (Hakim, 2000: 52). Therefore, to avoid a wholly institutional bias, I endeavoured to cross-reference where possible with other types of evidence that may offer different perspectives, such as Newspapers, Pamphlets circulated at the time, Parliamentary and Home Office reports. Using non-criminal sources alongside criminal sources gave me various perspectives. Moreover, a feminist narrative should seek the voice/agency of the girls, which one cannot get from the institutional records. There are no surviving letters or diaries written by the girls, either while at the reformatories or post discharge. Within the rules of the schools, it is stated that the matron reserved the right to check all letters so, even if these letters existed, it would be doubtful that they recorded genuinely how the girls felt, in case this led to repercussions and punishments. There is reference to letters written by the girls after they left the institutions in the discharge books, indicating that there were hundreds, if not thousands, of these. However, none of these are kept within the archives. The lack of inmates' original accounts, voices and narratives within the archival records means that we need to examine the actions of the girls within the daily records and reports. The girls absconding from the school, or rebelling against work, were demonstrating their modes of resistance and agency through their actions. These actions were documented in sources utilized, like Carpenter's personal journal and Minute Books. They highlight that they were not passive recipients of the institutions but had a voice that is essential to female penal history.

Moreover, bearing in mind that the research is drawing upon human history, any study that collects and presents any personal data raises issues of ethics. The digitization of the nineteenth-century school admission and discharge records means that many records are already within the public domain. However, the researcher needs to be sensitive and considerate of the fact that these archives are not just data but are the histories of young girls who were removed from their families and incarcerated. These girls were sometimes the victims of sexual and physical abuse, which can be painful histories to research and sensitivity needs to be employed in presenting this research. This leads me to the question of whether to anonymize the girls in this research and give them a pseudonym. The decision on whether to name, or to give the girls pseudonyms, depends on the potential social harm to their families. In light of the fact that the records are, in some instances, now over 150 years old and many records are often available online, I will use the original names in all cases. As Godfrey et al., maintain in *Young Criminal Lives*, these children

> were more than their official record; they were brothers, sons, fathers, and grandfathers. They were workers, soldiers, farmers, factory workers and shop

owners. They played as children, they were sometimes ill, they grew old and received pensions, and some died for their country.

(2017: 59)

I hope that naming the girls will illustrate that these were real lives and real histories and that their treatment and pathways will provide lessons for the future treatment of young female offenders within the criminal justice system.

Structure

Female juvenile Institutions, the pathways in and out of the institutions, are the organizing themes of this book. Chapter 1 contains a brief overview of the literature and research that has been conducted so far. I discuss the significance of the research to the history of youth, particularly the importance of adding female experiences to the existing scholarship on youth history, penal reform, criminology and gendered history. I highlight the locations and institutions that will be examined and note their significance in this research before discussing the sources and methods utilized for this book.

Chapter 2 contains an analysis of the historical representation, gendered 'ideology' and discourses around femininity, respectability and domesticity. It charts the fears and concerns around delinquent and wayward girls and their proximity to urban areas which were associated with vice, criminality and 'immoral' behaviour. In this chapter, I explore the stereotypes and representations associated with working-girls and their families broadly and the localized concerns during the nineteenth century. I highlight why these discourses were central to the national agenda of Empire building, and how they were central regarding the control of populations, highlighting Foucauldian theory from a feminist perspective.

Chapter 3 examines the networks and locations of the three institutions researched in this study. The chapter will examine the local networks and the management and running of the institutions, highlighting the various sectors of society involved with each institution in each location. This chapter highlights that the reformatory and industrial schools for girls in Manchester and Bristol sought to place girls in domestic service, despite the growth of factories and mills in these locations. This reflected the moral objectives of the institutions that sought to position girls in the private sphere, within domestic servitude.

Chapter 4 utilizes original admission records of the pathways of girls into the three female juvenile institutions. It will examine the institutional admission records for both the reformatory and industrial schools together with the crimes that the girls committed and the Victorian conceptions of what constructed girls 'at risk' that led to their admission. The admission records are rich in qualitative details about the girls' lives and the circumstances surrounding their pathways, highlighting the complex factors related to victimization, abuse and their family background. This chapter will highlight the intersection between gender and class, demonstrating how Victorian gendered 'ideology' of an idealized femininity and respectability played a significant role in the criminalization of working-class girls and their families during the nineteenth century.

Chapter 5 examines the Institutional cultures, the specific gendered discipline and regulation within the three female institutions. The ideal of 'respectable femininity', constructed around the 'ideology' of a chaste, passive female in the private sphere, was reinforced through the discourses of domesticity. These discourses justified gender-specific disciplinary practices within the female institutions, in which every aspect of the girl's appearance, character and behaviour had to conform to the deemed standards of acceptable, appropriate and respectable feminine behaviour. The dynamics of class also played a central role within the institutions. Middle-class women ran the institutions, dictating the ideals of respectability. The chapter examines the day-to-day experience of the girls within the institutions, including their training, discipline and punishment. I will seek to examine the intricate power dynamics within disciplined spaces and uncover the voices of the girls through their actions, probing their modes of resistance within these constricted environments.

Chapter 6 follows the lives and destinations of juvenile girls after they left the reformatory and industrial schools. Utilizing the discharge records, which traced these girls for three years after their departure (or, in some cases, longer), I assembled, coded and analysed the data to explore the lives of these working-class females, to identify whether or not they came into further contact with the law, their employment routes and their family life. Examining the lives of working-class girls on licence, exploring their experiences beyond youth custody to investigate whether they had been 'reformed' and successfully reintegrated back into society. In the context of the girls, the dominant discourses of respectability and domesticity that were used to regulate female behaviour within the institutions were used as a criterion for success within the licence period, thereby reflecting the aims of the female institutions that sought to place girls in domestic servitude in the private sphere under close surveillance and social control.

Finally, chapter seven will conclude the book by revisiting and drawing together all the central themes. It will evaluate the main findings and, in so doing, consider the contribution that this research makes to the field of crime history and feminist criminology. I will reflect on the process of conducting archival research and present possible future research avenues that have come to light as a result of doing this research.

Conclusion

Utilizing a unique dataset about juvenile girls within a 66-year time-frame who entered female reformatories and industrial schools, the book rests on an analysis of the intersection between gender and class, examining female institutions in specific locations, that have not been fully considered previously. I explore the girl's lives and show that their individual experiences and social background impacted on all aspects of their passage through the Victorian juvenile institutions and their subsequent discharge. The available sources allow us to piece together the experiences of a documented few, that helps us to identify the common factors and experiences of the many girls who entered reformatory and industrial schools during the Victorian and Edwardian period.

This research is significant for the fields of Feminist Criminology and Youth justice policy and practice. It provides a detailed analysis of the historical institutions established for females, which laid the foundations for the youth justice models that exist today. It is also significant in light of the Police, Crime, Sentencing Courts Act 2022, which has proposed to introduce secure schools as a 'new form of youth custody;' however, they are essentially a re-configuration of the institutions that had been tried and tested in the past. Linking the past to the present will inform the feminist theoretical criminology and policy for the future. As Garland postulates: 'The point is not to think historically about the past but rather to use that history to rethink the present' (Garland, 2001: 2). The past incarceration of females and the 'ideology' within the institutions surrounding the reform of 'criminal' and 'at risk' girls can inform the present about the traditional conceptions that were held and embedded in the very foundations of the penal and care institutions for girls.

2

Deviance, immorality and ideal femininity

The female reformatories and industrial schools were not conceived in a vacuum but shaped by the contemporary attitudes and discourses around gender, sexuality, delinquency and the ideals of femininity, that were themselves influenced by numerous ingrained contemporary ideologies in the Victorian period. In 1857 Carpenter wrote:

> Girls of the criminal class are far more degraded, dangerous to society, and difficult to control, than boys; this is well known to those whose experience has enabled them to compare the two sexes. The proofs and causes of this state of things cannot be here entered on; the fact is in part referable to the greater natural delicacy and susceptibility of the nature of girls, which renders them open to a deeper impress both of good and evil. They have also been more directly exposed to the evils of bad homes, and the affections, which are very strong in these girls, and therefore in close sympathy with vice.
>
> (Carpenter, 1857: 38)

The depiction presented encapsulates how criminal and 'at risk' girls were constructed in the reform 'ideology'. This ideology played an influential role in the construction of 'ascribed' and 'deviant' femininity and masculinity. This chapter will examine gender and the multiple feminizing discourses that operated around sexuality, domesticity and respectability at this time. I would argue that these representations of females in the nineteenth century, particularly the criminalization of working-class, delinquent girls, are significant for exploring how the ideologies and discourses were central in the gendering of deviance and the development of the carceral estate for juvenile girls in the nineteenth century.

In the nineteenth century, multiple discourses stemmed from the social, cultural and economic changes that were occurring during this period. The changing roles of females in Britain's newly industrialized economy, particularly the working-class females who had entered the many factories, mills and even mines as (low-paid) workers, were seen as threatening the traditional roles of women and the gendered social order (Zedner, 1991a; Gomersall, 1997; Cossins, 2015). Cossins maintains:

> Nineteenth-century society in England and Wales was highly morally regulated, with moral campaigns and their inherent moral standards constituting individual identities by encouraging women, in particular, to engage in self-regulation in relation to a variety of activities.
>
> (2015: 4)

In particular anxiety was expressed about the 'immorality' and prostitution in the urban industrial towns and cities, ironically the economic spaces which working-class females occupied, which were categorized as places of vice, depravity and sexual danger (Howell, 2009; Archer, 2011; Cossins, 2015). D'Cruze (1998) maintains that the 'Victorian preoccupation with the symbolic role of the prostitute in society as the personification of a disorderly female sexuality and the cultural counterbalance to the chaste middle-class wife' (D'Cruze, 1998: 3). Notions of the 'ideal woman', chastity, marriage, motherhood and domesticity became associated with 'respectability' and females' God-given place as the 'angel in the home', reinforcing the gendered order and patriarchal structure of society.

Feminist criminologists maintain that the constructions of 'deviant sexuality' and gender are central to understanding how they were used for the social control of females within society and the law (Newburn and Stanko, 1994; Rafter and Heidensohn, 1995; Walklate, 1995; Heidensohn, 1996). Heidensohn (1996) argues that male dominance is sustained mainly through the private sphere, marriage and the control of female sexuality and reproduction through the construction of gendered roles, in which, Foucault argues, gender has to be scrutinized as an apparatus with 'a dominant strategic function', that 'at a certain historical moment has the major functioning of responding to an urgency' (Foucault, 2001: 299). Victorian society is located as that period of urgency, when the discourse of gender was linked with the sexual apparatus. In *The History of Sexuality* (1980), Foucault argued that the 'sex lives of ordinary citizens became a matter of governmental concern'. In the nineteenth century, sexuality and the 'ideology' of deviant sexuality became a key element in the governance of the population, being incorporated into the fields of medicine, psychiatry and criminal justice (Foucault, 1980). Indeed, laws such as the Contagious Disease Acts 1864, Infant Preservation

Act 1872 and the Criminal Amendment Act 1885 are all examples of how the law regulated sexual and reproductive behaviour. Representations of the sexual, argues Mort (2000), are linked to the themes of ill health, immorality and environmentalism (Mort, 2000: 75). As well as statutes and excessive concern about sexuality and sexual precocity, simultaneously the ideals around the family began to take shape, and ideal femininity and respectability were actively promoted by the church, medical discourse and the state. Ideal masculinity and femininity became socialized and conditioned into expected roles (Wiener, 2004; Tosh, 2005). Thus, analysing gender, sexuality and the social constructions of femininity is important when mapping out the representations of deviant females to understand how the reform 'ideology' presented these discourses.

This chapter will first map out the gender constructions and the different representations in turn to examine the factors around why these discourses took place over the nineteenth century, linked to social and economic changes. Second, we will examine the Foucauldian arguments around the power of these discourses, particularly in shaping the reform of juvenile girls.

Gender – construction of femininity

The nineteenth century witnessed an explosion of discourses from multiple areas of the church, the state and the medical field. The unprecedented social, industrial and political transitions that occurred during the nineteenth century imposed a creed of Puritanism, evangelism and a moral crusade for the reform of vice in Victorian life. The working class become a target for reform, particularly the youth. Females represented social disintegration and chaos, as highlighted in the review of the literature. Females, namely deviant girls, caused alarm and apprehension. Sharpe maintains, 'When we place women's history into a long-time frame we can see the Victorian Epoch as a historical aberration – a time when incredibly powerful ideological forces laid a particular cast on gender roles and family forms' (Sharpe, 1998: 10).

This distinction between sex and gender, which Sharpe advises is important to explore, has allowed feminists to analyse how gender roles have been socially constructed. Barrett (1980) argues that gender is the representation of sex, the construction of sexed bodies into specific roles, norms and expectations. Gender and gender roles, then, are not predetermined by sex but have been culturally and historically produced through the construction of binary opposites: masculinity and femininity. Simone De Beauvoir's comment that 'one is not born a woman, but, rather, becomes one' (1973: 301) suggests that, under cultural compulsion, one becomes a woman, in which discourses and representations are integral in the development of these gendered codes of conduct. Joan Scott, in *Gender and the Politics of History*, also highlights the significance of gender in demarking the differences between men and women. Scott maintains that 'gender, as a culturally produced, historical category is one of the recurrent references by which political power has been conceived legitimized and criticised' (Scott, 1996: 173). Gender is an epistemological concept that is the hallmark of the feminist project (Newburn and Stanko, 1994; Rafter and Heidensohn, 1995; Walklate, 1995; Heidensohn, 1996). West and Zimmerman (1991) who use the phrase 'doing gender' advance understanding of gender embedded in everyday interaction. Butler (1990) maintains that gender is culturally constructed, which involves consolidation and normalization, that governs behaviours and bodies (1990: 8).

The nineteenth century was a pivotal period in which both gender and sexuality of females were being moulded into expected roles. The model of ideal femininity was located 'in the middle-class wife and mother whose asexual, morally uplifting influence was … a vital bulwark against the sordid intrusions of industrial life' (Zedner, 1991: 11). Stereotypical roles, which were embedded and normalized into our way of being, have been constantly reproduced and consolidated over the last two centuries. Williams points out that 'even in the twenty-first century, the experience of what it means to be a man or a woman can be heavily shaped by our nineteenth-century roots' (Williams, 2016: ix). Indeed, both masculinity and femininity underwent changes in the nineteenth century. According to Wiener (2004), a 'civilising' of masculinity also occurred. Within the literature, there has been a great deal of contribution regarding masculinity and crime (Messerschmidt, 1993; Newburn and Stanko, 1994; Connell, 1995, 2000, 2013). However, Cossins argues that 'a similar epistemological framework that interrogates femininities is needed to explain the diversity and the differences between women and their relationship to crime' (2015, 10).

Femininity, in this period, was being represented and idealized, argues Vicinus, in terms of 'delicacy and dreaminess, sexual passivity, and a charmingly labile and capricious emotionality' (Vicinus, 1972; quoted in Bardo, 1992: 16). Bardo argues that these notions were formalized and scientized in the work of male theorists from Acton and Kraft-Ebbing to Freud, who described 'normal' mature femininity in such terms. This 'normalising' and presentation of expected roles were being laid down. The feminine code of conduct was moulded into an ideal form, centred around the ideals of domesticity, dependency and delicacy. Bardo states that the construction of femininity involves concrete, exaggerated at times and even caricatured presentations of the feminine ruling mystique as opposed to the bodies of disordered women. Thus, the ideal female is also constructed and reinforced through the ideal and through her 'fallen' other. Gorham agrees that 'Victorian negative images of girlhood arose from two sources. In part they simply reinforced the image of a good girl through the portrayal of her opposite; positive images were presented for emulation and negative images they should avoid' (Gorham, 1982: 49). Thus, what we see is dual representations throughout the nineteenth century: the domestic angel in the home is promoted and what they should aspire to, while the deviant prostitute is the negative, within the public sphere and should be avoided. Thus, these representations not only created an ideal image but also cited where the ideal woman should be located within the private sphere. The gender code was constantly recreated and regulated the body and mind psychologically to accept that a female's place is within the home, as a wife and mother. Auerbach argues that the contradictory meanings of Victorian women – as old maid, fallen woman, and angel in the home, all rolled into one – capture the complicated effects of the era's attempt to control the representation of women's nature. She points out that, in fact, 'women's very aura of exclusion gave her imaginative centrality in a culture increasingly alienated from itself' (1982: 188). Paradoxically, this suggests that the ideological divide meant that women were both eroticized and condemned simultaneously.

These descriptions, in turn, became extended to the reform 'ideology' of juveniles. Young girls were presented as either innocent children who required protection, or sexually corrupt molls who needed reform. Shore argues that the Victorian preoccupation with morality ensured that girls' delinquency and sexuality were closely linked (Shore, 2002b). Girls' morality became 'policed' and girls who were deemed at 'risk' were incarcerated in industrial schools to prevent them from falling into vice and crime. Mahood posits that the 'incarceration of girls and adolescent women' indicates that sexual practices were the key marker of their 'delinquent' status' (Mahood, 1995: 102). Cale (1993) argues that 'sexual immorality, not criminal delinquency, was the failing most feared for working-class females, such girls were discussed more by those who sought to control prostitution than those who sought to control criminality' (1993: 15). The representation of working-class girls in the reform discourse was that they were 'at risk' and once fallen, would slip into prostitution. Social purity campaigners such as Ellice Hopkins highlighted the concerns about prostitution in society and the negative influence of children in close proximity to it during the campaigning for the passing of the Industrial Schools Amendment Act

(1880), which permitted the removal of children from homes which were frequented by prostitutes or associated with prostitution (Cale, 1993). Once fallen into prostitution, they were deemed as 'depraved' and 'irredeemable'. Thus, an analysis of the representations of prostitution, 'the fallen woman', is important to reveal how this played a significant part in the reform discourse.

Corrupting, sexually deviant females – the prostitute

Within the literature, there is a wealth of both primary and historiographical material highlighting the nineteenth-century obsession with prostitution, labelled by contemporaries as 'the Great Social Evil' (Mayhew, 1868; Acton, 1857; Walkowitz, 1980; Bartley, 2000; Rowbotham and Stevenson, 2005). The prostitute became associated with other social evils, such as illegitimacy, infanticide and venereal disease; a pollutant in society that needed to be removed (Joyce, 2008). The social anxiety and fear expressed by the social purity groups, articulated by the middle-classes, was that women engaging in 'immorality' failed to meet the social and gender ideals, thereby threatening the moral order and health of the nation.

The prostitute was represented as 'The Great Social Evil', so instantly this concept alludes to social sin threatening the existence of moral society. Historically, the corrupting influence of a woman, based on the biblical notion of a sinful woman, Eve, is presented through centuries of discourse. However, in the nineteenth century, pamphlets presented the prostitute as utterly 'immoral'. Caricatured images of evil-looking prostitutes appeared in Penny Dreadful papers and illustrated in Police News reports. Women who were associated with or known to run a house of disrepute, a brothel, were considered devoid of any morality. Wiener argues that this represented a perpetual battle between good and evil, order and anarchy (Wiener, 1990: 21). The totality of a woman's reputation is encapsulated within her sexual reputation. Descriptions of crimes frequently referred to the female offender's past sexual conduct, marital status and ability as a wife and mother (Zedner, 1991b: 321). Deviant sexuality subsumed her whole character, unlike men, which the following passage illustrates:

> The man's nature may be said to be hardened, the women's destroyed. Women of this stamp are generally bold and blushing in crime, so indifferent to right and wrong, so lost to all sense of shame, so destitute of the instincts of womanhood that they may be more compared to wild beasts than to women.
>
> (Owen, 1866; quoted in Zedner, 1991b: 321)

In society, the representation of the prostitute was the public symbol of female vice, in stark contrast to the feminine woman. Medical discourses presented sexually corrupt females as a source of disease and infection, posing a threat to the future of the empire. The spread of contamination, venereal disease and the reproduction of a criminal class were represented as a female problem, thus reflecting the double standard regarding prostitution, whereby men were not associated with disease, nor criminalized for seeking out prostitutes. Lord Ashley, a Tory government member in the nineteenth century, wrote, 'in the male the moral effects of the system are very sad, but in the female, they are infinitely worse … It is bad enough if you corrupt the man, but if you corrupt the woman, you poison the waters of life at the very fountain' (Ashley cited in Weeks, 2012: 72). This representation of the poisoning of life, which was reflected in the public health discourses, led to the establishment of lock hospitals and the Contagious Disease Act of 1864. The Contagious Disease Act (1864) required that 'common prostitutes' should be identified, registered, subjected to fortnightly examinations and if found to be infected with venereal disease, placed in the lock hospital for nine months, highlighting the double standard of the Victorian era. Weeks maintains 'stigmatised poor women as the source of infection – left male clients off the hook' (2012: 28).

The introduction of the Contagious Disease Act (1864) in port and garrison towns led to the distortion of the number of prostitutes in these locations, heightening the surveillance of working-class females. Walkowitz (1980) maintains that the regulation of sexuality was a central target of state policy and law enforcement. The state involvement in prostitution and the Contagious Disease Act was motivated by the potential harm caused to men by sexually transmitted diseases. Walkowitz argues that before the Contagious Disease Act was passed, working-class women could pass in and out of prostitution as their economic circumstances demanded, whilst remaining accepted as part of their working-class communities (Walkowitz, quoted in Arnot 2001: 4). Lee (2013), in *Policing Prostitution*, argues that, alongside the increasing authority of the medical profession, the image of the prostitute as an 'agent of decay and contagion' became widely disseminated, in which the association with venereal disease infused the debates around contagion (2013: 3). Lee argues that the image of the prostitute as a source of infection alongside the civic project to clean up the streets in the second half of the nineteenth century meant there was a web of surveillance and policing of females who were suspected of engaging in prostitution. Working-class girls who were on the streets going about their work, or travelling to and from their jobs, would be suspected of being streetwalkers.

Lee maintains that it is important to bear in mind that the Contagious Disease Act was about controlling working-class women, as 'measures brought to bear upon marginally poor whose way of life and public behaviour deviated from prescribed standards and norms' (2013: 12).

The representations of the prostitute were a symbol of the degraded and threatening the social order with it spread over respectable society (Walkowitz, 1980: 2–4). According to William Tait, by 1840 prostitution had spread its influence over Victorian society, and there was 'no bound to its extent' (Tait, quoted in Joyce, 2008: 11). Patrick Colquhoun, magistrate and founder of the first preventative police force, estimated that 50,000 prostitutes resided in London alone (Cited in Sturma, 1978: 6). However, Sturma argues that one must be wary of taking these numbers at face value. He argues the identification of prostitutes was shaped by the moral attitudes of the ruling class, which were very different from those of the lower orders. Thus, a woman living with a man outside marriage was regarded as a 'prostitute' (Sturma, 1978: 6). Sturma maintains it is worth noting the definition of prostitution given by contemporaries Henry Mayhew and Bracebridge Hemyng:

> Prostitution … may be done either from mercenary or voluptuous motives; be the cause however, what it may be, the act remains the same … prostitution, then does not consist solely in promiscuous intercourse, for she who confines her favours to one may still be a prostitute.
>
> (Mayhew and Hemyng, 1862; cited in Sturma, 1978: 6)

Sturma maintains 'in short, the woman labelled a "prostitute" might be guilty of no more than cohabitation' (1978: 6). Cohabitation practices were common in working-class communities in the nineteenth century and were becoming represented as 'immoral' (Frost, 2008). Within the Manchester admission records, we see mothers cohabiting labelled as 'prostitutes', or 'immoral', as in the case of Emma Avery, who was described as 'cohabiting with a Mr Hatherton'. Her daughter Jane Avery was admitted in 1888 for not attending school and wandering the streets (Manchester Sale Admissions, M369/4/18/2: 374, MRO). Mothers who allowed their daughters to wander the streets were regarded as neglectful and children could be admitted into an industrial school under section 14 of the Industrial School Amendment Act if found wandering, loitering, or not attending school (Gear, 1999).

However, deprivation and poverty drove those females onto the streets to try to earn money by singing, selling flowers and running errands, to help boost the family income. Chinn (2006) maintains that women and girls of the urban poor were living in poverty and hunger. Moreover, the need to provide for their family led them to work outside the home, so any job, no matter how low, or how low the wages, was preferable to none. The middle-class gaze failed to acknowledge the connection with poverty and prostitution, but tended to represent them as failing to follow the 'ideal' virtues of femininity. Paradoxically, the high standards that the feminine code prescribes mean that these ideal codes are always going to be broken, due to the ridiculously high expectations of the behaviour of an ideal lady, particularly with regard to the working class. Cossins (2015) maintains that 'paradoxically, working-class women's battle with poverty saw the criminalisation of prostitution, soliciting, vagrancy and homelessness' (2015: 66). Chinn argues that contemporary middle-class commentators such as Henry Mayhew in *London Labour and the London Poor* (1868) represented the working class as 'immoral', 'dirty' and 'diseased'. Chinn maintains:

> The standardised image of a slum woman was a person whose appearance and habits were commensurate with the miserable, squalid districts in which she lived. She was regarded as a foul-mouthed slut, over-fond of drink, careless as to her appearance.
>
> (Chinn, 2006: 16)

Chinn argues that it is important to recognize how the urban poor were stigmatized and blamed almost for their position. As Cox puts it, 'questions of poverty, and propriety, of class and conduct, were closely linked' (Cox, 2013: 4). Therefore, without a doubt, poverty was the strongest link with prostitution. Ellen Reese, during her trial, stated that 'she did not become a regular prostitute till shoplifting failed – was miserable both ways, but going on the streets was more profitable' (Tobias, 1972, 62). This encapsulates, at first hand, the lack of options and resources available to these girls. Structural and economic barriers left girls with limited options to earn a living. Attention was turned instead to controlling young girls in the public sphere, in factories, mills and mines, limiting their options further.

Although significant research by Walkowitz, Finnegan and Lee on the impact of the Contagious Disease Act on women in Victorian cities, the implications for juvenile girls have not yet been fully explored. The exaggerated representation of prostitution in society led to a moral panic, thereby igniting a moral crusade to protect girls from becoming prostitutes by any means (Cossins, 2015). The protection of girls from sexual 'immorality', particularly the threat of child prostitution, became a focus of philanthropists and reformers. Child or juvenile prostitution, which is a contested term, became a representation that was associated with the nineteenth century and the paternalistic 'ideology'.

Child prostitution – paternalism and the infantile image

This term 'child prostitution' is controversial, and within contemporary discourse the term 'child prostitution' would be referred to as child abuse. However, the legal age of consent up until 1885 was thirteen years. Jackson (2000) states that this term, 'child prostitution', is another euphemism – along with 'moral outrage' and 'corruption and immorality' – for what we now describe as 'child sexual abuse'. Jackson maintains that although it is usually acknowledged that sexual abuse was both discovered and constructed in the 1970s, however what was happening to these girls was child abuse by fathers, neighbours, employers or strangers. Jackson argues that framing this abuse as 'child prostitution' did not open the emotional and moral can of worms that a narrative of incest, or rape would have involved (Jackson, 2000: 16).

The number of girls who were involved in 'juvenile prostitution' is obviously difficult to ascertain. However, Ian Sparks (Chief Executive of the Children's Society) claims that, in 1848, almost 2,700 girls in London, aged eleven to sixteen years, were hospitalized due to venereal disease (Guardian, 24 May 2000). This may represent only the tip of the iceberg, as we are only aware of the girls who both contracted and sought treatment for venereal disease, so the true figure for those affected by venereal disease may be far higher. The moral purity represented these girls as the innocent, passive victims of the evil men, or older female prostitutes who were contaminating them. Cox (2013), who examines gender, sexuality and Victorian childhood, highlights a Pall Mall Gazette article, in which a girl aged between thirteen and fourteen was purchased to be used for sex. Cox argues that the moral panic about the extent of prostitution and the supposed 'white slave trade' of girls abroad spurred the child-saving movement of the nineteenth century. This concept of 'moral panic' was defined by Stanley Cohen as follows:

> [A] condition, episode, person or group of persons emerge to become defined as a threat to societal values and interests; its nature is presented in a stylised and stereotypical fashion by the mass media; the moral barricades are manned editors, bishops and other right-thinking people; socially accredited experts pronounce their diagnoses and solutions [and] ways of coping are evolved or (more often) resorted to.
>
> (Cohen, 2011: 9)

The exact number of young girls working on the streets and in brothels is difficult to ascertain in this period. Finnegan, in *Poverty and Prostitution: A Study of*

Victorian Prostitutes, cites a *Report on Female Prostitution* (1857), in which it was estimated that in '1857 there was at least 200 regular prostitutes under 12 years of age on the streets of the port' (1979: 81).

In particular, brothels were numerous in port cities, due to the constant influx of soldiers, merchant traders and travellers. Archer argues that most seaports, like Liverpool, had a large sex industry, with brothels being active and tolerated. However, Archer argues that enticing of young girls was frowned upon. He cites a newspaper report entitled 'ENTICING YOUNG GIRLS' (*Liverpool Mercury*, 8 November 1869) as follows:

> A mother and daughter Catherine and Selina Smith who owned a brothel, were charged with enticing four girls newly arrived from Dublin looking for lodgings. The mother fed the girls, and told them to go out and look for men. If they winked at by one these men they were to bring them back to the house.
>
> (Archer, 2011: 208)

Archer argues that the attitude of Detective Superintendent Kehoe towards magistrate Mr Mansfield was striking: 'It was not intended to prosecute the keepers of all the houses of ill fame in the town, and it was necessary that in some places they should be tolerated' (Archer, 2011: 208). In this case, it was the age of the girls that warranted attention and punishment. Moreover, it was the enticement of working-class Irish girls that was also significant in this case. Although gender was important, we should bear in mind the fact that females were not a homogenous group. D'Cruze points out that it was clear that criminal justice was 'raced and classed as well as gendered' (2009: 11). In particular, Irish working-class girls, who were perceived as wayward, or at risk of sexual deviance, were seen as a threat to the civilizing project. A large number of young, unaccompanied Irish girls entered Liverpool and other port cities, particularly during the Great Famine, seeking employment (Swift, 1997). Father Nugent, Catholic Chaplin at Liverpool Borough Gaol, commented that Catholic women in 1865 accounted for 62 per cent of all female prisoners, 'with a considerable proportion committed for prostitution' (Cited in Neal, 1991: 178). Nugent was of the opinion that few girls went to Liverpool to take up prostitution, but the opportunities for labour and employment in the second half of the nineteenth century led females into prostitution. The implications of port locations, such as Bristol for young juvenile girls, are also important to explore. Locations such as Manchester, Salford and Lancashire were mill towns and could offer employment opportunities in the factories, but in port locations such as Liverpool and Bristol, in the mid-nineteenth century, it was claimed that there were as many as 30,000 sailors in the port at any one time. Father Nugent claimed that the demand for prostitutes meant that the girls could easily make £2–3 a week, compared to the 10s they could make from sewing (Neal, 1991: 186). Carpenter refers in her diaries to coming from Bristol to Liverpool to collect girls to be admitted into Red Lodge Reformatory (Red Lodge Journal, 12693/1: BRO).

Thus, it is important to bear in mind the representations of race, as well as class and gender in this period. Neal argues around the height of concern of Irish migration in the 1870s, around 23,826 boys and girls were admitted to reformatory schools during the period 1875–9, 25 per cent of whom were Catholic. Over the same period, 39,826 were admitted to Industrial schools 26 per cent of whom were Catholic (Report of the Department Committee on Reformatory and Industrial Schools, 1896, cited in Neal, 1991: 183). Thus, port environments in particular were deemed 'immoral' places for young working-class girls, particularly Irish girls, who were, like the situation described above, arriving in port cities, unsupervised, looking for work and were being enticed into prostitution. The fear of girls being enticed into prostitution heightened concerns around protecting girls from 'immorality' and 'waywardness'.

The moral concerns of Juvenile prostitution had gradually increased over the second half of the nineteenth century. The social purity movement of the 1880s, inspired and led by Ellice Hopkins, brought the 'sacrifice of the girl child' into sharp focus (Cale, 1993: 47). In 1881, a select committee, set up to investigate the issue, reported that child prostitution was widespread. One police officer informed the committee that, in London, children above the age of thirteen could be procured 'without any difficulty whatsoever' (Guardian, 24 May 2000). The protection of girls from 'sexual immorality', particularly the threat of falling into child prostitution, became a focus of the philanthropists and reformers. The investigation and moral reformers set in motion a campaign to increase the age of consent from thirteen to sixteen years. The Parliamentary Select Committee in 1882 indicated juvenile prostitution from an incredibly early age was increasing to an appalling extent in England, and especially in London (1882: 4). Also, the Parliamentary Report of the Contagious Disease Act 1882 highlighted the public order of the streets and young females being exposed to prostitution:

> As juvenile prostitution is the principal source by which the supply of fallen women is kept up, it is evident that the Acts, in diminishing the number of youthful prostitutes, are operating effectually to diminish the number of adult women abandoned to an evil life.
>
> (1882, Parliamentary Report of the Contagious Disease Act)

These fears were also heightened by the campaign launched by Newspaper editor William Stead, when he exposed the problem of 'child prostitution' in the article entitled 'The Maiden Tribute of Modern Babylon' in the *Pall Mall Gazette*. Stead, launched an investigative campaign to uncover the extent of child prostitution by visiting brothels and actually procured a 'child prostitute'. He claimed that countless girls were being sacrificed to the insatiable 'London Minotaur'. Stead was prosecuted and imprisoned for his purchase of thirteen-year-old Eliza Armstrong. Nevertheless, the publication caused outrage and Stead's practical journalistic study both exposed the horrors of juvenile prostitution and contributed to the enactment of Criminal Amendment Act 1885 (Gorham, 1978). The Criminal Amendment Act 1885 was designed to make provision for the protection of girls, raising the age of sexual consent from thirteen to sixteen years and for the suppression of brothels. Although the age of consent was changed and the vulnerability of girls exposed, the structural barriers in society to employment and the feminization of girls, which overwhelmingly led them into poverty and so, in turn criminality, were neither addressed, nor regarded as contributory factors leading girls into prostitution. Gorham maintains that seeing these girls as victims suited the 'ideology' of that time:

> [H]ad they allowed themselves to see that many young girls engaged in prostitution not as passive, sexually innocent victims but that because their choices were so limited, the reformers would have been forced to recognise that the causes of juvenile prostitution were to be found in an exploitative economic structure.
>
> (Gorham, 1978: 355)

Gorham maintains that, instead, philanthropists chose to focus on the 'moral uplift' of the girls and saw these females as innocent as well as in need of protection and reform. According to Carpenter, to instil good virtues in the girls and to 'rouse a consciousness in them' (Carpenter, 1853), the philanthropists sought to protect them and guide them like children, even if that meant incarcerating them in order to 'save' them. Barton (2005) argues that deviant females were perceived as irresponsible, childlike and in need of protection: 'The perceived infantile nature of women, along with their own incapacity for self-governance, made them appropriate beings for the reformatory supervision' (2005: 4). This paternalistic approach that dominated the reformatory discourse remains embedded in contemporary society. Chesney-Lind and Sheldon maintain that within current paternalistic 'ideology' juvenile institutions – the police, courts and institutions of correction – exercise the repeated need to protect girls (Chesney-Lind and Sheldon, 2014: 237). Gelsthorpe and Worrall (2009) agree that the historical continuity surrounding expectations of 'lady-like' behaviour and feminine conduct – fears around 'sexual promiscuity' resulting in unwarranted repressive tendencies in the name of 'protecting' girls – leads to the criminalization of girls' behaviour.

Thus, today as in 1850, the categorization of girls as both a 'threat' and a 'victim', 'virtuous' and 'vicious', is evident in the penal and welfare reform (Carlen, 1983; Goodfellow, 2019). This dichotomy serves as a means of regulating females' bodies and sexuality, but also acts as a means of social control. Feminist theorist Lerner (1986) maintains that, in both the past and present, the majority of female delinquency is placed within a context related to girls' sexual behaviour. Lerner argues that these gendered constructions are critical for understanding how girls' crime and deviance were constructed as a moral problem and how the constructions of deviant sexuality relate to women's oppression and control (Lerner, 1986; Mackinnon, 1987, 2005). This paternalistic 'ideology' that deems females as 'child-like' and in need of being saved, has been constructed in the child-saving 'ideology' and is embedded in the response, to justify the control and regulation of delinquent females to conform to the ideals of femininity, the 'angel in the home', which I now explore.

The Angel in the Home

The polar opposite representation of the prostitute was the 'angel in the home', a phrase drawn from Coventry Patmore's famous poem. 'Angel in the House' became a phrase that encapsulated ideal womanhood; the perfect woman, who cared for her children and husband and lived a moral, domesticated life. According to Hall, the dichotomy between the public and the private was reworked in the transitional period of the late eighteenth and early twentieth centuries: 'Men placed firmly in the newly defined public world of business, commerce, and politics; women were placed in the private world of the home and family' (Hall, 1990: 52). Indeed, the family, and particularly women, become a metaphor for societal issues. The regulation of moral behaviour was part of a wider formation of class identity, nation and empire, in which females played a central role in the formation of public morality/purity at home. Weeks (2012) argues that this moral crusade against society was a conscious 'ideology': 'the product both of a political crisis and the fear of social disintegration for which the breakdown of female and sexual order became a striking metaphor' (Weeks,

2012: 31–2). Weeks maintains that the 'ideology' of the family was motivated by the state and the ruling dominant class' desire to preserve their position in society. Due to the moralizing of society, especially working-class communities, urban locations became sites of regulation to seek to promote working-class respectability. D'Cruze agrees that the Poor Law Amendment Act 1834, particularly through its direct attack on the working class, forced the political radicals to go on the defensive and led them to formulate a political rhetoric, based around the moral status of respectable working-class domesticity and social roles of male breadwinner and female household manager. D'Cruze argues that both 'working-class masculinities as well as femininities were refracted through the prism of domesticity' (D'Cruze, 1998: 17). Indeed, the reformatory and industrial schools became sites where working-class boys and girls were socialized and disciplined along gendered lines at an early age, in the hope that they would mould them into respectable individuals, useful to society – an ideal that was presented to all as attainable through self-regulation, moral work and living.

Respectability

Respectability was a central 'ideology', an ideal to which all should aspire. It was presented as an ideal, attainable by all through self-regulation and moral living. However, Skeggs argues that 'respectability was a central mechanism through which the concept of class emerged' (Skeggs, 1997: 3). Conley (1991) in *The Unwritten Law* argues that respectability was a fundamental concept in the late nineteenth century. Conley maintains that respectability was a 'social category posing as a moral category' – meaning that the middle classes were born respectable while the poor had to earn it (Conley, 1991: 4). For the working classes, to be respectable, the criteria included a male breadwinner with a wife who kept up the housework and cared for the children well (Griffin, 2020). For men, they derived their 'masculine respectability' from the workplace, as head of a family and from their public identity (D'Cruze, 1999: 40). Women, on the other hand, became associated with the private sphere 'as domestic beings, "naturally" suited to the duties in the home and with children' (Nead, 1988: 29). However, there were class differences in the cultural expectations of the family unit. Begiato (2020) maintains that a respectable, working-class Victorian home would have the mother at its heart, but expectations of respectable domesticity differed from middle-class ideals. For a family to be thought respectable and 'happy', the husband and father should be hard-working, affectionate and non-violent towards his wife and children (2020: 21).

Moreover, the practical reality of working-class lives was that wives, as well as daughters, worked outside the home to ensure the family's financial survival. Bailey (2012) argues that the expected standards of respectable behaviour were well-established in lower-class culture. They had their own recognized conventions and knew how society expected them to behave in order to be considered respectable (2010: 15–16). Mahood and Littlewood (1994) maintain that this was considered by working-class parents to be a proper initiative as, when a daughter sang outside a bar, or sold flowers, this was seen as leading to 'immorality' and prostitution by the middle-classes. Working in the public sphere, as a street seller, factory worker, or miner, was accepted within working-class culture as contributing to the household. However, over the nineteenth century, females within the public sphere were perceived to have contributed to their downfall. This reflected the different interests in society; moral philanthropy and religion on the one hand and the needs of capitalism on the other.

Alexander argues that: 'The working woman emerged as a "social problem" in the 30s and 40s. Indeed, it is as though the Victorians discovered her so swiftly and urgently did she become the object of public concern' (Alexander, 1983: 60). Parliamentary commissions investigated working conditions in the factories and mines. There were concerns about the sexuality of the working class, particularly girls. The Sadler Commission (1832) and the Children's Employment Commission (1842) exposed the degrading and 'immoral' working conditions for females in traditional trades and pictures emerged of them half-dressed, to expose 'the condition of England'. The 1832 Commission claimed that: 'It would be no strain on his conscience to say that three quarters of the girls between fourteen and twenty years of age are unchaste' (Weeks, 2012: 72). The Commissions, which reflected the male gaze, focused on sexual depravity. Mort argues that it was the perception of female depravity which filled page after page of the sub-commissioner's book. Questions about the women's physical suffering, or specific division of labour (issues central to the concerns regarding the male workforce) were subordinated to this obsession (Mort, 2000: 107). Public Louche locations, bars, pubs and dancehalls were places associated with corruption. Thus, the representations of the 'Angel in the House' reinforced the ideal that the private sphere was the place for 'respectable females'. This ensured the regulation and social control of women within the confines of the home and domestic life. Thus, an examination of the implications for class as well as gender highlight how these dominant codes of conduct around respectability were an 'insidious form of moral regulation' of working-class lives (Cossins, 2015: 64). The middle-class ideals of 'respectability', the male in the public sphere and the female within the home, had become more prominently defined by the end of the nineteenth century (Weeks, 2012). The 'middle-class' family was seen as the 'respectable' model, considered vital for the moral order of society.

Wohl (2016) maintains that, if there was one image which evoked the essential fabric of Victorian society, it would be the family. He points to the quote by Lords Shaftsbury, a Tory member of government in the nineteenth century, stressing the vital importance of the family unit to society:

> There can be no security to society, no honour, no prosperity, no dignity at home, no nobleness of attitude towards foreign nations, unless the strength of the people rests upon purity and firmness of the domestic system. Schools are but auxiliaries. At home the principles of subordination are first implanted and the man is trained to be a good citizen.
>
> (Wohl, 2016: 9)

Thus, the representations of respectability served to socialize and normalize females' role regarding their domestic and childcare responsibilities. The ideals of respectability not only reaffirmed the gender roles of femininity and masculinity, but also sought to place females in subordinate positions within the family and in society. The revisionist literature (Rush, 1992; Weeks, 2012; Case and Smith, 2020) has highlighted that many of the changes made towards juveniles were in response to economic changes, so it is important to understand why these representations in this particular period became so critical.

Patriarchy, capitalism and empire building

In the nineteenth century, the health of the Empire became dependent on the health of the nation. Bates argues that 'the process of empire-building, over the course of the nineteenth century the state increasingly emphasised the value of social order and the importance of children to the nation's future' (2016: 10). The representations of 'dangerous', incorrigible juvenile offenders and the reproduction of a 'criminal class' became an 'emblem for social breakdown and domestic instability' (Shore 2002a: 1). The middle-class home became idealized as the symbol and heart of civilized society (Tosh, 1999). The home became a seat of patriarchal dominance for men, as well as women, who were judged on their ability to maintain an efficient, respectable household. The representations of ideal femininity, respectability and 'angel in the home' acted to control and regulate females in society within a patriarchal unit (Tosh, 2005). Women's labour and sexuality were institutionalized within the nuclear family. Walby (1990) argues that the gendered 'ideology' of the home, family and private sphere coincided with the patriarchal and capitalist changes occurring in nineteenth-century society.

The transition from feudalism to capitalism led to the creation of separate public and private spheres. Fredrick Engels (2004), in *The Origin of the Family, Private Property and the State*, argues that the subordination of women is a result, not of her biological disposition, but her social relations. Engels argues that the widespread fixation with sexual morality and chastity aimed to ensure that inheritances were passed only to legitimate offspring. Marxist feminists argue that the patriarchal 'ideology' is rooted in capitalism and economic structures. The advent of capitalism brought about male-dominated public spheres and the private sphere was designated as relevant to female workers' domestic work. Morton (1971) maintains that gender oppression is linked to the capitalist system where women are assigned to the domestic sphere, where the labour (cooking, cleaning, child-rearing) is reproductive, unrecognized and unpaid, whereas men's work is productive and has monetary value in the form of a paid wage.

Girls within the reformatories and industrial schools were regulated and disciplined in domesticity engaging in laundry, cleaning and cooking and sent to complete their licence period as domestic servants, which was seen as ideal preparation for their future roles as wives in their own homes. According to Weeks, in the 1851 census, there were 847,000 domestic servants but by 1881, 1.3 million (Weeks, 2012: 80). Despite the problems related to census data collection in the nineteenth century, domestic service constituted the largest single category of employment for women until well into the twentieth century (Higgs, 1983; Steinbach, 2011). Undoubtedly, females' domestic role as part of the labour force was crucial to an industrializing nation. Domestic service within the home for reformatory girls completed the reform into feminine subjects, productive for society. Weeks argues that regulating the family was a necessary instrument for capitalism. It regulated the workforce and the health of the nation. The 'ideology' of separate spheres and the domestic 'ideology' were instrumental in constraining women in the private sphere (Weeks, 2016).

However, Mort argues that male professionals who adhered to the separate sphere' 'ideology' saw the importance of an alliance with female philanthropists as critical to politics at a local level (Mort, 2000: 122). Females were complicit in this 'ideology', which would suggest that class dominance was of central importance. Mort argues that male experts had female allies who cemented the programme of social disciplining (Mort, 2000: 114). Alexander states how Elizabeth Fry, Mary Carpenter and Octavia Hill, all advocated industrial training in the form of housework for their fallen sisters. Mrs Austin, an ardent advocate of industrial education, wrote in 1850: 'our object is to improve the servants of the rich and the wives of the poor' (Alexander, 1987: 61). Purvis agrees that upper class women were assigned roles as the moral arbiters of the domestic sphere (Purvis, 1989: 53).

Philanthropists such as Carpenter and Fry legitimized their place within the public sphere, in reformatories through adopting positive, motherly, charitable positions. The need to save working-class girls and their philanthropic causes gave them prominence and secured their position in the public sphere: 'While the philanthropic work contributed to the widening of middle-class women's sphere of influence, it was often directly opposed to the interests of the women in the class below them' (Mort, 2000: 21). Prochaska in *Women and Philanthropy in Nineteenth Century England* (1980) argues that middle class bourgeois freedom depended on a responsible servant class. The need to be free from domestic chores meant that philanthropists needed a servant class. Thus, the 'ideology' was for women to be in the home but for working-class females, it was to be servants in other people's homes. Thus, the reformatory and industrial schools sought to provide trained domestic servants as a servant class for the ruling classes. Thus, the role and power of philanthropists, including upper class females' access to a position in the public sphere, would suggest that explanations of capitalism and patriarchy are too sweeping (Rowbotham, 2015).

Moreover, the philanthropic reformers and institutions also became involved in youth emigration, whereby working-class children and youths were also removed from their harmful environments and relocated in the new world. Between the 1860s and 1920s, philanthropic institutions across Britain sent approximately 90,000 orphaned, criminal, and 'friendless' British children to Canada to start a new life in the settler empire (Boucher, 2014; Lamont et al., 2020).

Whether the forces of capitalism and empire building were responsible for the 'ideology' of the family or the influence of philanthropy and religion, what is clear is that contradictory and multiple representations were at play during the nineteenth century. Mort argues that the nineteenth century was a pivotal period, in which moral environmentalism together with the social and political transformation of morality and sexual behaviour, as well as the position of women, were central to the expansion of industrial capitalism (Mort, 2000: 122). He argues that discourses, such as the formation of a masculine professional expertise, like that of Edwin Chadwick, were part of the expanding state. The discourse on gender, domesticity and sexual regulation through to the medical discourse on disease and contagion were bio-powers and bio-politics, which Foucault argues were crucial to how power operated in society. Foucault argues that 'power' and 'knowledge' were implicitly related and indeed mutually constitutive (D'Cruze and Jackson, 2009: 9). Foucault (1979) argues that 'discourse' and 'knowledge' were integral in regulating sexuality. Barton agrees that these 'dangerous sexualities' were controlled through the mobilization of discourses which served to label and categorize women as 'immoral', thus bestowing on them an 'outcast' status (2005: 15). Discourses around the ideal feminine role, the values of motherhood, domesticity and the denigration of prostitution, which constructed females as in need of regulation, became codified in the formal state laws. In utilizing Foucauldian theory, one can see how power was produced/exercised and made legitimate, at particular historical moments. A brief examination of the arguments of Foucault allows us to critically engage with how these multiple representations and discourses contributed to the establishment of juvenile institutions.

Foucault and the representations of females in the nineteenth-century discourses

Foucault, in the *History of Sexuality*, identified sexuality as one of the defining bio-political technologies of the nineteenth and twentieth centuries. Foucault emphasizes how sexuality emerged as a discourse in Western bio-politics (Repo, 2014: 6). According to Foucault, power operates around two main ends; first, through the construction of particular knowledge, which is bio-power, in which an efficient government manages and regulates like a social body; and second, through 'disciplinary power', which manipulates and trains the 'body' through institutions, such as hospital, prisons, schools and factories. Within the institutions, perpetual surveillance through the panoptical structure is internalized and individuals then discipline themselves. In applying Foucault's principles of power and discourse, one can assess historical events and periods critically and begin to understand how events unfolded. For instance, how it was possible for the state to remove children into juvenile institutions and how this come to be accepted by the public. Foucault's genealogies demonstrate that this occurred as a result of discourses and bio-powers. The reform discourse in the early nineteenth century investigated the 'problems' and solutions related to how best to deal with delinquent youth. The 'problematization' of a subject and discourse on its solutions became normalized and unchallenged. Foucault maintains:

> Problematization doesn't mean the representation of a pre-existent object, nor the creation through discourse of an object that doesn't exist. It is a set of discursive and non-discursive practices that makes something enter into the play of the true and false, and constitutes it as an object for thought (whether under the form of moral reflection, scientific knowledge, political analysis).
>
> (Foucault, 1989, quoted in Besley, 2006: 10)

In the first half of the nineteenth century, the problematization of youth produced 'saviours' and competing discourses from the religious, health and philanthropic arenas. Philanthropists, such as Carpenter, became 'experts' and asked to present before a Parliamentary Committee on delinquent children. Hence, Foucault argued that the discovery of problematic populations, and the discursive construction of problems, became central to the art of the European government. The philanthropists who wished to set up these institutions framed their practices as 'benevolent' and 'child-saving'. Cox maintains that 'locking up children of the poor thus became a humanitarian gesture, an emblem of a civilised society. Which in fact masked incarceration of a child by the state' (Cox, 2013: 87). The establishment of Reformatory and Industrial schools in 1854 was a means of forging these young people into 'docile bodies' and useful citizens to the nation. Training the youth to enter industrial, or domestic service, meant that they would become integrated and useful in society and not fall into criminality or vice. These institutions introduced a continuous routine in a panoptical space, which meant that the bodies would monitor and regulate themselves:

> The disciplinary apparatus of the institution takes as its target all aspects of the individual inmate: physical exercise and labour; general conduct; moral and mental attitude. It provides, in other words *a total education.*
>
> (Foucault, 1977: 236)

The construction of childhood, akin to that of insanity, saw the establishment of juvenile institutions and asylums. Foucault argues that the environment of both was protective and paternal, with enforced sexlessness, restriction of movement and constant subjection to authority (Foucault, 1967: 253–5).

Thus, the female reformatories became a disciplinary site for regulating females through public/private and domestic 'ideology'. Foucault argues how the eighteenth and nineteenth century public discourses' emphasis on heterosexual monogamy and the scrutiny of 'unnatural' forms of behaviour (masturbation, homosexuality, perversity) led to the 'policing' and regulation of sex. 'Repression has indeed been the fundamental link between power, knowledge and sexuality' (Foucault, 1979: 5). Sexuality becomes a key element in the governance of the population and is incorporated into the fields of medicine, psychiatry and criminal justice. Indeed, during the nineteenth century, we see an upsurge in the number of reports on the health of the nation. Notable examples include Edwin Chadwick's sanitation and public health, and the Malthusian consequences of over-population. Poovey, *In Making a Social Body*, analysed this period and maintains that: 'The "diseased" (unproductive, criminal, plague-ridden) members, the poor were considered inimical to the health of the body politic' (1995: 7). Poovey argues that, as a result of the discourses and regulation, the British social domain had been reconceptualised by 1860 into 'similar, self-regulating individuals' (1995: 22). Medical knowledge, as a bio-power, provided a new mechanism for power regarding the management of 'life'.

Constructions of gender and space became regulated, resulting in stereotypical forms of masculine and feminine identity being produced and re-produced. Foucault suggests that individuals' behaviour is controlled through standards of normality. The social control of women normalizes the view that their place is within the domestic sphere. These technologies of discipline along gendered lines were a regulatory power over females. According to Butler, gender identity then is 'a set of repeated acts within a highly rigid regulatory frame that congeal over time to produce the appearance of substance, of a natural sort of being' (Butler, 1990: 33).

However, Feminist critiques have been cited against Foucault's theory. Primarily, he is accused of androcentrism and of failing to be specific about the sexual differences between male and female bodies, or between masculine or feminine disciplinary practises. Additionally, Fraser argues that Foucault's reduction to 'docile bodies' leaves no room for resistance. Moreover, Mort argues that, although Foucault points usefully to the productive nature of regulation, he leaves unanswered the class articulations at play (2000: 104). Nevertheless, despite the many critiques to which Foucault has been subjected, McLaren argues that his work provides important theoretical recourses for feminism (McLaren, 2002: 17). Diamond and Quinby agree, and identify the convergence between feminism and Foucault, arguing that both identify the body as a site of power and both emphasize discourse (1988: 1). Repo (2016), in *The Biopolitics of Gender*, argues that by utilizing the Foucauldian approach, it is possible to identify how 'Sexuality made it possible to control forms of behaviour in order to make use of it socially, economically and politically' (Repo, 2016: 13). Butler argues that Foucault's work provides feminists with the means to think beyond identity politics. To understand how females are conditioned and socialized, according to their sex, into gender-defined roles.

Indeed, examination of Foucauldian arguments highlights the need to be sceptical and interrogates bio-powers and knowledge-producing agents, although questions still remain regarding why men become those wielding power. Bartky maintains that the female, since childhood, knows that she is 'subject to the evaluating eye of the male connoisseur' (Bartky, 1990: 28). This idea that there is a panoptical patriarchal society, in which women are under surveillance and regulate themselves, is an interesting way for feminists to apply power and social control over females in society. The constructions of the nineteenth century have become embedded in society, which continue to present the 'ideology' of ideal femininity closely related to sexuality. Analysis of the historical representations is significant for understanding the criminalization of girls in the past and in the present.

Conclusion

Representations and discourses were important in the extension of bio-powers that justified the incarceration of problematic, deviant individuals in prisons and reformatories in order to regulate and discipline their behaviour. The multiple representations examined in this chapter, the prostitute at one extreme and the 'angel in the home' at the other, were depicted as polar opposites. The rhetoric and representation of the prostitute come to reflect permissiveness, uncontrollable sexuality and breeding, which were framed within the medical discourse and sexual regulation. The representation and rhetoric of the 'angel in the home' and domesticity operated to regulate the mind, body and soul. The ideal female was a wife and mother in the domestic sphere. These socially constructed codes of ideal feminine roles pushed females into subservient positions within both the public and private spheres.

By utilizing Foucauldian arguments, we can consider how power was dispersed through 'experts' and other regulatory powers' medical discourse, that served to justify the incarceration of girls. Repo maintains that, by examining the

Foucauldian approach, it is possible to identify how 'sexuality made it possible to control forms of behaviour in order to make use of it socially, economically and politically' (Repo, 2016; 13). The presentation of the 'child-saving' rhetoric to save 'at risk' girls established the reformatories under the guise of humanitarian institutions (Cox, 2013). This establishment of reformatories and industrial schools, in a sense, become microcosms of the aims of the wider society: to exert sexual control and ensure that girls were trained in domesticity, removed from the public sphere and kept within the private confines of the home. The regulation of girls continued into their 'situation' and their everyday life in domestic service, which pushed girls into low paid, subservient employment, often for life.

Feminists argue that although Foucault has much to offer, ultimately, he fails to explain why predominately, in most societies, it is men who wield the power. Although patriarchal relations alone do not explain the social control of women, it does elucidate a panoptical society that regulates females through a constant male gaze (Bartky, 1990). The representations that were embedded in the nineteenth century still play a dominant role in the criminalization of females today. Sexuality was and remains a significant marker of their deviance. The double standard by which a female's sexual behaviour is judged means that her whole character can be destroyed by categorizing her as promiscuous, whereas a man may publicize his promiscuity with no stigma being attached to his behaviour. In moving forward into the future, it is crucial, within criminology and gendered responsive justice, that we understand how, historically, gendered stereotypes have been constructed if we are to move away from criminalizing girls for their sexuality or disciplining females along gender ideals of femininity, which merely serves to reproduce the gendered power relations within society.

3

The institutions, location and networks

The nineteenth century witnessed the increasing size of the Victorian towns and cities. Industrialization also brought with it rapid urbanization, for which the infrastructure was not only unprepared but also ill-equipped to accommodate. The rapid growth of cities doubled the population from 8.3 million in 1800 to over 16.8 million in 1850, with half the population aged below twenty in the 1830s (Godfrey et al., 2017). Particularly in the urban cities, there was a fear of overpopulation and the financial burden represented by the poor, who were thought to be 'racially degenerate' 'dangerous and infectious' and likely to undermine the nation with their prolific breeding and inferior offspring (Nead, 1988: 31). The visibility of the youth on the streets in the urban towns and cities, alongside the introduction of mass media reporting and popular literature such as Charles Dickens' *Oliver Twist* (1837), purporting to show the social reality for 'child criminals' as the members of street gangs led by figures like Fagin, fuelled the anxiety about juvenile crime and delinquency in the major cities, such as London, Liverpool, Manchester and Bristol.

Although the concern about juvenile boys was high on the agenda, it was the presence of young girls that created both fear and sympathy. Notably, the character of 'Nancy' in *Oliver Twist* was a gang member and young prostitute, although Dickens never makes this explicit in the book. Nancy was situated at the periphery of crime, in the context of the sexual threat that she posed to the boys and the fact that she consorted with thieves. In the end, she was brutally murdered by Sikes, a malicious criminal, with whom she was cohabiting, presenting Nancy as both a threat and a victim. Although fewer girls than boys came before the courts, the reformers, along with the local government and philanthropists, deemed it imperative to 'save' girls before they fell into a 'depraved' way of life, and so established the female reformatories and industrial schools in the major cities across England (Rimmer, 1986; Cale, 1993; Cox, 2013). This chapter will examine the local development, networks and management of the three female institutions assessed in this study.

An investigation of the networks, charitable donations and organizations involved is important in order to build up detailed profiles of the juvenile institutions within their localities (Jackson, 2000). This study will foreground the particularities of the institutions in the two urban locations of Manchester and Bristol. Both cities were undergoing significant economic and social changes during this period. Research has tended to focus on these locations, without referencing working-class females and the interplay between class, gender and deviance (Briggs, 1963; Messinger, 1985; Kidd, 1993). In examining two major Victorian cities, this will facilitate micro-research regarding what was happening on a macro-scale in terms of the socialization and social control of young juvenile girls in the reformatory and industrial schools in the nineteenth century.

This book examines one reformatory school (Red Lodge) and two industrial schools (Carlton and Manchester Sale). Although historians have frequently considered these schools together, as part of one reformatory school system, there were distinctions between them (Gear, 1999; Godfrey et al., 2017). The 1854 Reformatory Schools Act and the 1857 Industrial School Act (together with further amendment acts) codified the circumstances in which a child could be committed to these two institutions. The industrial and reformatory schools were both designed to house juveniles, but the latter were reserved for those who had committed crimes and had served a mandatory prison term prior to entering the reformatory. Both the reformatory and industrial schools were inspected annually by Home Office officials after 1860. Gear (1999) maintains that this joint inspection by a single government department has led historians frequently to consider the schools together, as part of one reformatory school system, without noting the clear distinctions between them. However, Johnston (2015) argues that: 'while there appeared to be quite clear boundaries on paper between these schools and reformatories, in practice the lines were little more blurred. This was partly because of the changing categories of young people who could be committed to industrial schools' (2015: 145).

The Industrial Schools' amendments increased the categories for which a child could be sent to an industrial school. Shore (2011) argues that as a result of the Industrial Amendment Acts, the distinction between the schools was blurred, suggesting that 'magistrates by the late 1860s inclined to use the industrial school for both criminal and destitute children' (2011: 8). Moreover, the removal in 1899 of the mandatory prison term prior to admission to a reformatory resulted in further blurring between the two schools. The growth of the schools fluctuated for both reformatory and industrial schools. By the eve of the First World War, there were 43 reformatories, and 132 industrial schools (Radzinowicz and Hood, 1990: 182). Although, initially the reformatory schools began with ten institutions in 1855, by 1860, there were forty-eight reformatories, hosting 4,000 young offenders. The number of industrial schools grew from twenty-five in 1866, to fifty by 1871 and ninety-nine by 1884, encompassing over 20,000 children in 1885 and 24,500 by 1893 (Radzinowicz and Hood, 1990). Furthermore, although more boys were admitted to both reformatory and industrial schools, Gear (1999) argues that the Industrial Amendments Acts, introduced in the 1880s, saw the proportion of girls increase, with 22 per cent of the children in industrial schools being girls, compared to just 13 per cent of those in the reformatory schools (1999: 213).

Although the establishment of female reformatory and industrial schools for girls marked a watershed in the incarceration of young girls, they also now formed part of a network of institutions to regulate women who were deemed 'fallen', or 'immoral'. Institutions for females were not new in England, where Magdalenes and penitentiaries had a long history. The first was the Magdalen hospital, established in Whitechapel, London in 1758. There were also numerous organizations alongside the Magdalenes, including Waifs and Strays and the Salvation Army as well as the Church of England penitentiaries, of which by 1885 there was over fifty (D'Cruze and Jackson, 2009: 74). However, the reformatory and industrial schools specifically designed for Juvenile girls were certified in England, Scotland and Ireland during the nineteenth century (Mahood, 1995; Kelly, 2016; Curtin, 2020). Internationally, in the United States, reformatories and training schools for juvenile girls were established throughout the country; notably, the New York House of Refuge was the first reformatory for juvenile offenders in the United States (Giallombardo, 1974; Brenzel, 1983; Alexander, 1995; Odem, 1995). The establishment of reformatories in port and urban locations is an important similarity between the two countries that warrants further research, and points to the importance of the institutions and their geographical locations.

I now examine in detail the three female institutions assessed in this study, exploring the institutions, their management and their networks within their localities. I first explore the networks and institutions in Bristol (namely, Red Lodge Reformatory and Carlton Industrial School), and then proceed to examine Manchester Sale Industrial School.

Bristol – Red Lodge Reformatory and Carlton Industrial School

As briefly explored in Chapter 1, Bristol, as an industrial port city, gives us a clear example of a location facing economic decline and its effects. Manton describes the effects that the declining port had on the city in the nineteenth century. The old houses, once occupied by the wealthy merchants and ship-owners in the eighteenth century, had been let out as tenements and lodging houses, inhabited by the drifting populations, sailors, prostitutes, beggars and gangs of children who lived by scavenging (1976: 72). The desolate area stretching from the docks to Lewin's Mead was 'notorious as being among the worst slums in Britain' (Manton, 1976: 72). Manton argues that around the docks, the boys were scavengers of coal and breakers of crates, while the girls were sellers of watercress, matches and flower-girls, growing up to engage in back-alley prostitution (1976: 81). Horn, in *The Victorian Town Child* (1997), argues that, in particular, theft by juveniles from docks was widespread in ports like Liverpool and Bristol. In Bristol, she maintains that the 'police reported boys of six and seven taking bits of old iron, copper, brass and ropes left on the quays' (1997: 183). Port locations became particularly associated with juvenile delinquency. According to the 1849 Prison Commissioners figures, 17,126 young people under the age of seventeen years were in prison: 2,557 girls and 14,569 boys nationally, two-fifths from London and three-fifths from seaports and large cities (Manton, 1976: 99). Within this climate of uncertainty and change, bourgeois attention turned towards the poor populations and swelling number of unsupervised children on the streets. As Goldson (2020) maintains, 'child-saving' initiatives developed in tandem with moral anxiety and political concerns stating:

> Prominent philanthropists were moved by their revulsion at the appalling conditions endured by the children of the poor, while the Establishment was concerned with the prospect of the 'criminal classes' and the 'dangerous classes' (increasingly organised sections of the working class) joining forces and destabilising the social order.
>
> (2020: 318)

The most prominent reformer in Bristol, Mary Carpenter, was involved in all aspects of Bristol's street children, devoting her full attention 'to the dark world of the very poor, and among them, to the suffering and degradation of convicts' (Manton, 1976: 44). Carpenter established Bristol's First Ragged School (schools set up for the poorest children to provide free lessons before the introduction of free schooling) in August 1846 in Lewin's Mead, with the support of local surgeon John Bishop Estlin. Carpenter's Unitarian network provided crucial 'material, intellectual and moral support' (Watts, 2000: 43). Her ideas gained the support of a wealthy resident of Bath, Russell Scott, who purchased a building in an industrial village in the great Bristol coalfield in 1852, where she and Scott opened Kingswood Reformatory. Businessmen (such as Russell Scott) invested in the reformatory and industrial school movement, which reflected an interest in producing an industrious labour force. The reformatory school they stated was designed to offer education and training 'to extirpate acquired habits of idleness and vice, and to replace them with habits of industry and a sense of moral responsibility' (Kingswood Report cited in Gray, 2016: 191). Carpenter's experiment at Kingswood was initially a mixed establishment, but there was serious concerns about the mixing of boys and girls, after several incidents of girls absconding and riotous behaviour which, according to Manton, 'had seriously shaken the confidence of the founder, Russell Scott' (1976: 121). In 1854, a committee of Management was formed who distrusted Carpenters 'unorthodox beliefs' and were 'unwilling to keep fifteen rebellious girls any longer' (Manton, 1976: 122). This led Mary Carpenter to found the first girls' reformatory school in England: Red Lodge.

Red Lodge Reformatory

Red Lodge Reformatory, the first certified reformatory for girls, in Bristol was opened on 9 October 1854, with Carpenter as its superintendent. On 9 December 1854, the establishment was officially certified to accommodate fifty-two girls. Carpenter received support from local philanthropists, networks of those who supported her cause. Lady Noel Byron, widow of the distinguished poet, offered financial help to purchase a house and property in Park Row, known as Red Lodge, an Elizabethan-style house, dating back to the sixteenth century (Manton, 1976). The image below shows the reformatory from the main street, the high walls wrapping around the side and garden to prevent the girls from escaping. The front door keys were with the matron at all times (Red Lodge Journal, 12693/1: BRO).

The census records for the school reveal that girls were admitted to the reformatory from Liverpool, Manchester, Wales, Plymouth and Portsmouth, as well as Bristol (Census Returns of England and Wales, 1881, Piece: 2176; Folio: 5; Page: 3; RG11–2477).

Image 1 Red Lodge Reformatory street view (40826/BUI/80, BRO).

Miss Carpenter undertook the sole management of Red Lodge and managed the institution for twenty-three years. In 1856, a local newspaper described the school and Carpenter as follows:

> The Red Lodge is now a little convict depot for female children, who having each committed some offence which rendered them amenable to the law, have been sent hither from various courts, magisterial, sessional, and assize, to see if a kind but firm course of instruction could not prove more potent than punishment with incarceration, in effect their reform. It is in fact an experiment whether the school may not prove a more efficious agent for good than the goal, with young offenders. For the present its chief control (a talented matron and mistress, having the management and superintendence under her), is in the hands of one of the most remarkable women in England, MARY CARPENTER, whose intimate knowledge and successful treatment of juvenile criminals has been acquired in a life of incessant, untiring, disinterested, and almost Herculean labour amongst the class of offenders.
>
> (*Devizes and Wiltshire Gazette*, 10 January 1856)

Red Lodge, similar to the other female reformatory schools (Toxteth Reformatory), was established in an urban location (Rimmer, 1986). Ploszajska

(1994), in *moral landscapes and manipulated spaces: gender, class and space in Victorian reformatory schools*, argues that the reformatory strategy was shaped by contemporary assumptions about gender and class, whereby Carpenter maintained that girls 'must be prepared for domestic life, either in the houses of persons in the respectable portion of society, or eventually in their own families' (Carpenter, 1857 quoted in Ploszajska, 1994: 420). Red Lodge developed close networks related to the domestic service of girls in the growing bourgeois districts of Clifton and Redlands, where trained servants were in high demand (Miss Sullivan's Discharge book, 5137/1, BRO). Red Lodge also had an adjoining cottage for older girls, where they prepared for their immediate release on licence into domestic service. The institution, with the aid of a matron, schoolmistress and assistant laundress, trained the girls in laundry, cooking and domesticity, which is explored in more detail in Chapter 5.

Within the institutions, the girls were expected to be trained how to provide laundry service. This industrial training not only regulated the girls regarding domesticity but also provided an activity that was financially profitable for the institutions (Carlebach, 1970: 58). Thus, the industrial training not only provided sufficient income to pay the wages of the staff of the schools, but also the girls provided a service to local, middle-class, private customers. Rimmer maintains that fashionable middle-class women of the time had 'endless petticoats, underskirts, overskirts, tucks, flounces and trimmings' (1986: 54).

Alongside the income generated by this industrial work, Red Lodge was funded by the treasury and voluntary contributions. Parental contributions were also required by law, but these were often extremely difficult to obtain. The payments from parents were recorded in the Home Office report for each location. For the year ending 1870, the total amount obtained from the reformatory and industrial schools in Bristol was £24. 5s.1d. in contrast to schools in Manchester, with £156 19s.0d. (14th *Report of Reformatory and Industrial Schools*, 1871: 260–1). Nevertheless, from the opening of Red Lodge, Carpenter managed the costs efficiently. Turner reported, in 1862, that 'Red Lodge was the cheapest girl's reformatory' (6th *Report of Reformatory and Industrial Schools*, 1863: 28–9). The annual cost per girl was £14. 15s.0d., compared with the national average of £18. 16s.5d. (Carlebach, 1970: 54). The financial running of the school was so efficient that, by 1862, the original subscriptions and donations had been transferred to charity:

> The management of the reformatory was inexpensive and independent of extraneous pecuniary aid. The original subscriptions and donations being no

longer needed, a considerable sum having being saved annually and funded for the institution, these were transferred to form a new fund for neglected and destitute children, a second time doing a work of charity.

(*Leamington Spa Courier*, January 1862: 9)

Carpenter remained superintendent of Red Lodge until her death in 1877. Inspector William Inglis, who inspected Red Lodge, following her death reported:

The report on this school could not be submitted without a notice of the death of Mary Carpenter, its founder and supporter. The cause of Reformatory and Industrial Schools ever found a highly experienced and able advocate in Miss Carpenter. Very few besides herself were so well acquainted with the principles on which such schools were originally founded, and with the most approved methods for their due regulation and management. Her life was one of unswerving devotion and self-sacrifice for the successful development of those principles, and to the establishment of kindred institutions throughout the country at large.

(21st Report of Reformatory and Industrial Schools, 1878: 56)

On her death, Carpenter left a will, in which she set out instructions for how Red Lodge should be run (Hodgson, 2017). A trust was formed to be responsible for the school, but no member of the committee was allowed to be a member of the trust. Mr Herbert Thomas (Mary's brother-in-law) formed a small committee to preside over the overall management (Saywell, 1964: 7–8). The trustees were Mr Philip Worsley and Mr Herbert Thomas, and the committee members Mr William Terrell, Mrs Terrell, Mrs Whitwell, Miss Evans, Miss Sturge, Mrs R Forbes Carpenter, Miss Elizabeth Duck and Miss Catherine Duck (Red Lodge Minutes, 12693/7, BRO). Several women served on the committee, and it is striking that these did not form a separate Ladies Association but were part of the Management Committee. Hannam and Dresser (1996), in *The Making of Modern Britain*, maintains that philanthropic, religious and political activities frequently overlapped, with men and women of different persuasions working together (Hollis, 1987).

In 1880, Elizabeth Langabeer was appointed Matron and her younger sister, Sarah Langabeer, schoolmistress. Their parents ran Park Row Industrial School for Boys, which was located in Bristol and had been established by Carpenter. The Langabeer sisters managed the day-to-day running of the school from 1880 until its closure on 9 July 1919 (due to the decrease in the number of girls sent to Red Lodge). Manton maintains that the Langabeer family 'ran the school as a pious memorial to its founder, consulting the rules she laid down 1854 and even applying them 60 years later' (Manton, 1976: 247). However, in 1896, Home Office inspector Legge, from the Prisons Commission, was critical in his report of Carpenter's methods that were still being followed at Red Lodge:

> The school … still venerates the memory of Miss Mary Carpenter. There is, consequently, apt to be a tendency to rely too much on old methods and the fact is overlooked that methods which may have been suitable and perhaps advisable forty years ago may be the reverse now.
>
> (*40th Report Reformatory and Industrial Schools,* 1897: 155)

Carpenter was central in establishing Red Lodge and it was run according to her rules and principles to the very end. The strict rules and principles laid down for Red Lodge and other reformatory schools in 1854 were established to deal with youths when no other provisions for them existed. The development of industrial schools, intended for the 'perishing classes' without the stipulation of imprisonment prior to entering, had expanded and saw an increase in admissions into industrial schools and a national decline of youths being sent to reformatory schools. The introduction of compulsory schooling for all children beginning with the Elementary Education Act (1870) and the proceeding acts (passed up until 1893) also reflect a growing interest in how children developed. The proceeding acts (passed up until 1893) also reflect a growing interest in how children developed (Hendrick, 1997). Moreover, the development in 1883 of the Liverpool Society for the Prevention of Cruelty to Children (LSPCC) became the NSPCC in 1889. Thus, by 1896, the child and welfare and wellbeing of the child were at the forefront of youth policy. Carlebach maintains that 'by the end of the century the trend of development was thus the opposite of what the prototypal institutions had found to be effective' (2013: 81).

Nonetheless, the reforms that Mary Carpenter helped secure argues Behlmer (1982) gave 'latter-day Child Savers a base to build upon' (1982: 11). The significance of her contribution to the reformatory movement cannot be understated. Saywell maintains 'the pioneering work which she began in 1854 at the Red Lodge, in Park Row, Bristol, proved remarkably successful and provided a model for many of the institutions which were later established in other parts of the country' (1964: 1). Red Lodge not only provided a blueprint for other female institutions but Carpenter's standing within the reformatory movement allowed her to form networks, both locally and across England. Hodgson (2017) argues that Liverpool businessman Frederick Chappell was so impressed with Mary's success with Liverpool girls who had been sent to Red Lodge Reformatory that he bought Lunsdale House in Park Row so that she might open an industrial school for boys. These business class interests in the reform of juveniles are particularly significant in the network of schools. As Cale maintains 'this altruistic motivation was also underpinned by good economic sense: if the criminal tendencies of a youthful offender could be checked early in their development, then the nation would be saved the cost' (1993: 10). Case and Smith (2020) also maintain that the changes were happening during a 'dramatic period of restructuring of capital and its requirement for new forms of educated, healthy and physical capable labour, which necessitated a reshaping of the relationship between the dominant economic interests and generation of children' (Case and Smith, 2020: 5). The local business interests were also reflected in the management of the schools, the school board members and the trustees of the institutions, and the members of the school committees were also businessmen. This is significant as it highlights the vested interests in the accumulation of profit by using child labour within industrial capitalism. As becomes evident, the opening of Carlton Industrial School in 1874, after the introduction of the Elementary School Act of 1870 and the introduction of school boards, gave local businessmen an opportunity to be elected to the school board committees, thereby allowing them to play a more official role in the management of the industrial schools (Lawson and Silver, 1973).

Carlton Industrial School

Carlton Industrial School opened in 1875 in Southwell Street, St Micheals Hill, Kingsdown, and was certified for fifty-five girls, twenty years after the establishment of Red Lodge. It was established by the Bristol School Board under the management of Mark Whitwell, JP magistrate and chair for many years of the Bristol School Board, overseeing the running of Park Row and Clifton Industrial School for Boys, as well as Carlton. It closed on 13 March 1924 and became Bristol Maternity Hospital. The building, similar to Red Lodge Reformatory, was a large Victorian home, surrounded by gardens and a high wall. Inspector William Inglis reported 'buildings which twenty years ago would have received a certificate without remonstrance would not be considered satisfactory now' (38th *Report of Reformatory and Industrial Schools*, 1895: 10).

The schoolmistress, Miss Catherine Combe, oversaw the day-to-day running of the school and was succeeded by Miss Katherine McFarlane in 1881. The Bristol School Board, which was set up in 1871 under the provisions of the public Elementary Act of 1870 to deliver the state system of education (21131/BSB, Bristol Record Office), oversaw the management of Carlton and contributed

Image 2 Carlton Industrial School (37006/Ph/1, BRO).

to the purchase of the building. The school board in Bristol met monthly, consisting of local gentlemen, politicians and men associated with the church. Lawson and Silver highlight the importance of the school board positions in the nineteenth century, stating that 'a seat on the school board was a highly-coveted honour' (1973: 318). Lewis Fry, grandson of Joseph Fry, founder of the chocolate company in Bristol, was elected the first chair of the Bristol School Board, highlighting the link between industry and social philanthropy among the expanding middle classes (Hall and Davidoff, 1987).

As well as the direct financial contributions by the middle classes to philanthropic causes, Higginbotham (2017) also points to the 'veritable army of women' from the middle-classes who assisted charities' administration and fundraising efforts (Prochaska, 1980; Hall and Davidoff, 1987). It was from this cohort of women that the schools drew their staff and ladies' committees. Hartley maintains that the 'evangelical emphasis upon duty and service as well as the domestic experience of women was a further qualification which made them ideally suited to the internal management of institutions and missions' (Hartley, 1986: 22). The Ladies Committee of Carlton, chaired by Mrs Whitwell, played an active role in the household management of the school and met monthly to discuss admissions, discharges, the health of the girls and resources that the school needed (Visitors' Records, 21131/SC/CAH/V/2, BRO). Mrs Whitwell, along with Miss Sturge, was also on the committee established for Red Lodge

Reformatory in 1877, highlighting the close networks between the two schools (Red Lodge Minutes, 12693/7, BRO). The admissions records indicate a connection with Bristol Female Missionary, a preventive branch, where the mission aimed to 'save girls from falling' (Prochaska, 1980; Bartley, 2000). There are instances in which the Bristol Female Missionary brought the girls to the attention of the magistrates and to the school in the records (Carlton Admission records, 21131/SC/CAH/A/1/1, BRO).

As manager, Whitwell was actively involved in the school, particularly the discharges of the girls. Whitwell, a local shipbuilding merchant, owner of the Great Western Steamship Company, was also part of the Bristol Emigration Society. The society set up a receiving and distribution home to receive children. Canadian immigration officials allowed the Bristol Emigration Society to take children to Canada. Parker (2010) states that 'he was clearly a man who played a variety of interlocking roles and who had similarly interlocking interests, among which was the encouragement of emigration' (Parker, 2010: 121). Parker argues that he appeared to be a driving force behind the Bristol initiative of the emigration of children from industrial schools, even bearing part of the cost. *The Bristol Mercury* stated that the aim was 'to stop any opposition on the grounds of expense' (10 February 1883, quoted in Parker, 2010: 121). The discharge records indicate that sixty-eight girls (32 per cent) of the 212 Carlton discharge cases examined were sent to Canada (see Chapter 6). Mr Whitwell is mentioned frequently in the records as visiting the girls in Canada (Carlton Discharge books, 21131/SC/CAH/A/2). Although there has been a considerable amount of literature on children sent to Canada from children's homes across England in the nineteenth century (Parr, 1994; Murdoch, 2006; Boucher, 2014; Lamont et al., 2020), there remains a gap in the literature regarding the number of industrial and reformatory girls who were sent to Canada. This number increased after the Amendment Act of 1891, which granted extensive powers to the managers of juvenile institutions to dispose of children without their parents' consent. Bean and Melville (1989) maintain that Britain was negotiating its place within the Empire, claiming that 'philanthropy took second place to unadulterated imperialism (and children) were thought of as "Bricks for Empire Building"' (Bean and Melville, 1998: 78). Bates (2009) agreed and maintained that, despite their benevolent representation, philanthropists, social reformers and government officials increasingly emphasized the contribution that these 'gutter' children, once relocated, could make to the Empire. Bates states:

> Juvenile emigration has been interpreted as a form of rescue that rested upon
> middle-class values of domesticity, underpinned by Malthusian principles,

peppered with a strong dose of Evangelicalism, and neatly situated inside the largely cultural move towards disciplining the poor.

(2006: 145)

As well as emigration to Canada, Whitwell's business interests in Bristol helped to find places for the girls on discharge (Hodgson, 2017: 197). There were numerous examples of girls who went to work in the local factories. It is important to analyse the local business interests in the industrial schools and the employment of working-class girls, who often constituted a cheaper option with regard to providing labour for the wide range of industries: cotton, tobacco and chocolate. However, to date, few studies have investigated the presence of females in the factories and their contribution to industrial growth in the nineteenth century (Pollert, 1981; Tilly, 1994). *Bedminster's Tobacco Women* (Thomas et al., 2018), a local study conducted in Bristol, collected oral testimonies from twenty-three women who worked at Willis Tobacco Factory, which dominated the tobacco trade both in Bristol and nationally in the nineteenth and early twentieth centuries. They highlight the thousands of women whose labour over the decades generated enormous wealth for the Willis Tobacco Factory. Nineteenth-century experiences, particularly those of young girls from juvenile institutions and their contribution to the growth of these industries, have not yet been fully explored within the literature.

The records for Red Lodge and Carlton indicate that the girls went to work in two factories in particular: Fry's Chocolate Factory and Willis Tobacco Factory, both of which were located close to the schools, as in the case of Ada McCarthy, who left Red Lodge in July 1891, and was placed in domestic service on licence. However, she left her position shortly afterwards, and visited the matron of Red Lodge to ask about getting a job at Fry's Chocolate Factory. The licence records then highlight that Ada worked in Fry's Cocoa works from 1893 until 1898 (Miss Sullivan's Discharge book, 5137/1: 67, BRO). The records would indicate that the matron was instrumental in helping Ada to obtain employment at the factory, thereby contradicting the preference of the schools to send girls into domestic service. However, many local factory owners shared the moral views of the industrial and reformatory schools and adopted social investment practices within the factories. Factory owner Joseph Fry, a Quaker, sought to provide a workplace that offered the best facilities, investing socially in the workforce; holding morning prayers, further education classes and recreation for boys and girls. It is believed that, when the girls left the factory to get married, they received a copy of *Mrs Beeton's Book of Household Management* (Chrystal, 2022: 94). However, Marxist writers Rusche and Kircheimer (1938) have pointed to the significance of the welfare 'ideology', the demands of capital and naked class interests. They argue that the primary purpose of the reform was to implement more sophisticated methods of domination and discipline to serve, the needs of developing industrial capitalism.

Examining the links between the local industry and girls who left the reformatory and industrial schools to work in these factories highlights how these 'child-saving' institutions sought a productive labour class to serve the local needs. The records indicate that, during the period 1880–1920, 46 of the total of 325 girls (14 per cent) from Carlton went to work in local factories. Red Lodge, between 1880 and 1920, listed 32 of a total of 331 (10 per cent) girls as going into factory work. Nevertheless, it was domestic service that constituted the majority of the discharge destinations for the girls, reflecting the demand in the labour market and the discretion of the institutions to place girls in suitable work environments. The records indicate that girls sent to work in the factories were not considered suitable for domestic service, as in the case of Mary Carter, who was considered 'too bad tempered for service' and went to work in a factory (Carlton Discharge books 21131/SC/CAH/A/2, BRO). Domestic service was the preferred employment for girls in the nineteenth century, as described in the Home Office Reformatory and Industrial schools report:

> In most parts of the country the demand for the girls is so large that the school authorities are able to pick and choose, and great care is exercised to find the right place for a particular girl, seeing that the character or disposition of the mistress has to be studied just as much as that of the girl … One of the great difficulties was stated to be the liking of the girls for employment in factories or mills. The reason why domestic service is preferable is that the majority of these girls, coming as they do from undesirable homes, the employment to be found for them should, so far as possible, combine a new home with occupation.
>
> (1897: 47–8)

The institutions would seek to place girls in domestic service first and foremost, even if this meant relocating them. A total of 56 (13 per cent) girls of the 420 girls discharged from Red Lodge were relocated to take up domestic service in Hull, Birmingham, Wales and London. This re-settlement reflected the demand for domestic service but also the institutions' preference for placing girls in service rather than factories in the local community. Employment in domestic service was seen as a central factor in ensuring probationary surveillance over the girls. The surplus of girls from the reformatory and industrial schools, who were regulated and disciplined, provided a solution to what Schwartz termed the 'servant problem' in the final decades of the nineteenth century. Schwartz (2019) argues that 'the "servant problem" should not be dismissed as a trivial middle-class gripe but pointed to deeper and widespread anxiety over the rising worker militancy' (2019: 3). Schwartz maintains that the 'servant problem' can be traced back to the second half of the nineteenth century.

The invisible labour within domestic service constituted, according to Higgs (1983), the largest occupational group in the economy during the second half of the nineteenth century. Steinbach (2011) contended that, by the 1880s, a third of all women between the ages of fifteen and twenty-one were in service (2011: 146). D'Cruze and Jackson (2009) maintain that, to understand women in low-waged occupations' oppression in society, we must examine the historical process of how capitalism and patriarchy shaped the contemporary world (2009: 5). Domestic service and its implications for working-class girls, who made up the servant class, helped to reaffirm not only the power structures but also the gendered divisions of labour for working-class girls in the nineteenth century. Skeggs (1997) argues that the 'cult of domesticity' was central to middle-class consolidation, the self-defining of the middle-classes and the maintenance of ideas of an imperialist nation (1997: 12).

Working-class girls, both during their time in industrial training and their long-term domestic service roles while out on licence, provided a low-paid service for middle-class ladies, which freed up the latter's time (Rafter, 1985: 54). Rafter (1985), in *Partial Justice: Women in State Prisons and Social Control*, argues that working-class girls provided a pool of cheap domestic labour, which was a central aspect of the reformatory movement in North America in the period 1800–1935. Rafter states:

> Two groups of women – the working-class offenders and the middle-class reformers – met, so to speak, at the gate of the women's reformatory. The struggle between them was economically functional in some ways to the reformers: it helped maintain a pool of cheap domestic labour for women like themselves, and, by keeping women in the surplus labour force, it undergirded the economic system to which they owed their privileged position. But such purely economic explanations do not account adequately for the dedication with which the reformers went about their tasks of rescue and reform. The struggle also involved the definition of gender. Reformers hoped to recast offenders in their own image, to have them embrace the values … of the lady.
>
> (Rafter, 1985: 175)

Both gender and class operate together; working-class girls trained as domestic servants served the labour demand for low-paid service workers in middle-class homes. This conformed to the gender politics of removing working-class girls from corrupt public spheres and the feminizing 'ideology', whereby respectable femininity required females to be within the private sphere (Hall and Davidoff, 1987). Domestic service work reinforced the inequality and servitude of working-class girls. Rose (1993) maintains that gender is a cultural process, distinguishing females and males in all social relations, including economic or production relations. In this way, she argues gender is an important aspect of the cultural construction of class relations: 'employers and workers have been gendered, and the jobs they done have also become gendered' (1993: 191).

The economic and social changes happening in Bristol, the networks, the demands for capable, healthy labour and the gendered divisions of labour (Lown, 1990; Humphries, 1991) reflected the changes happening in other urban cities, particularly in the industrial town of Manchester, which I now examine.

Manchester

In nineteenth century Manchester, there were similar social and economic changes occurring in the port city of Bristol. However, Manchester, dubbed 'Cottonopolis', was the centre of the world's cotton industry (Farnie and Jeremy, 2004). Growing from no textile mills in 1780, to 108 working mills in 1850, Manchester became the largest mill town in the world (Nevell, 2017: 4). The industrial rise was matched by a significant rise in population from around 75,000 in 1801 to over 300,000 by 1851 (Kidd, 1993). The new population created a huge demand for housing, which increased the number of dwellings substantially from 3,446 to nearly 50,000 by 1851 (Nevell, 2017: 4). The image of the heart of Manchester, depicted by Fredrick Engels who visited the city in the mid-nineteenth century, was as a place of 'filth, ruin, and unhabitableness'; presented as 'Hell upon earth'. The literature published by Engels points to the role of crime and class struggle in the nineteenth century in *The Condition of the Working Classes in England*, 1845:

> The clearest indication of the unbound contempt of the workers for the existing social order is the wholesale manner in which they break its laws. If the demoralisation of the worker passes beyond a certain point then it is just natural that he will turn into a criminal – as inevitably as water turns into steam at boiling point. Owing to the brutal and demoralising way in which he is treated by the bourgeois, the worker loses all will of his own and, like water, he is forced to follow blindly the laws of nature … consequently the incidence of crime has

increased with the growth of the working-class population and there is more crime in Britain than in any other country in the world.

(Engels cited in McDonald, 1982: 411)

This image presented highlights the fears and concerns around criminality and the working-class populations. Kidd maintains that 'the massive urban growth brought enormous problems of organization, provision of amenities and amenities of public order' (Kidd, 1993: 36). Overcrowded, unsanitary homes, neglectful parents, alcohol and vice were believed to lead to juvenile crime. Concern around the juveniles on the streets, particularly engaging in criminality and violence, was highlighted in moral panics around Scuttlers (Davies, 1999, 2009). The breakdown of social order was connected to the changing economic structures. Work in Manchester was dominated by the cotton mills and factories, which employed numerous women and believed to turn homes and marriages 'upside down', as married women primarily went 'out' to work (Holmes, 2017). Gomersall maintains that the patriarchy was challenged, as not only did the factory system confront the cultural norms of women's social position, but also employing the cheap 'competition' of working women was seen to threaten men's job security and status, both as workers and as 'honourable' men and husbands (1997: 4). Female economic independence (albeit marginal), gained through their employment in the mills and factories, enabled them to start to lead independent social lives. Mothers were expected to be preservers of morality and respectability. Davies maintains that in late Victorian Manchester and Salford 'working class notions of respectability incorporated central components of the middleclass ideal of womanhood' (1999: 76). Female drunkenness was of particular concern in industrial Manchester (Stafford, 2018). Overcrowded, unsanitary homes, neglectful parents, alcohol and vice were believed to lead to juvenile crime.

The local fears and anxiety about juvenile delinquency contributed to the need to establish institutions to reform and regulate children on the streets. Similar to the establishment of ragged schools in Bristol, Manchester established the Manchester Ragged School in 1851, at St Johns Parade in Byrom Street. However, Gear (1999) argues that ragged schools were cramped and overcrowded because of their poor teaching standards and relied almost entirely on insufficient voluntary aid (1999: 31). Following the passing of the 1857 Industrial Schools Act, the school relocated to Ardwick Green to provide residential lodgings and industrial training for up to 100 children of both sexes. However, as the numbers grew, the shortage of accommodation and difficulties related to supervising boys and girls were reported to pose serious problems (31st Annual Report, 1877, 22). A separate industrial school for girls, Manchester Sale, was certified in 1871, opening in 1877.

Manchester Sale Industrial School for Girls

Manchester Sale Industrial School for Girls was certified in April 1871. Unlike Red Lodge and Carlton, which were formerly large Victorian family homes, this school was purpose-built to accommodate up to 100 girls. Originally, the girls were part of Ardwick Green Industrial School for boys and girls. The girls were transferred to their own purpose-built premises at 429 Northenden Road, Manchester Sale, Cheshire. The land on which the school was erected had been gifted to the institution by Mr R. B. Clayton, Justice of the Peace (JP) of the county of Lancashire. The Manchester School board contributed £3,000 and the Salford School board £1,000 towards the cost of the building (Manchester Times, 17 July 1875). The first inspection report in 1878 stated that 'the arrangements of the buildings are excellent, compact, convenient, well ventilated and in every respect suitable, some trifling things remain to be done to render it one of the most perfect schools in England, of the size, it is situated in the country, about six miles from Manchester' (21st Report of Reformatory and Industrial schools, 1878: 142).

Image 3 Manchester Sale Industrial School, Northenden Road (Source: Peter Higginbotham, www.childrenshomes.org.uk).

The school continued to fall under Ardwick Schools' Board Committee under the management of J. T. Anderson Esq., and was managed by Miss Emma Pettit. The 1881 census records reveal that 102 girls attended the school, with the majority from locations in the North West, Manchester, Salford, Chester and Liverpool (Census Returns of England and Wales, 1881, Piece: 3507; Folio: 35; Page: 36; RG11). The Manchester Industrial Schools Committee for Manchester Sale was responsible for both Ardwick Green and the Barnes School. Politicians and philanthropists were all involved in the Ardwick, Barnes and Manchester Sale Schools. The schools had four patrons: Rev Lord Bishop of Manchester, the Dean of Manchester, Algernon Egerton MP and Edward Hardcastle MP. Their presidents were the Mayors of Manchester and Salford. The committee consisted of forty-two members, all of whom were males, except for Miss Becker. She and John Watts were nominated by the Manchester School Board. Henry Hodgson was the chair. The school was financed by government grants and School Board grants, as well as donations and subscriptions, in which the Ladies Association Committee played a large part (Manchester Sale Annual Reports, M369/4/37/1, MRO).

Alongside the School Committee, Manchester Sale had a separate Ladies Association Committee, consisting of twenty-two members, a treasurer and a secretary, which organized the collection of contributions from each district. The Ladies Association of Manchester is notable, as it comprised of around 600 women who would collect miscellaneous gifts for the girls, attend the school to give bible readings and gather donations and subscriptions for the school (Manchester Sale Annual Reports, M369/4/47/1, MRO). The Annual Reports list how this was organized. The Association had main collectors, each of whom was responsible for the collections of around twenty members (Annual Reports M369/4/47/1: 44). The financial contributions were listed annually: in 1878, 207 donations and subscriptions were collected, amounting to £461. 8s.4d. (Treasurers Accounts 1878, Annual Reports M369/4/47/1: MRO). Some of the donors to the school were also linked to the major industries/local farms in the North-West. The monetary donations made to the schools were cross-checked against the British Industrial History records (www.graceguide.co.uk). Notable names included Armitage and Rigby (cotton manufacturers) and Ryland and Sons (cotton spinners).

However, despite the donations from cotton manufacturers and the concentration of textile factories in Manchester, these were deemed unsuitable locations for young, unsupervised females. Davies (1999) maintains that, during the period 1870–1900, there was concern about street violence in urban Manchester, which females attended in 'scuttling gangs'. Davies argues that the girls associated with scuttling typically enjoyed a degree of freedom and a disposable income that were associated with female factory workers (1999: 74). Davies maintains that domestic servants had a less independent lifestyle, lower wages and were 'significant by their absence from the ranks of those charged with scuttling' (1999: 78).

The licence records for Manchester Sale are similar to those for Carlton and Red Lodge. The 'ideal destination' was domestic service and girls would be relocated to these situations to prevent them from returning to corruptive families or environments. Manchester Sale developed networks in order to place girls in domestic service, often outside the city. Of the Manchester discharge sample, 30 per cent of the girls were sent on discharge from Manchester Sale to Wales to engage in domestic service (see Chapter 6). Howells (2014) maintains that, during the second half of the nineteenth century, domestic service expanded in Wales, particularly in Carmarthen, in South-West Wales (2014: 44). D'Cruze and Jackson argue that girls', like adult women, movements were circumscribed within the public space (2009: 147), the continued employment of young women as domestic servants meant that the household hierarchies continued to structure and discipline their lives. Thus, the female reformatory and industrial schools played a pivotal role in the regulation and social control of working-class girls, relocating them upon release to employment and locations that would ensure they led 'respectable' lives.

The networks of schools were essential in not only providing employment but also supervision of the girls licenced to work in domestic service, particularly when the girls were relocated. The licence records highlight the numerous networks existing between the schools, employers, and the places of service, who took a vested interest in the aftercare of children who had been discharged from the schools. The Ladies Committee was also active in visiting discharged girls to obtain knowledge about their circumstances. The importance of these networks was acknowledged by the schoolmistress, Isabella Stewart, in the 1885 Committee's Annual Report:

> I gratefully acknowledge the assistance given by members of the Ladies' Association, and various clergy and ladies in distant towns, in the supervision of discharged girls, and the kind of interest they have taken in their welfare. This branch of our work is rendered difficult and discouraging by the interference of parents and friends, who persuade the girls to leave comfortable situations and return to their homes, thus bringing them among undesirable associates, and hindering the well-being of the girls.
>
> (Annual Reports, M369/4/47/1: 520, MRO)

Manchester Sale maintained high standards and received positive reports. In 1902, twenty-five years after opening its doors, Inspector Legge reported, in the annual report: 'It is gratifying to find that this school keeps up steadily in all departments to the high level it has reached in previous years … Industrial training seems to be receiving more diligent attention than ever' (Inspection Report 1902, *Manchester Courier and Lancashire General Advertiser*, 29 March 1902).

Manchester Sale Industrial School, similar to Carlton Industrial School, and Red Lodge Reformatory were all established at different times during the nineteenth century and each differed in terms of their management. However, the networks involved in each of the institutions were composed of local businessmen, philanthropists, educationalists, politicians and members of the church. Collectively they supported the schools financially by providing subscriptions and donations and gave their time voluntarily to contribute to the school boards, school committees and Ladies' Associations. Godfrey *et al.,* (2017) maintain that the emergent youth system was developed and shaped by the involvement of all these groups, describing it as an 'early social investment state' (2017: 42). However, it is important to note that, for females, these institutions reflected the state-sponsored patriarchal, paternalistic regulation of females, reinforcing the idea that their place was within the private sphere as domestic servants and eventually wives. These discourses and 'ideology' continued well into the twentieth century, laying the foundations for subsequent female juvenile institutions, with the development of Borstals in 1908 under the Children's Act, also known as the Children's Charter, and later, in 1933, with the establishment of Approved Schools, which later became Community Homes with Education (CHEs), under the control of the local authorities (Giller, 1982). Thus, charting the establishment, management and networks of juvenile institutions for girls in the nineteenth century is central to understanding the foundations of penal welfare for juvenile girls, which continued well into the twentieth century and up until the present day (Gelsthorpe and Worrall, 2009).

Conclusion

The development and management of the reformatory and industrial schools assessed in this study came about as a result of social investments and they received considerable voluntary and charitable support from many sectors of society. Each of the schools' buildings was funded by private philanthropy. The management boards, which were committees who donated their time to overseeing the running of the schools, were largely in the hands of private individuals, who were drawn to the work for a combination of social, welfare and altruistic reasons. Godfrey et al., (2017) argue that 'the emergent system epitomized local liberalism … developed by local interests to suit local needs' (2017: 41). This chapter has highlighted the local networks and numerous sectors of society who had a shared interest in the development of the reformatory and industrial schools. The significant socio-economic transitions that occurred during the nineteenth century contributed to both their development and the support of local businesspeople, who also saw a need for healthy, physically capable labour (Case and Smith, 2020). Shore (2011) maintains that youth justice reflected 'overlapping practices, strategies and ideologies that have shaped juvenile justice over the two centuries in which the modern system evolved' (Shore, 2011: 131).

However, this chapter has highlighted that in relation to females, both gender and class interests were reflected in the management and networks of the institutions, as demonstrated by the overall running of the institutions, in which all the staff of the schools were females. Moreover, the ladies' associations played a greater role in the committees and visits to the schools and the girls out on licence. Girls released on licence primarily were sent into domestic service, whilst boys were prepared for the labour force, farm work and the armed forces (Godfrey et al., 2017). There was evidence of girls going to work in factories, but the number of these was marginal in comparison to the domestic service sector jobs. The managers of the female institutions sought, above all, to place the girls in respectable occupations that would continue their training in feminine skills and duties. Domestic service was seen as the ideal employment for working-class girls, a life-cycle position between employment and marriage. The networks within and outside the schools reflected the aim to position girls in respectable locations. The gendered reform and regulation of working-class girls is central to the youth history of the nineteenth century. The next chapter will examine the pathways of the girls into the three institutions explored in this chapter.

4

Juvenile girls' pathways into the institutions

The pathways of juvenile girls into the reformatories and industrial schools between 1854 and 1920 are the central theme of this chapter, which examines both how the authorities defined the pathways of females into the institutions as well as the individual personal and family circumstances of the girls who were sent there. The chapter will highlight the gendered pathways and risk factors that brought juvenile girls within the public gaze and into contact with the criminal justice system and state authorities. The emergence of feminist research (Daly, 1992; Holsinger and Holsinger, 2005; Pasko, 2008; Chesney-Lind and Sheldon, 2014) suggests that the girls' life experiences and pathways into law-breaking need to be taken into consideration when attempting to explain their offending. They argue that there are risks and needs associated with female offenders that substantively differ from those of male offenders, such as victimization and a history of sexual or violent abuse (Daly, 1992, 1994; Belknap, 2007). This chapter will highlight the intersection between gender and class, demonstrating how Victorian gendered 'ideology' of 'respectability' played a significant role in the criminalization of working-class girls and their families in the nineteenth century.

The pathways into offending within criminological research have focused on male data sets and samples, so there remains a lacuna regarding female pathways into crime, particularly those of juvenile working-class girls. The major criminological pathways research by Glueck and Glueck focused on the criminal careers of 500 male offenders who were committed to reform schools in Massachusetts compared to 500 non-offending males to identify why they began law-breaking and their pathways into and out of crime (1930, 1934, 1950, 1968). In London, Farrington et al.'s classic Cambridge study on delinquent development is a prospective longitudinal survey of crime and delinquency among 411 males who were born in South London that identifies particular 'risk' factors that have been associated with criminal pathways (Farrington et al., 2007, 2013). The work of Godfrey, Cox and Farrall (2007) in *Criminal Lives* is a significant contribution in pathways research in developing an understanding of how life experiences are vital in crime and offending. Their study of over 300 individuals in the Cheshire town of Crewe, between 1880 and 1940, outlined the factors that most led to persistence and desistance in crime. More recent research, *Young Criminal Lives* (Godfrey et al., 2017), adopts a similar retrospective approach that entails examining the pathways of 500 juvenile boys who passed through a certified Victorian institution. However, the focus of this research is juvenile boys and the research to date on female juveniles' experiences, the risk factors that may be associated with their delinquency and law-breaking in the nineteenth and early twentieth centuries has not been thoroughly examined to the same degree as in the case of males. Feminist scholars have questioned whether the theories developed about males can account for the females' experiences (Daly and Chesney-Lind, 1988; Daly, 1994; Pasko, 2008; Chesney-Lind and Sheldon, 2014).

My research, utilizing the admissions registers of three female institutions, examined the pathways into the institutions in the Victorian urban and a port city. When navigating the archival data by adopting a contemporary criminological lens, it is essential to bear in mind that the archival records are imbued with moral judgements of female 'immorality' and Victorian standards of 'respectability'. This research demands the adoption of a critical lens, as the research undertaken by Barton (2005), Cox (2013) and Williams (2016) has ascertained that it requires the deconstruction of the dominant discourses around respectability, domesticity, motherhood and sexuality that were used to categorize and mobilize nineteenth-century society. Moreover, Rose (1993) argues that, to understand gender we need also to examine class and the economic structures. Gender is a cultural process, distinguishing females and males in all social relations, including economic or production relations.

Intersection of class and gender

Working-class families in this period were denigrated and often seen as exerting a corrupting influence on children, leading to the onset of criminal behaviour. Young children, particularly girls in these corruptive environments and families, were categorized as at 'risk' and needed to be 'saved' before they fell into a 'depraved' way of life. Taylor (2019) maintains that 'Victorian society collectively worried (much as modern commentators do) about the fragility of family units, with "nomadic husbands" who moved from family to family, alcoholic parents, wandering wives and working-parents all featuring in social investigations from the 1860s' (Taylor, 2019: 3). The establishment of reformatory and industrial schools in 1854 was a means of forging the working-classes into 'docile bodies' and useful citizens (Foucault, 1980). Training the youth to enter industrial or domestic service meant that they would become integrated and useful in society and not fall into criminality or vice. Cox maintains that 'locking up children of the poor thus became a humanitarian gesture, an emblem of a civilized society. Which in fact masked incarceration of a child by the state' (Cox, 2013: 87). The investigation of the causes of juvenile criminality in the nineteenth century, the 1816 *'Report of the Committee for Investigating the Causes of Delinquency in the Metropolis'*, interviewed and considered several hundred boys in Middlesex prisons and houses of correction, in which family background and poor parenting were cited as central factors in juvenile delinquency. However, no female juvenile offenders were interviewed and 'typically girls were referred to only in the context of prostitution' (Shore, 2002b: 178). Thus, it is important to understand the intersection between gender and class and how this impacted the pathways into the female institutions.

Within criminology, the penology around 'risk' and the view that risk factors for offending can be measured, and those deemed 'risky' can be prevented (Farrington and Welsh, 2006), has been debated and contested (O'Malley, 2010). The risk factor paradigm, that focuses on family dynamics, poor parenting, social inequality and corruptive environments, has led to the view that criminal justice can, by means of social and economic re-distributive policies, deal with the root causes of crime. Feminist criminologists Stanko (1997) and Walklate (1997) argue that it is important to note that the criminological and victimological embracing of risk is deeply gendered. In the nineteenth century, young working-class girls in public spaces were presented 'at risk' and perceived to be highly susceptible to 'sexual immorality'. This construction of 'at risk' of what they may do increased the likelihood of their pathway into an industrial school, particularly after the introduction of the Industrial Amendment Act (1880) which permitted the removal of children from homes which were frequented or associated with prostitution (Cale, 1993). Figure 1 highlights admissions across all female reformatory and industrial schools in England and Wales between 1854 and 1912.

There was a steady growth of female admissions into both institutions, but after 1880 there was an increase in admissions into industrial schools, highlighting early investment into social welfare, rather than penalism (Cox, 2013). I now turn to examine the pathways into the institutions in this study.

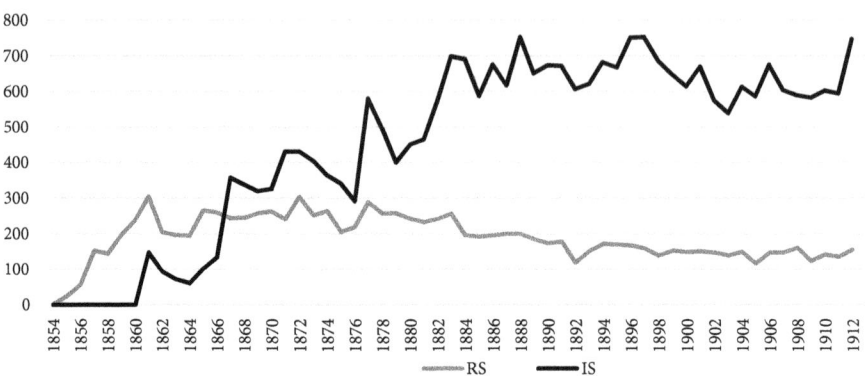

Figure 1 Female admissions into reformatory and industrial schools (1854–1912).

Data taken from Home Office Reformatory and Industrial School Reports 1854–1912 (*56th Report of Reformatory and Industrial Schools, 1914*).

The pathways into the institutions

The girls admitted into Red Lodge Reformatory, Carlton and Sale Industrial School were audited in the same way in the admission records. Reformatory Schools were reserved for children who had committed a criminal offence and had to undergo a short prison term of fourteen days, prior to admission. Both Carlton and Manchester Sale were industrial schools reserved for children who were believed to be 'at risk' of falling into 'delinquent' or 'immoral' behaviour. However, there were also admissions into the industrial schools of girls who had committed a criminal offence under section 15. Also, within the Red Lodge admissions were girls who had been admitted for vagrancy and wandering the streets. Thus, there is a significant blurring between the criminal and non-criminal admissions into both schools. Table 1 highlights the formal reasons stated for entry into the industrial schools, while Table 2 outlines the admissions to Red Lodge Reformatory.

The data for the Manchester Sale and Carlton Industrial Schools reveal that 60 per cent and 78 per cent of their admissions between 1875 and 1900 were for status offences, such as begging, wandering, being on the streets and truancy and being placed in institutions under section 14/12 due to being in 'want of proper guardianship'. However, the figure was smaller for Red Lodge Reformatory, where only 10 per cent of the girls were committed for vagrancy or wandering the streets; and as Table 2 shows, 90 per cent for property crimes, such as theft and petty larceny, usually related to items of relatively small value. This is reflected in the cases of Annie Doyle and Maggie Butt, who were sent

Table 1 Classification and admission into the industrial schools of Carlton and Manchester Sale (1875–1900).

Industrial Legislation	Offence	Carlton (per cent)		Sale (per cent)	
Section 14	Begging, wandering, destitute, frequenting or bad company	128	(60)	112	(78)
Section 15	Convicted of a felony (first offence)	34	(16)	16	(11)
Section 12 Education Act 1872	Truant from school	44	(21)	4	(3)
Amendment Act 1880	Residing in a brothel, frequenting the company of a prostitute	6	(3)	11	(8)
Total number of girls		212		143	

Source: Carlton Admission records 21131/SC/CAH/A/1/1, BRO; Manchester Sale Admission Records, M369/18, BRO.

Table 2 Admission and offence profile of girls admitted to Red Lodge (1854–1900).

		Per cent
Pickpocketing/stealing a purse	31	(28)
Theft from shops/obtaining by false pretences	41	(37)
Stealing from parents	6	(5)
Burglary/found in a house	4	(4)
Stealing from domestic service	14	(13)
Public order/Vagrancy	11	(10)
Violence	1	(1)
Suicide attempt	1	(1)
Arson	1	(1)
Total	110	

Source: Juvenile Admission Register CAT/364, LRO, Historical Newspapers.

to Red Lodge for five years in 1882 for stealing flowers, but both claimed that they were unaware that picking flowers from a garden was theft (*Western Daily Press,* 1 June 1882). Within the Red Lodge Reformatory records, the most serious crime in the dataset was arson, nine-year-old Annie Syms was admitted in 1855 for setting fire to a farmhouse. There were no admissions to any of three institutions of females for assault or serious violence, which contrasts with the research results on juvenile boys (Godfrey et al., 2017).

The ages of the girls on entry to the institutions

Figure 2 shows the ages of the girls admitted to the institutions, as recorded in the admission records (Tables 1 and 2). The data show that the most frequent age for both Carlton and Manchester Sale was eleven years, with thirteen years for Red Lodge Reformatory. There were no girls admitted over the age of thirteen to either Carlton and Manchester Sale. Mary Carpenter also stipulated in the rules and regulations that no girls over the age of fourteen must be admitted (Rules and Regulations, 12693/3, BRO). The youngest admitted to Carlton was four years old: Annie Walters admitted under the 1880 Amendment Act (prostitute). The admission records read:

> This little one was taken from a house of prostitutes; the mother has been one since the child was born. The school board officer hearing of the case investigated it, the little one was remanded and sent to the union for two weeks but after some difficulty, the presiding magistrate Mr Whitwell got her sent here. The child was clean and well clothed.
>
> (Carlton Admission records 21131/SC/CAH/A/1/1, BRO)

The youngest girl to enter Manchester Sale was Eliza Harris, aged seven, in 1887, under section 14, in want of proper guardianship. Eliza's father had died and her mother was recorded as being a professional beggar and a 'drunk'. The younger the age of the girls when admitted, the longer they spent in the institution, as in the case of Mary Ann Western. She was admitted in 1879, aged six, under section 15 for pickpocketing. The admission record reported:

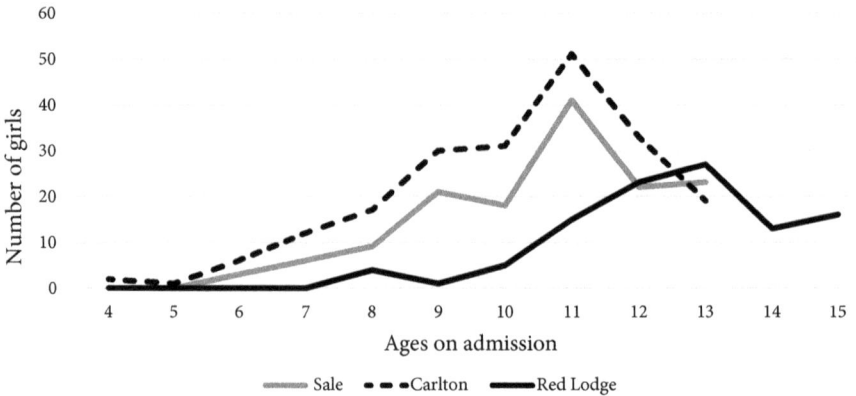

Figure 2 Ages on admission into Manchester Sale, Carlton and Red Lodge.

Source: Carlton Admission records 21131/SC/CAH/A/1/1, BRO; Manchester Sale Admission Registers, M369/4/18/2/3, MRO; Juvenile Admission Register CAT/364, LRO, Historical Newspapers.

*Totals recorded: Carlton 202, Red Lodge 104, Manchester Sale 143.

The father who the policeman states to have been a very respectable man and clerk at a church has been dead about a year. Since his death the mother has taken to drinking and in order to be supplied with money, has instructed the child in pick-pockets. As young as she is, different cases of pick pocketing were proved against the child.

(Carlton Discharge books 21131/SC/CAH/A/2, BRO)

Mary Ann Western remained in the institution until she was fifteen and was then discharged into domestic service on licence in 1889. The age of entry of the girls along with the factors around why the girls were admitted and the details on their family circumstances in the admission records allow us to build up a picture of what was considered to place girls 'at risk' during this period.

Girls 'at risk' admitted into the institutions

As well as the officially stated reasons in Tables 1 and 2 regarding the admissions into the schools, the records provide details of other 'risk factors' that helped to explain why the girls were on the streets in the first place. A closer examination of each of the admissions to both Red Lodge and the industrial schools highlights specific details about their families and environments, which are crucial for understanding the pathways into lawbreaking or 'at risk' behaviour. Girls being arrested for status offences and petty crime, from the Victorian period up until the present day, have been questioned by Feminist criminologists Gelsthorpe and Wright, who argue that, historically, the terms 'deviant' and 'delinquent' cannot be separated off from the study of how all women were defined and controlled in society. They argue that, within criminology, we must recognize nuanced accounts of women's pathways into crime (Gelsthorpe and Wright, 2015: 40).

Daly (1994) maintains that by far the most common pathway into female law-breaking is the so-called *Street Woman* scenario, which Daly describes as females on the street who commit a crime in order to survive. Daly maintains, 'whether they were pushed out or ran away from abusive homes, or became part of a deviant milieu, young woman begin to engage in petty hustle or prostitution' (Daly, 1994: 13). As in the case of Selina Nooflendew, aged nine, the admissions records stated:

This child ran away from home and was taken into a house and sheltered for the night and sent home in the morning. After leaving a watch was missed, which she had taken away and sold to another little girl for a half penny.

(Manchester Sale Admission Records, M369/4/18, MRO)

Similarly, in the case of Mary West, aged thirteen, the admission record stated 'this girl has been found wandering, having no home and associating with prostitutes and thieves in a common lodging home' (Manchester Admissions records, M369/4/18, MRO).

The 'Street Woman' scenario has dominated the feminist discussions of offending onset and persistence, although Daly is applying the 'street-woman' scenario to the present-day pathways into law breaking and it has not yet been applied to female criminality in the past. The 'Street Woman' scenario in Victorian society may prove a fruitful avenue to explore in order to examine the 'risk factors' associated with females in the nineteenth century. Victorian environmentalism deemed urban streets 'immoral' sites of vice and 'degradation'. Croll maintains that there was a 'civic project' which consisted of a collection of strategies developed to 'order, civilize and rationalize the urban experience' (2000: 3). Local concerns and anxieties in both Manchester and Bristol sought to regulate the public space, deeming children on the streets to be 'at risk' of criminality and vice.

In the dataset, I coded the admissions to the schools based on the historical 'risk' factors identified in the admission records. I constructed a questionnaire based on factors such as why the girls were admitted: their parental background, criminal convictions, alcohol abuse, poverty and abuse within the home and on the street. The remainder of this chapter now highlights each of the identified risk factors and pathways into institutions.

I commence with the 'risk' of 'immorality' and 'sexual depravity', which was officially administered 'under section 14', 'in want of proper guardianship', if girls were found on the streets wandering, or loitering.

The 'risk' of 'immorality' on the streets

Girls unsupervised in the public sphere were seen as both a 'risk' and in danger of 'depravity' and 'immorality' (Mahood, 1995). They were liable to be arrested for being on the streets, under 'section 14'. Within the admissions, this group makes up a significant majority of the admission records (60 per cent of the Manchester Sale admissions and 78 per cent of the Carlton admissions), girls found on the streets were deemed to be 'at risk'. Admissions could involve girls who had committed no crime and were simply found on the streets as in the case of Doreen Pound and Rosa Fry. Both were sent to Carlton in 1875, having been found wandering on the streets or having 'absconded' from home

(Carlton Admission records 21131/SC/CAH/A/1/1, BRO). There are many similar cases like this, which state that girls were found frequenting, loitering, singing, or selling on the streets. Criminologists Chesney-Lind and Sheldon (2014) maintain that, both historically and today, girls were more likely to be arrested for offences that are not actual crimes such as 'running away', being incorrigible, or being beyond parental control. Chesney-Lind and Sheldon (2014) argue that 'status offences' played a major part in bringing females in contact with the juvenile system.

In the dataset, status offences and cases in which the girl is referred to as 'wayward' are administered formally as 'section 14' and concern is expressed in terms of removing girls from 'risk' and 'immoral' streets, especially if they were in the habit of running away from home. One case involved Sabina Whale, whose admission record states that her 'mother and father has both most drunken and dissolute characters' and describes Sabina as running about the streets wildly, 'learning and seeing much that is impure and immoral' (Carlton Admission records, 21131/SC/CAH/A/1/1, BRO). I also came across the case of twelve-year-old Selina Poole, who was found wandering in Manchester and picked up in a lodging house (Manchester Sale Admissions Registers, M369/4/18, MRO). Lodging houses and brothels were associated with 'immorality' and 'promiscuity' in urban towns and port cities (Archer, 2011). Contemporary commentators such as Acton (1857) emphasized the link between prostitution and the urban environment; thus, the moral boundary between pure/fallen women became reflected in the private/public spheres. Juvenile children, particularly females who were wandering or suspected of being prostitutes, or 'at risk' of associating with prostitutes, were liable for arrest. The case of eleven-year-old Catherine Herdman is illustrative as she was admitted to Sale, where the record states she had been found in the company of a 'drunken' prostitute and taken to a lodging house by a man who found her wandering (Manchester Sale, M369/4/18 Admissions, MRO). Although there are no specific details regarding whether the girl was harmed in any way by the man, this risk itself was enough to have her committed.

Criminologists today suggest that the vast majority of juvenile girls who end up on the streets, running away or committing petty crime and come into contact with the criminal justice system are most likely to have experienced childhood abuse, particularly sexual abuse (Pasko and Chesney-Lind, 2010; Belknap et al., 2011). Daly (1992) argues that we must examine the life experiences of females in order to understand their pathways into law-breaking. Goodfellow (2019) maintains that a gendered perspective on female pathways into penal custody and institutions is essential in order to understand the gender-specific response needed today in custodial establishments. The direct correlation between being a victim of abuse and a pathway into law-breaking has also been highlighted more recently by the Corston Report (2007). Historical research data collected in this data set and research conducted by Glueck and Glueck (1934) on 500 delinquent women in Massachusetts ascertained that the majority of these women had experienced abuse at a young age. Thus, not only it is vital to explore gendered pathways in the present, but analysing and applying diverse cohorts in different historical periods can offer crucial information on the routes into offending and past custodial solutions for females. Historical criminological research (Cox, 2013; Godfrey et al., 2017) offers a continuity by linking the past with the present (Churchill et al., 2022). The cases which I now examine are all over a century old and highlight how abuse contributed to girls being on the streets and their pathway into institutions in the nineteenth century. Using real-life cases offers us crucial first-hand evidence from the past regarding the unique problems that juvenile girls face within families and society, particularly Victorian society, where girls had few options and little power. I now begin with abuse as a factor identified in the admission records.

Abuse as a pathway into offending and institutions

It is challenging to identify sexual abuse as a route into delinquency based on historical records and even today, it is often very difficult to detect. Goodfellow highlights how the abuse of girls can be a pathway into law-breaking where the perpetrators are often close to the girls, constituting adults in positions of trust. Consequently, this abuse can be hidden, hard to detect and can have severe and long-term effects for girls' emotional, mental and physical wellbeing (2019: 9). Sexual abuse in the nineteenth century was associated with female children and 'the legislation for prosecuting child sex abuse was confusing and complicated' (Jackson, 2000: 14). Jackson maintains that 'Victorians used a wide collection of euphemisms – "moral corruption", "immorality", "molestation", "tampering", "ruining" and "outrage" – to refer to sexual abuse' (2000: 3). Mahood (1995) maintains that all references to sexual abuse in the case notes were indirect prior to 1920, and these were often couched in terms of concern about the girls wandering or the number of beds in working-class homes, within the admissions. Cale (1993) argues that 'overcrowding was always used to suggest that indulgence in incestuous behaviour was rife among the poor working-classes' (1993: 43). Descriptions such as those presented by Mayhew who complained of working-class living:

> The promiscuous sleeping together of both sexes in urban working-class apartments and lodging houses corrupted young women, turning them from innocent girls to infanticidal mothers.
>
> (Cossins, 2015: 65 quoting Mayhew, 1985; 1851–2: cited by Homrighaus, 2001: 353)

Holmes (2017) maintains that, despite the contributions by Ross (1993), Clark (1995) and Roberts (1995) on working-class lives, working-class bedrooms are limited to 'salacious contemporary writings on sexual immorality – incest – arising from the overcrowded sleeping arrangements prevailing in the Victorian Slum' (2017: 11). Thus, deciding whether the information in our sources was implying abuse, or innuendo and denigration of the working-class' living and sleeping arrangements becomes a highly complex task.

However, within the admissions data, there were eight cases which make direct reference to sexual abuse and the perpetrator. Three cases in the sample referred to family members, as in the case of Charlotte Long, Bertha Wright and Blanche Lawrence, where the father was the perpetrator. The admission of eight-year-old Charlotte Long due to 'wandering' in 1887 recorded 'The Father is the most evil man, 3 years ago he was sent to prison for 18 months for "immoral" conduct to his girls, they were both sometimes in the infirmary afterwards sent out to Canada. This little one expressed herself very glad to be away' (Carlton Admission records, 21131/SC/CAH/A/1/1 BRO). The records often employed terms such as 'immoral conduct, indecent assault and outrage' when describing sexual abuse, but some cases were quite specific, particularly those which went before the police or magistrates and the girl had to be examined by a police doctor. Bertha Wright, for example, was admitted into Red Lodge in 1893 for stealing and living on streets two months after she reported being raped by her father to the magistrates. Although the case was dropped, it indicates why Bertha was on the streets. Cases of incest, in which there was a prosecution like this, were uncommon before it was officially made a criminal offence in 1908. The newspaper report below describes the charges that Bertha Wright had made against her father two months prior to her arrest in April 1893. The case went before magistrates and she had to undergo an examination by a police doctor. Medical practitioners increasingly contributed evidence in cases of suspected crime over the nineteenth century (Bates, 2016).

Serious charge against father

Charles Wright a labourer was charged on remand for indecently assaulting his daughter Bertha Wright aged 11 years. The girl alleged during the absence of her mother the prisoner took her upstairs and twice assaulted her. Mr Charles Homer, surgeon stated that he found no evidence whatsoever for the charge. The girl's statement had been concocted by his wife for the purpose of getting him put away. The chairman said he could not send the case for trial on the evidence before them and the prisoner would be discharged. If further evidence be brought up he might be brought up again.

(*Essex Herald*, 28 February 1893)

Similarly, the admission record for Clara Jones, who was sent to Carlton Industrial School in December 1889, merely hinted at an assault, reading as follows: 'Clara was sent here in consequence to outrage committed on her by a young man, lodger in the house' (Carlton Admission Records, 21131/SC/CAH/A/1/1: BRO). However, the specifics of the case were detailed in the newspaper record:

A shocking case

William Jones Banks, 25, Labourer took his trial on an indictment for an attempted offence with Clara Jones, aged 10, Aug, 3rd. Mr Metcalf Barrister, prosecuted the prisoner conducting his own defence. It appeared the little girl lived with her mother and sister in a lodging house in Little Ann Street, where the prisoner also lived with a woman passed as his wife. Having sent a militia man to pawn his shirt late on the night in question, prisoner called this child into his room. She made no complaint at the time, and first told her sister eight days afterwards. Evidence was given by the child and her sister Flora, both of whom were now in a home. The latter witnessed the occurrence but had said nothing about it. The girl's mother, in cross-examination, denied having offered to settle the matter for a florin. When accused of the offence, prisoner protested his innocence, but disappeared. Mr J Paul Bush, surgeon to the Bristol police force, detailed the inconclusive results of the examination. Prisoner denied the option of giving evidence but read a statement declaring that the only time he ever touched the complainant was to strike her with his belt in order to drive her out of his room. His lordship summing up, said that many persons in a higher position than the prisoner would shrink from going into the box, through fear of a cross examination as to their previous lives. The jury retired

to consider their verdict, and on return they found the prisoner guilty. He was
sentenced to ten months hard labour.

(*Bristol Mercury,* 13 December 1889)

The newspaper provided more details regarding the incidence. Importantly, it highlights how Clara Jones was admitted into Carlton Industrial School, despite the fact that she was a ten-year-old victim of indecent assault. This would suggest that many girls who were often victims found themselves arrested and committed into an institution (Jackson, 2000). Victim blaming was not uncommon at the time. Adolescent girls according to Bates (2017) were often labelled as sexually precocious, rather than regarded as vulnerable. In this instance, the character of Clara's mother, accused of accepting a Florin to settle the matter, was also brought into cross-examination in the trial and reported in the article. Thus, the newspaper reveals attitudes about who is deemed 'true victims' and sheds light of her family background, that she was the daughter of a single mother with a sibling. Clara was admitted when she was found wandering and admitted officially under section 14.

The cases in which abuse was involved were also compounded by other factors, as noted in the admission record for Blanche Lawrence, which stated that her:

> Mother died six months ago and the Father was a brute, not only did he neglect his wife and children but he behaved indecently towards at least one of his girls. He was a respectable man until he took to drinking. Two other of his children were admitted in 1890. His wife died practically of starvation and the girls looked halved starved and filthy, devoid of any clothing. What they were wearing had to be buried. They had been dependent on neighbours for food.
>
> (Carlton Admission Records, 21131/SC/CAH/A/1/1, BRO)

The cases of Bertha Wright, Clara Jones and Blanche Lawrence demonstrate clearly the link between victimization and pathways into institutions. The 'risk' of 'abuse' is also alluded to when a girl was admitted from a home deemed as 'ill-famed'. This was the case for eight-year-old Elizabeth Brain, whose mother had died and whose father had deserted her, so she was living in a house of ill fame and had been ill-treated (Carlton Admission records, 21131/SC/CAH/A/1/1, BRO). Although the details of her abuse are not specifically stated, the fact that she was living in a house of 'ill-fame' suggested that the girl was at 'risk' and she was admitted under the 1880 Amendment Act.

The admission records provide key details of the girls' life experiences that allow us to build up a picture of the risks in their lives during this period. Goodfellow (2019) maintains today that 'a consistent finding about girls in contact with the criminal justice system is the link between offending behaviour and experiences of victimisation and trauma' (2019: 6). Roberts also argues that 'the overlapping nature of law breaking and victimhood where women with experience of abuse, assault and sexual violence are frequently swept up in the Criminal Justice system as "offenders"' (2014: 9). During the Victorian period, the juvenile institutions would refuse to admit girls who had been sexually violated. Mary Carpenter refused to allow 'penitentiary cases' to enter Red Lodge; even if these girls were the victims, they were still blamed for the crimes that befell them. Jackson maintains:

> The sexually abused girl was seen as a polluting presence, and was a particular danger to other children. The construction of childhood in terms of sexual innocence was dependent on the association of adulthood with knowledge and experience. Girls who lost their innocence could no longer be deemed "children" and, instead, became social misfits who needed retraining and reforming in a specialist institution.
>
> (2000: 6)

Sexual abuse and histories of abuse are important factors in the female pathways with regard to explaining why the girls were on the streets and their pathways into law-breaking within the dataset. As well as evidence of sexual abuse in the data, the admissions pointed to the physical abuse, which resulted in girls running away from home. I now analyse evidence of physical abuse in the admission records.

Physical abuse

Within the admissions there were details of physical abuse which resulted in girls running away from home. Chastisement of a child was not illegal in the nineteenth century, but legislation to prosecute those accused of child cruelty came into operation in the 1880s. In the data sample, there were thirty-eight cases where there was specific reference to physical abuse of the girl. Evidence of physical abuse of a child, particularly over a prolonged period, can have a damaging psychological effect, as Gelsthorpe and Wright note, 'victimization' creates psychological sequelae that can lead to offending behaviour (Sheehan et al., 2011 quoted in Gelsthorpe and Wright, 2015). This is evident in the case of Jane Crawford, who was admitted into Red Lodge for stealing two bonnets. The court was informed that: 'The mother, incorrigible, had been in goal twice and in the habit of chastising the child with great cruelty. The father spent his pension in public houses. The child needed rescuing' (*Leeds Intelligencer,* 18 August 1855). Although the physical abuse is not described in detail here, there were cases in which this occurred, such as in the case of Keziah Moore, where both the admission record and newspaper highlight the severity of the physical abuse that she endured:

> *Florence Moore was charged with assaulting her stepchild Keziah. Mr Hugh Holmes Gore conducted the prosecution. In answer to the charge, defendant said she beat the child because of her thieving and dirty habits. Mr Gore said this was a particularly painful case. Defendant, the step-mother, appeared to be perpetually beating the child and acting with greatest cruelty towards her. Owing to the energy of Mr Bird, School board officer inquiries were made and the child examined. She was covered with bruises as the magistrates now saw on her hands, arms and shoulders … The child, whose nose and knees were broken told the magistrates that her mother frequently beat her with a stick and kicked her on the knees with her boots. Prisoner – 'of course she is tutored to say things by Mr Bird, it is nothing but his spite.' Prisoner's husband told the bench that he was not aware of his wife beating the child as had been represented – both of them told him that it caused by playing outside. The chairman said the prisoner was a most cruel and inhuman stepmother. In all the years of his sitting in that court he never saw a child so ill-treated and the woman must go to prison for six months hard labour. Being charged as not under proper control and guardianship, the child was sent to Carlton House industrial school till the age of 16.*
>
> (*Bristol Mercury*, 11 May 1889)

The case of Keziah Moore describes the physical abuse endured in particular detail; other cases highlight severe physical abuse. Frequently, as in the case of Eliza Tawkin, domestic abuse was suffered by both the parent and children, whose admission record notes:

> This child was born before wedlock, the man afterwards married the woman but took a great dislike to the child, consequently she had a sad life from which they were fast developing into a bad woman. The man is a cattle driver, the woman sells sticks. There are three children younger than this child. The man is most brutal to his wife and children, knocking them most unmercifully, the last occasion to this child, he lashed her 8 times on the back, making the bruises 6 inches long and broke the mother's ribs for which he was sent to prison for

21 days. Eliza would run away from home, first to one friend, then to another, stealing money or something else when she left, very troublesome girl before being sent here.

(Carlton Admission records, 21131/SC/CAH/A/1/1, BRO)

Alana Piper and Victoria Nagy maintain that within the criminological literature, family dynamics that are particularly disconnected, abuse, or unstable family relationships and domestic partnerships are highly correlated with female pathways into prison (2018: 279). Violence within the home, between parents, is detailed in a total of sixteen cases. However, this is not to say that abuse did not occur elsewhere, but often it was the cases that were brought to the attention of the police and magistrates that were substantially more detailed in the records. These cases were probably merely the tip of the iceberg but, nevertheless, highlight how abuse was a significant factor in the pathways to girls running away from home and also into law-breaking to survive the streets. Sharpe (2016) maintains that 'one of the most consistent findings of feminist pathways research is that justice system-involved young women have experienced extremely high rates of violent and sexual victimisation' (2015: 12). Moreover, Sharpe argues the relationship between victimization and criminal behaviour is undertheorized and the relationship may be neither linear nor one-directional (Smith and Ecob, 2007: 7).

Exposure to violence has significant negative repercussions for children's social and emotional functioning (Farrington, 2009). Intergenerational trauma was examined in a prospective study of a sample of 543 over a twenty-year period to test exposure to domestic violence between parents. The findings from this twenty-year prospective study suggest that childhood behaviour problems are among the most robust predictors of partner violence (Ehrensaft et al., 2003: 751). It was also found that in violent families, trauma can be transmitted over the generations, leading to the risk of individuals becoming a victim of intimate partner violence and trauma. In particular cases, where a parent is killed as a result of violence, this can be deeply traumatic and lead to later pathway into serious violence or criminality, as in the case of Annie Randy, who had witnessed the killing of her mother. The court records suggest that the mother's last words were to the child: 'Annie your father is murdering me' (Western Daily Press, 29 June 1893). Annie and her siblings found their mother dead following a violent attack by their father. The intergenerational transmission of trauma can affect children in the short term, especially in terms of hidden harm and self-harm. The admission recorded that Annie was a 'sad hearted girl' (Carlton Admission

Records, 21131/SC/CAH/A/1/1, BRO). Abuse within the home is also linked with neglect and in this case, Annie's father was sent to prison, which leads to Annie and her siblings being separated and admitted into different institutions in Bristol. The children also had to deal with the stigma of having a parent in prison.

Parents serving prison terms or having previous convictions are detailed within the admission records. Parents with criminal convictions were seen as corruptive influences on children. Criminal behaviour within families mirrors the key issues explored today within the field of criminology and often difficult to directly hold responsible alone for intergenerational criminality (Besemer and Farrington, 2012). The transmission of intergenerational crime from parents to children has been identified as a 'risk' factor of juveniles' pathways into law-breaking. I now highlight parents with criminal backgrounds or convictions within the dataset.

Criminalization of working-class families

The intergenerational transmission of criminality as a direct factor regarding why children may turn to delinquency has been explored in the criminological research (Besemer and Farrington, 2012). The results demonstrate the strong intergenerational transmission of criminal behaviour between fathers and their children. Historically, criminal parents brought families under the gaze of the local police and authorities. Within the dataset are examples of families that are known to the police or references to individuals coming from a 'family of criminals', as in the case of Mary Dillion who was admitted into Red Lodge in 1858, and dubbed in court as coming from a 'Family of Criminals' (*Liverpool Mercury*, 12 May 1856). Her parents and brother were all in prison and Mary was sent to Red Lodge Reformatory for stealing butter. In total, there are sixty-four admission cases where one, or both parents, had a criminal record when the girls were admitted into the school.

Table 3 above highlights the parents with criminal convictions. There were twenty-two fathers and forty-two mothers with a criminal conviction or actively in prison at the time of admission. In nine admission cases, both parents were recorded as being in prison at the time of admission. The admissions highlight girls were deemed more 'at risk' particularly if the mother had a criminal background. In Manchester Sale, twenty-two mothers had criminal convictions on the admission of the girls into the school, the majority of which were for

Table 3 Parents with criminal convictions – Manchester Sale, Carlton and Red Lodge (1854–1900).

	Mother	(per cent)	Father	(per cent)	Both	(per cent)	None	(per cent)	Total
Sale	22	(15)	8	(6)	3	(2)	110	(77)	143
Carlton	16	(8)	11	(5)	3	(1)	182	(86)	212
Red Lodge	4	(4)	3	(3)	3	(3)	100	(90)	110
Total	42	(9)	22	(5)	9	(2)	392	(84)	465

Source: Carlton Admission records 21131/SC/CAH/A/1/1; Manchester Sale Admissions, M369/4/18, MRO; Juvenile Admission Register CAT/364, LRO.

theft and larceny. Matilda Tomkins, whose mother was admitted into prison twenty-two times, was admitted for neglect and the case notes detailed how her mother took the girl from lodging to lodging, where putting her to bed in closets (Manchester Sale Admissions, M369/4/18, MRO). In three Manchester Sale admissions, both parents were in prison, as in the case of Amy Jones, whose parents were imprisoned for keeping a brothel. Amy had committed no criminal offence but was left without a guardian (Manchester Sale Admissions, M369/4/18, MRO). This was similar to the case of Catherine Radford, both of whose parents were serving twelve months in prison for keeping a 'disorderly house'. Catherine was admitted into Carlton on the 4 January 1876 and her mother died in prison on 23 January 1876 (Carlton Admission records, 21131/SC/CAH/A/1/1, BRO). Disorderly houses/brothels were deemed the most corrupting and dangerous environments for young girls.

Criminal families were known to the police and authorities, which often meant they were labelled and the children were already deemed 'at risk', as in the case of eleven-year-old Augusta Taylor, who was admitted into Carlton Industrial School in 1875. Both her father and her step-mother were in prison, the former for assaulting a police officer and the latter for being drunk and disorderly and stealing a watch and chain from a lady. The admission record shows that Augusta's mother had died and that her father and step-mother had 'the most disrespectful characters known'. Augusta, left alone and neglected, was arrested under Section 14 and was described as 'half-starved and very cadaverous in appearance and in a most filthy condition' (Carlton Admission records, 21131/ SC/CAH/A/1/1, BRO). Admitting these girls into the institutions was believed to be removing them from criminal environments and bad moral examples (Godfrey et al., 2017).

Evidence of criminal parents training their children in crime, as was believed to occur, is relatively limited. In all sixty-four cases in which a parent had a criminal conviction, the majority of the admissions were made under section 14, with the girls deemed to be 'at risk' and only a handful had committed a crime. Regarding Manchester Sale, only one admission record notes that Alice Hill's mother was sent to prison for two months for receiving and encouraging the girl to steal. In four further admission cases for Red Lodge, the parents were actively involved in the criminal offence of the child. In the cases of Charlotte Howell and Caroline Fletcher, the parents received goods, knowing them to have been stolen and pawned them (Bath Chronicle Gazette, 15 October 1857). In the other two instances, the mothers received custodial sentences and were sent to prison and the daughters to the Red Lodge at the same time, as in the case of Thomasine Adams in Bristol and her two daughters (*The Western Times Exeter*, March 29th 1856). Also, Ann Roberts taught her daughter, Martha Roberts, to steal. The mother was sent to prison and the father ordered to pay maintenance for his daughter while in Red Lodge (*Liverpool Daily Post*, 14 November 1856). Thus, the evidence suggesting that criminal parents lead to 'onset' and pathways into crime for children is relatively limited. This correlates with the data compiled by Godfrey et al.'s figures for boys in *Young Criminal Lives* of twenty-nine parents. The researchers conclude that 'there was no army of Fagin-like parents training their children in the arts of criminality' (Godfrey et al., 2017: 73).

However, criminal parents and criminal environments brought families to the attention of the police, magistrates placing families under surveillance and labelling children as 'at risk'. In the nineteenth century, we see the emergence of what Mahood (1995) calls the 'disciplinary society', in which there was an intensification of the social discipline of private life and 'increasing intervention in family life by outside agencies' (1995: 7). Donzelot, in *The Policing of Families* (1979), maintains that the policing, regulation and strategies related to the working class were not philanthropic pastimes but a political act, intended to depoliticize poor communities and introduce non-familial agencies into the family nexus (1979: 16). Carrington and Pereira (2009) also argue that, during this period, it was about policing families through children, and it was also about regulation and reorganization. They maintain that '[T]he punishment of children for non-criminal conduct under status or welfare offences, such as being uncontrollable or exposed to moral danger, permitted the criminalisation of immorality, poverty and cultural difference' (2009: 2). Carlen argues that 'it was their poverty, rather than their law-breaking that made working-class children prime candidates for incarceration' (1988: 5). It is essential to understand the intersection between class, as well as gender in the nineteenth century. Working-class children, particularly girls, in these corruptive environments and families were categorized as at being 'risk' and so needing to be 'saved' before they fell into a 'depraved' way of life. Williams and Godfrey (2014) argue that to understand the onset of offending, we need to examine the wider environmental and socio-economic conditions that families in poverty experienced during the Victorian period.

Poverty, deprivation and family structure

Poverty, deprivation and family structure are significant risk factors in the context of female offending and criminality. Piper and Nagy (2018) maintain that 'during the nineteenth and early twentieth century, poverty was not only a significant mitigating factor for female offending but was also, itself, effectively the "crime" for which most often imprisoned' (2018: 275). Girls were admitted on charges on vagrancy and begging, such as seven-year-old Sarah Mcloughlin, who was admitted for begging and whose parents were described as 'tramps' (Carlton Admission records, 21131/SC/CAH/A/1/1, BRO). There is a total of forty-four cases in which poverty, deprivation or begging is explicitly stated, although poverty and deprivation were a factor that was alluded to throughout a significant majority of the admissions. The descriptions and details contained within the cases provide a window into the depth of poverty and deprivation that the families were experiencing at this time. The table below provides some indication of the economic circumstances of the girls' families, through exploring parental occupations. I listed and coded the occupations detailed within the admission records, into marginal, unskilled, and skilled akin to the categories adopted by Godfrey et al., in *Young Criminal lives* (2017).

Table 4 Parental occupations for Carlton and Manchester Sale (1875–1900).

Carlton	Marginal	(per cent)	Unskilled	(per cent)	Skilled	(per cent)	Total
Fathers	46	(46)	32	(32)	22	(22)	100
Mothers	54	(74)	17	(23)	2	(2)	73
Manchester Sale							
Fathers	38	(44)	34	(39)	15	(17)	87
Mothers	21	(54)	18	(46)	0	(0)	39

Source: Carlton Admission Records 21131/SC/CAH/A/1/1; Manchester Sale Admissions, M369/4/18, MRO (details of parental occupations are omitted in the Red Lodge admission records).

The fathers' occupations are listed for 187 admissions for Manchester Sale and Carlton. Where the occupations are not listed, the parents were recorded as being dead, deserted, or in prison. Strikingly, the number of fathers listed as being unemployed with no occupation for Manchester Sale was only 5 out of the 143 admissions, with 10 fathers of 212 admissions at Carlton. Among these unemployed fathers, ill health was specified, as in the case of Lillian Silvester, who was admitted in 1889 for stealing. It was stated that her father was 'too ill to work, bad chest'. Similarly, for Harriet Prince, admitted in 1892 under section 14 after she was found wandering, it was recorded that her father was 'blind, could not work' (Carlton Admission records 21131/SC/CAH/A/1/1).

Table 4 highlights that, in both the Manchester Sale and Carlton admission records, the majority of the fathers were in marginal occupations, such as hawker, street trader and labourer. For Manchester, this was 38 per cent and slightly higher for Carlton (46 per cent), which correlates with the employment patterns in port towns such as Bristol, where there was a concentration of casual employment, such as dock labourers, which was often seasonal and rarely provided a stable form of income. This is in contrast to Manchester, an industrial town, in which the fathers were employed in the local factories and mills, working in jobs such as machine operative. These occupations were not necessarily better paid, but provided a regular, stable income for the families. Unskilled occupations, such as porter, sailor and factory worker, made up just over 30 per cent of the listed occupations of the fathers in both locations. The findings also show that, in both locations, there were fathers who were employed in skilled occupations, such as joiner, blacksmith and carpenter. The findings show that 22 per cent of the fathers from Carlton and 15 per cent of those from Manchester were employed in a skilled occupation.

Within the working-class communities, working-class men's work was uncertain, periodic, seasonal and/or poorly paid and thus insufficient to support the family, which meant that females were forced to work (Holmes, 2017). The majority of mothers in the admission records are listed as having no occupation or having 'home duties'. However, there were 112 occupations listed for mothers, which were mainly marginal work. The findings show that, for Carlton, 74 per cent of the mothers were in marginal work, such as charwoman, laundress or hawker. Mothers hawking, which meant selling wood chips, fruit and flowers on the streets, contradicted the domestic 'ideology' of the institutions and was not deemed a suitable home influence for the girls. Jankiewicz (2012) examines Street Sellers of the nineteenth century and maintains that 'street sellers posed a continual threat to the discipline, values and rhythms of the larger capitalist economy' (2012: 391).

Within the findings, only two mothers were listed as being in a skilled occupation: both were nurses. Minnie Bastaple was one of the cases. She was admitted to Carlton in 1879, and her mother Maria Bastaple left Bristol and worked at an infirmary in London as a nurse (Carlton Admission records 21131/ SC/CAH/A/1/1). There were also girls whose mothers' occupations were listed as making a living from 'immoral means' or 'prostitution'. Manchester Sale lists three mothers as prostitutes and three more as brothel owners. At Carlton, this number was far higher, as twenty-six mothers were listed as earning their living by prostitution, or 'immoral means'. This corresponds with the finding of Archer (2011) that brothels during this period were active and tolerated in port towns such as Bristol and Liverpool. Examining the occupations of the parents of the girls in this study offers insights into the economic circumstances of the girls' early lives, prior to their entry into the institutions.

As well as occupations of parents of the girls, the records also highlight family background in which poverty and household income are closely related to family structure and dynamics. Table 5 below lists the deaths of parents, parents who deserted and single mother families.

The data set shows that death, desertion or separation can leave families financially dependent on one parent and lead to a lack of parental supervision, which may be a key factor arising from the lack of family resources. Research by Mahood and Littlewood (1994), Alker (2014), Williams (2014, 2016), Davies (1999) and Archer (2011) highlighted the dynamic of working families during the nineteenth century. The children of working-class families often took to the streets to sell whatever they could in order to help their family. Both boys' and girls' labour contributed to the family income but the concern was that it brought children into contact with 'vice' and 'immorality', Manton (1976) argues that girls in Bristol were 'sellers of oranges or watercress-bunches, ballad singers, match sellers, flower – girls, growing up to back-alley prostitution' (1976: 81). Emsley (1991) argues that the street life of the poor, and public behaviour that had been previously tolerated, was now subjected to an 'unprecedented degree of scrutiny and control' (1991: 59–60). Working-class girls were seen as more at

Table 5 Family household structure, Carlton and Manchester Sale (1875–1900).

	Father dead	Mother dead	Both parents	Father deserted	Mother deserted	Single mothers
Carlton	42	38	8	11	14	55
Sale	26	23	2	19	6	52

Source: Carlton Admission records 21131/SC/CAH/A/1/1, BRO; Manchester Sale Admissions, M369/4/18, MRO.

risk of 'moral danger' and in need of 'saving', particularly if they came from single mother families, which were deemed 'immoral', or living outside a marriage (Cale, 1993).

Working-class mothers

Character descriptions feature heavily in the admissions records' descriptions of parents. Mothers were expected to preserve morality and respectability, so female 'immorality' and 'drunkenness' among mothers were deemed as setting a corrupt example and creating a negative environment for their young daughters. As Johnston (2019) argues that 'bad parents, but notably "bad mothers" were often blamed for the criminality of their offspring' (2019: 220). Davies maintains that in late Victorian Manchester and Salford, 'working class notions of respectability incorporated central components of the middle class ideal of womanhood' (1999: 76). Fears and concerns around female 'immorality' and 'drunkenness' in the urban cities led to a fear of family breakdown and social disorder.

Girls who were associated with 'criminal', 'immoral' or 'drunk' mothers were regarded as being 'at risk' of falling into corruption and depravation. As shown in Table 6 below, in the admission records for the industrial schools, Manchester Sale and Carlton, sixty mothers are described as being 'drunkards' or 'fond of drink'. The qualitative comments also add details on the nature of the alcohol-related problems within the households. The admission record for Elizabeth Godfrey, for example, who was admitted into Carlton at the age of eleven, states that 'the father of the child deserted the family nine months ago because of the drunken habits of the mother' (Carlton Admission records, 21131/SC/CAH/A/1/1, BRO). Also, in the case of Ada Holldsworth in 1875, the record states: 'Ada's Mother is a widow, employed chiefly at public houses as a charwoman, and drinks too freely' (Carlton Admission records, 21131/SC/CAH/A/1/1, BRO).

Girls with single mothers who drank were overwhelmingly admitted under section 14 (want of proper guardianship) but, when the father's character was associated with drinking, it was not a reason alone for a girl to be admitted

Table 6 Character of mothers recorded in the admissions (1875–1900).

	Alcohol	Immoral	Single	Total
Manchester Sale	24	15	52	143
Carlton	36	25	55	212

Source: Carlton Admission records 21131/SC/CAH/A/1/1; Manchester Sale Admissions, M369/4/18, MRO.

into the industrial schools. Piper and Nagy maintain that 'gendered expectations for female drunkenness was problematized in ways that males excess was not, encouraging more severe policing and punishment of female drinkers, as well as increased media scrutiny of them' (Piper, 2010, quoted in Piper and Nagy, 2018: 281). Alcohol was a main factor for the imprisonment for mothers, as in the case of eight-year old Mary Jane Lee, who was admitted into Sale, where it was recorded that 'the mother is an incorrigible drunkard in prison' (Manchester Admissions records, M369/4/18, MRO). The child was left parentless, as no father is recorded in the admission record. Fifty-five admissions for Carlton and fifty-two for Manchester Sale were associated with single mothers. 'Immoral mothers', who were considered 'prostitutes', were deemed unfit parents, as in the case of Rose Moore, where the Admission records stated:

> Rose is a dear little one saved from an awful life of evil as her mother is described as one worst in life; she leads as a prostitute. Rosie was taken from the house by Miss Sanders and placed for three months in the country. When the mother requested the child to be returned to her, Miss Sanders then requested the school board officer to meet the child and have passed into an industrial school, Miss sanders requests that the mother may not be allowed to see the child.
>
> (Carlton Admission records, 21131/SC/CAH/A/1/1, BRO)

Rose Moore, at the age of six years, was the youngest admission to the school in 1884. She was discharged in 1894, thus remaining within the institution for ten years. In total from both Carlton and Manchester Sale, forty mothers were described as 'immoral'. Seventeen girls were removed under the 1880 Industrial Schools Amendment Act. In contrast, as Cale (1993) has highlighted, such circumstances were deemed less significant in boys' admissions, pointing out: 'for example, of the 43 boys committed to Stockport Boys' Industrial School in 1891, only two were recorded as having prostitutes for mothers' (Cale, 1993: 205).

The removal of children from association with 'immoral' living, or mothers considered to be 'prostitutes' was made clear in the 1880 Industrial Schools Amendment Act. Walkowitz (1980) argues that the Industrial Schools Amendment Act 1880 gave the authorities the power to remove children from any home, or dwelling, associated with 'prostitution', thereby granting them huge leverage over working-class households. Walkowitz (1980) maintains that the removal of children from 'immoral' mothers was a radical effort to remake working-class culture in which 'control of children was the key to this radical transformation' (1980: 251). Carrington and Pereira (2009) argue that punishing mothers and holding them responsible for their children's conduct remained a feature of the child welfare discourse throughout most of the twentieth century. They argue that 'it was based on subjective perceptions of the mother's morality and competence, particularly if she was a lone parent' (2009: 32). We see mothers in the sample cohabiting or separated from their husbands, daughters being removed under section 14 due to the 'want of proper guardianship', and mothers being regarded as unsuitable to raise daughters due to their 'immoral' character. In so doing, they contributed to society's construction of a mother and what constitutes a good and bad mother, respectively, thereby facilitating its continuing control of women.

The construction of ideal motherhood stigmatized unwed, unfit mothers. The 'ideology' of the ideal feminine role and ideal mother was being constructed and enforced. Children on the street were seen as reflecting the 'depravity' of their mothers. As Stansell has argued of the antebellum in New York, the reformers represented motherhood as an expression of the female identity. The mothers of children who were admitted to the industrial schools were portrayed as being 'outside the bounds of humanity by virtue of their inability or unwillingness to replicate the innate abilities of true womanhood' (Stansell, 1987: 119). Roberts (1995) maintains that the special relationship between motherhood and crime should be a prominent subject of feminist inquiry (1995: 99). This is also an area that warrants further investigation that is beyond the scope of this chapter. In Chapter 6, motherhood and crime are investigated further. The 'ideology' and idealization of motherhood meant girls who reconvicted after becoming mothers, such as Ada Cope, were likely to receive a harsher punishment for failing to conform to the conventional models of femininity.

Beyond control

The main focus of this chapter has so far been on the pathways into crime, exploring abuse, family backgrounds and the risk factors associated with their admissions. However, in some instances, there are examples of families themselves turning to the police to enforce their authority over 'uncontrollable' girls. Within the admission records, some girls are described as beyond the control of their parents, 'incorrigible' or 'leading a criminal life'. Criminologist Davis (2017) argues that we should examine the girls' lives within this context to illuminate how the girls' actions may be seen as an attempt to gain a sense of power and status from their marginalized positions. Females' pathways into law-breaking as a means of gaining status or navigating society have not been explored in the same way as male criminality. Within the dataset, there are were twenty-three admissions which involved parents reporting their children themselves and turning to the courts to enforce their authority, as in the case of Mary Ann Glastonbury's father, who described her as '[I]ncorrigible and beyond his control' (*Bristol Mercury*, 7 December 1872). Similarly, Lillian Erskene, who was admitted into Manchester Sale as 'incorrigible and beyond control', was the daughter of a policeman and the admission record describes her as a 'bad and untruthful' girl. Social control within the family and females defying control, being active and being on the streets with 'bad associates', trying to gain status, is a pathway for girls which remains underresearched.

Davies' work on young women in Salford (1999) marked a shift in the literature and his research is particularly notable for suggesting that girls participated in gangs and violence in Manchester in the 1830s. Research by Miller (2001) also provides an original examination of the structure and activities of female gang members in an urban environment, highlighting their active positions. Miller situates these girls as having control and making decisions under their communities' cultural and economic conditions. Both Davies (1999) and Miller (2001) highlight females' active participation in criminality in the local urban environments these girls were navigating. The different 'cultural' standards are central for understanding deviance and the context of their lives in relation to class as well as gender. Females' active involvement in criminological theories has been sidelined. Indeed, some girls in the dataset navigated their marginal positions and took an active role in criminality. Rosina Soley, for example, who was admitted into Red Lodge in 1890, was found to have no less than thirty-five purses when her mother's house was searched (*Worcestershire Chronicle*, 17 May 1890). There was the suggestion that her mother had also received stolen goods and was involved. Rosina was obviously trying to navigate her local environment and marginalized position, which correlates with the case of Dorothy Horsey who was admitted into Red Lodge in 1913 after stealing, running away from home and masquerading as a boy. The newspaper article below describes the case in detail:

Girls masquerade: worked as a boy after disappearing from home
The adventure of a twelve-year girl who masqueraded as a boy and obtained work was recounted in the children's court at Old street, London. The girl Dorothy Horsey or Searles, who had been reported as missing, was charged with stealing a purse containing 9s and some pawn tickets from her house in Dunlace Road, Clapton. The evidence of her father showed that she stole the purse and contents on Monday of last week and left home. As nothing

was heard of her the witness communicated with the police and made an application to the press for assistance. Detective P.S Smith said that when he arrested the prisoner, she was dressed as a boy. Apparently, on leaving home, she cut her hair short and bought some boy's clothes. Having dressed herself in these she went in a coffee-house at 3s per week. She found a lodging elsewhere and it was because she failed to put in an appearance there on Saturday, when her rent became due, that inquiries were made which led to her arrest. It was added that on two previous occasions, the prisoner had masqueraded in a similar fashion, and had also passed as 'Dorothy Mott.' A remand was ordered.

(*Dundee Evening Telegraph*, 30 April 1913)

Dorothy's masquerading as a boy proved more injurious than her stealing. Females in this period had to navigate their limited power and place in society. Although we do not know why Dorothy took the decision to run away from home, she cut her hair and disguised herself as a boy, which suggests that boys were able to navigate society more easily than females. Dorothy's masquerade was about survival in what was a 'man's world', in a quest to make a living for herself.

Indeed, in the nineteenth century, there existed substantial social expectations for young girls, who were expected to assist mothers within the household, looking after younger children and domestic chores (Griffin, 2020). Females who displayed 'uncontrollable' behaviour were deemed 'beyond control' or 'incorrigible' leading to 'waywardness'. The pathway into the institutions has highlighted the Victorian prescribed ideals of femininity-problematized girls' behaviour, while the concern around urban and port 'immorality', particularly around prostitution, heightened the surveillance and the need to protect 'at risk' girls. The data set examined in this chapter highlights that girls were admitted to juvenile institutions for non-violent and status offences, and the need to 'save' and 'protect' 'at risk' girls overwhelmingly led to the pathways of working-class girls into the institutions.

Conclusion

In this chapter, I have readdressed the gap in the literature around female juvenile girls' pathways, highlighting victimology as well as the other 'risk factors' into law-breaking and institutional care during the nineteenth and early twentieth centuries, and thereby contributing a unique scope of data and research to the criminological literature. Current feminist contributions have sought to readdress aspects of criminality from a gendered perspective, including victimology pathways into criminality (Naffine, 1997; Walklate, 2001; Carlen, 2002). Examining the admissions in-depth highlights key details regarding the risk factors in female juvenile lives which bear some similarity with the present-day pathways (Chesney-Lind and Sheldon 2014). The chapter has demonstrated that in the nineteenth century there was 'blurred boundaries' between victimization and offending (Pasko, 2008). Goodfellow maintains today 'a consistent finding about girls in contact with the criminal justice system is the link between offending behaviour and experiences of victimisation and trauma' (2019: 6). The admission records highlight that a majority of girls had experienced victimization or trauma, or had come into contact with violence within the home, or on the streets.

The chapter also demonstrated the significance of the intersection between class as well as gender in the nineteenth century. Working-class children, particularly girls, located in these corruptive environments and families were categorized as being at 'risk', needing to be 'saved' before they fell into a 'depraved' way of living. The admission records demonstrate that the family life experienced by females in particular, such as inadequate parental supervision, poverty and deprivation, was believed to place girls 'at risk'. Carrington and Pereira maintain that 'the punishment of children for non-criminal conduct under status or welfare offences, such as being uncontrollable or exposed to moral danger, permitted the criminalisation of immorality, poverty and cultural difference' (Carrington and Pereira, 2009: 2). Working-class families were policed through their children; it was about the regulation and reorganization of the working classes.

The Victorian gendered 'ideology' of the period played a significant part in the pathway of females into institutions. The delinquent girl was seen within the nexus of 'prostitution' or at risk of 'immorality', so reformers sought to remove them from these 'at risk' environments before they fell into 'depraved' ways of living. Females in the public sphere were curtailed and working-class girls were re-moralized according to the middle-class code of respectability, domesticity and motherhood. The admission records are imbued with the moral judgments of the period which, in themselves, provide an interesting way to explore the 'ideology' and nature of the social control of young females and working-class mothers. Since the Victorian period to date, we find girls being arrested for less serious offences than their male counterparts (Goodfellow, 2019). Terms such as 'incorrigible' and 'wayward' girls continue to be used as justification for placing females into institutional and penal care (Chesney-Lind and Sheldon, 2014). The institutions framed the admissions into the schools as 'saving' or 'protecting' girls which, in the 'ideology' of Victorian morality (Odem, 1995), reflects a double standard that remains manifested today in terms of the attitudes and discretion referred to as 'judicial paternalism' (Chesney-Lind, 1977; Daly, 1989).

This need to 'save' and prevent 'immorality', or a pathway into criminality, led to the blurring of the division between the penalization and welfare established for juvenile girls, for which Pat Carlen proposed the term 'penal-welfarism', as well as the direction of the treatment of women which included 'discipline, infantalize, feminize, medicalize and domesticize' (Carlen, 1983: 182). This stigmatization of 'immoral', 'wayward' girls and label of 'at risk' females created a gendered 'ideology' of the female role. Mahood (1995) maintains that the institutions for females had a hidden curriculum, with an agenda of teaching female's domestication and their expected place within the private sphere. The next chapter explores the regulation and disciplinary regimes cultures within the Victorian institutions for girls.

5

Institutional cultures

Red Lodge Reformatory, the first female reformatory in England, was established in 1854, almost twenty years prior to Carlton and Manchester Sale Industrial School. Arguably, the reformatory regime was intended to be more punitive, in order to reform those who had committed crimes. However, notwithstanding the main distinction between the reformatory schools, reserved for children who committed a crime, and industrial schools, for those 'at risk' of criminality, all three institutions shared the same gendered institutional cultures. Carpenter advocated for separate institutions to address female needs stating:

> A school for boys is necessarily different in many respects from one for girls. They are to be fitted for independent, active life ... But girls are to be fitted for *home*; and while the same preparation for an independent life is not required for them, a far greater degree of neatness, order, and propriety of demeanour is desirable.
>
> (Carpenter, 1857: 38)

The prescribing of Victorian ideals of femininity, constructed around the 'ideology' of a chaste, passive female in the private sphere, was reinforced through the discourses of domesticity (Cale, 1993; Cox, 2013). This chapter examines the specific gendered discipline, regulation and culture within the three female institutions. These discourses justified gender-specific disciplinary practices, in which every aspect of the girl's appearance, character and behaviour had to conform to what were deemed the standards of acceptable, appropriate feminine behaviour. I will examine the day-to-day experience of the girls within the institutions, together with their training, discipline and punishment. I will also seek to uncover their voices through their actions, examining their modes of resistance within these carceral environments.

Examining the carceral space of the female institutions adds to the feminist and criminal history literature on female institutional regimes (Brenzel, 1983;

Carlen, 1983; Knupfer, 2000; Cox, 2013; Bush and Moore, 2019). Whilst extensive detailed research has emerged on boys from the same period in similar institutions – for example, *Young Criminal Lives* (Godfrey et al., 2017) – very little research has been carried out on female experiences (Cale, 1993). Godfrey and Lawrence maintain that it is essential to explore not only female deviance, but also how conceptions of 'respectable femininity' conditioned the criminal justice responses (2005: 128).

This chapter builds upon the feminist investigations of the importance of gender and the disciplining of females in penal and semi-penal institutions (Carlen, 1983; Cale, 1993, Bosworth, 1999; Rafter 1990; Barton, 2005; Haney, 2010; Cox, 2013). All three of the institutions examined, despite the differences between the reformatory and industrial schools explored in Chapter 5, shared a common characteristic, namely the identical gender-specific discourses and 'ideology' upon which they were based. The ideals of 'respectable femininity' were deeply integrated and embedded in the day-to-day running and operation of the institutions, reflecting wider societal ideas around gender and class. Inmates were expected to undertake feminized industrial labour and were primed to fulfil the traditional gendered roles of servant, wife or mother. I examine the historical evidence to analyse how these gendered discourses played a central role in regulating the working-class girls within the institutions.

This chapter examines how the institutions sought to replicate the gendered ideologies of the home, by exploring the entry process, daily regimes, discipline, regulation of sexuality and how females navigated the institutions and their forms of resistance. Whilst there appears to have been compliance with the ideals imposed upon the girls, I offer some evidence of the modes of resistance available to the females within the institutions, which not only provides evidence of subcultures and agency, but also, in the absence of personal diaries and letters, it is only through their actions that we can access their voice.

Replication of gendered ideologies of the home

We desire to reproduce to our children, the home, to place them nearly as possible in the position of the honest working-class family. This can never completely be done.

(Carpenter, Reformatory and Refuge Journal, December 1869)

The adoption of a family style system within the institutions was a middle-class response to the perceived cause of juvenile delinquency, the breakdown of family discipline in disorderly, working-class households. Murdoch maintains that, at the heart of the philanthropic movement, lay the middle-class belief that 'in order to be saved, children had to be transplanted to a new kind of domestic space' (2001: 151). Such an approach served to legitimize removal, while undermining the biological structures of working-class households (Murdoch, 2001: 161). In the nineteenth century, the middle-class home became idealized as the symbol and heart of civilized society. Tosh (1999) maintains that the ideal of the home was part of every Christian denomination. Bridgen (2011) argues that the ideologies of domesticity, 'angel in the home', were fashioned from the religious discourse. Carpenter stated that 'the home is the natural sphere for the woman', stating that girls must be prepared 'either as domestic servants or themselves hereafter the mothers of the next generation' (Carpenter cited in Ploszajska, 1994, 425). The institutions' gendered 'ideology' of the home, family and private sphere coincided with the patriarchal and capitalist changes occurring in nineteenth century society (Walby, 1990). The institutions sought to emulate the gender and class structures in the wider society. This 'ideology' of public/private spheres dictated how the female institutions were organized and governed (Davidoff et al., 1999).

The governance within all three institutions I examined reflected the micro-politics of the domestic home. As Barton noted: 'similar to the Victorian family, reformatory regimes were, to a great degree, established around paternalistic forms of governance' (Barton, 2011: 90). The female institutions were staffed entirely by women, but the senior management was male-dominated and oversaw all of the overall important management decisions. The Home Office Inspectors were males, notably Sydney Turner, as were the school doctors. The middle-class 'gentleman' on the institution committees would take care of the business and financial arrangements and provide a form of 'fatherly' authority. In contrast, the day-to-day running was undertaken by female superintendents and matrons, who would fulfil the daily domestic duties (Cale, 1992). This supervision by a 'matron-mother', whose purpose was to provide a good moral role model, produced a form of the 'mother-daughter' model of social control (Barton, 2005: 4). Carpenter, the superintendent of Red Lodge, frequently described herself in her journals as a 'mother':

> The girls seem to greatly enjoy my nightly visits to them when in bed. I can indulge the little ones in their warm embraces, which I think necessary to children, and the older ones take the opportunity to tell me their little secrets and feelings. These visits make them feel what I tell them – that I love them like a mother.
>
> (Red Lodge Journal, 12693/1: BRO)

The institutions' gendered 'ideology' of the home and the private sphere was central to their structure and governance, and normalized gendered identities. Hamlett (2015), in her book *At Home in Institutions*, maintains that domesticity was deployed in these spaces and central to the inmates' experiences within them (2015: 2). Cox posits that even the spatial organization was central to their reform:

> Certified schools – of all kinds – tried to reproduce the atomised space of the idealised middle-class family home. Dormitories, dining rooms, kitchens, laundries, bathrooms and recreation rooms were clearly demarcated … these spatial arrangements helped to foster middle-class domestic power relation, which were emphasised further by patriarchal patterns of authority.
>
> (Cox, 2013: 89)

These remaining photographs of Red Lodge Reformatory in the archives (Images 4-6) give us a glimpse of how all of the living areas were demarcated into separate spaces. Unfortunately, there are no internal pictures or floor plans of Manchester Sale or Carlton.

Image 4 Reception Room of Red Lodge Reformatory (1920s) (PicBox/3/Bint/58a, BRO).

Image 5 Great Oak Room of Red Lodge Reformatory (PicBox/3/Bint/60, BRO).

Image 6 Red Lodge Reformatory garden (PicBox, 17563/1/898, BRO).

The images above illustrate how the accommodation was demarcated into separate spaces. As well as the spatial organization, Hamlet (2015) points out that the material culture was important, in the form of the furnishings and decoration of the rooms. Red Lodge was a historic Elizabethan house with splendid oak panelling, a winding staircase, and a walled garden. The house dated back to Tudor times and Queen Elizabeth I is believed to have stayed there on one occasion. Carpenter was concerned that the residence was 'very unsuitable for the residence of young persons whose past and future lives belong in the labouring classes of society' (Carpenter, 1857; cited in Ploszajska 1994: 421). Red Lodge, similar to Carlton Industrial School, was previously a Victorian household that was significantly different from the living spaces from which the girls admitted to the schools came. In some cases, the admission records detailed the living conditions of the girls admitted to the schools. As in the case of the sisters Fanny and Ellen Richards, aged eight and eleven, admitted in 1876. The admissions record stated that 'the police sergeant stated in court that the only bed the children had to lie upon was a heap of bags in the corner of the room' (Carlton Admission Records 21131/SC/CAH/A/1/1, BRO). Similarly, Emily Manning, aged eleven, was admitted to Carlton, where the living and sleeping arrangements were commented on as follows: 'the family consists of the father, a son of 16, and two girls aged 13 and 11. The only bed the police sergeant found in the room was a heap of straw and rags on 4 chairs which was evidently shared by the whole family.' These records highlight the living spaces of the girls prior to their entry to the schools, highlighting how these Juvenile Victorian schools were both a marked improvement on their previous home, but were also a carceral space, away from their family, which the girls could not leave, in some cases for up to five years. Hamlet maintains that 'the agency of the material world – the controlling capacity of locked doors, barred windows or walled airing grounds – was an essential part of the institutional environment' (Hamlet, 2015: 9).

The evidence in the discharge records would suggest that these spaces made a lasting impression on the girls even after they left. The Great Oakroom (Image 5) had impressive oak panelling and a huge carved stone chimneypiece. Hamlet explores material culture within the schools and institutions and the significance attached to it by their inmates (2015: 8). The Great Oakroom was mentioned frequently in the discharge records. In one record, on 16 January 1906, Mary Ann Halcombe wrote a letter from Montreal, over a decade after her discharge, to say she had lost her little girl, nine years of age, and that she was in a good situation as a nurse, but had been left a widow a few years previously. She wrote: 'Please matron will you say a prayer in the Old Oak room for me, although I will not hear you, oh all favour I shall' (Miss Sullivan's Discharge book, 5137/1: 12, BRO). This suggests that prayers were held in the Oakroom and that it was a spiritual place of significance within Red Lodge for the girls. It may have given them hope but religiosity was also a panoptical form of surveillance, like an all-seeing eye in the sky (Schwan, 2001). Hamlet argues that the material world could create both opportunities for the inmates but also be used to control them (2015: 10).

The 'ideology' of the home, the ordering of space and the gendered governance was utilized to regulate and normalize females to accept that their place lay within the private sphere, performing domestic duties and feminine industrial labour. I will now explore how these regimes regulated the girls on a daily basis, beginning by exploring the archival evidence regarding the entry process of the girls into the institutions.

Entry process – the sanitization, cleansing and stripping off of the girls' former lives

As part of their entry procedure on arrival, the girls underwent a medical and decontamination process. On arrival, they were medically examined and had to be certified by a doctor as being in 'good condition' and free from disease. The admission process entailed checking for any signs of disease on the body, including venereal disease. The invasive style of checking female bodies through internal examinations by a doctor also extended into the reformatory and industrial schools, with girls required to undergo a medical examination to certify that they were 'intact'. Rodgers points to how the medical examination, entailing the use of the speculum, was seen as an aid to reform, even if this involved shaming the girls (Rodgers, 2006: 141), thereby regulating their sexual activity. Girls who had lost their 'chastity' could no longer be deemed 'children' and instead became social 'misfits' who needed reforming in specialist institutions. Even if these girls were victims of abuse, they were regarded a 'polluting' presence and a danger to other children (Jackson, 2000: 5–6). Girls who were deemed 'penitentiary cases', defined as girls who were not chaste, were deemed unsuitable for the reformatory and industrial schools. Carpenter, of Red Lodge reformatory, was quite vocal in her opposition of schools that accepted 'penitentiary cases', saying that 'the mere presence of a girl who has a mysterious and forbidden knowledge is a most dangerous stimulant to evil, and excites in other girls their latent passions' (Carpenter, 1861: 4–5, cited in Cale, 1993: 206). Invasive sexual health checks, which distinguished between pure and impure bodies, were particular to females' entry into the reformatory and industrial schools. The schools employed a doctor to check and certify that the girls were 'intact' and therefore eligible for enrolment. The use of the speculum by a doctor was a 'disciplinary technology' to regulate and police female bodies. Foucault maintains that medical knowledge, as a bio-power, provided a new mechanism for power regarding the management of 'life' (1977: 136). He states that the role of institutions is to define an inmate as 'abnormal', thus individualizing them in order to be observed and analysed by experts. In turn, they also define what was normal and abnormal, making power and knowledge co-dependent (Pembroke, 2013: 54). Red Lodge refused 'penitentiary cases', in effect labelling them as 'abnormal' (Jackson, 2000). These medical interventions were mechanisms of control. The checking, medicalization and policing of female bodies are gender-specific mechanisms of sexual control, regulating females' sexuality and their bodies.

However, the admission records for Carlton Industrial School admitted cases of girls who were believed to be 'at risk' of abuse, as in the case of Elizabeth Brain. Aged ten, her mother had died six years previously, she was later deserted by her father and was living in a 'house of ill-repute'. Elizabeth was removed under the Amendment Act (1880) which deemed it lawful to remove any child under fourteen found to be living in a brothel, or living with or associating with common or reputed prostitutes. The admission notes recorded that Elizabeth was:

> Suffering from an itch ... There is a still trace of the disease. The poor child appears to have been more than half-starved ... She is deaf, and at first seemed to be almost idiotic in her manner, but this is doubtless the effect of the severe treatment to which she has been subject.
>
> (Carlton Admission records, 21131/SC/CAH/A, BRO)

Similarly, another case, Catherine Radford admitted in 1876, aged eight, was also admitted under the Amendment Act (1880). Both of her parents were in prison for keeping a 'disorderly house' and the admission notes describe Catherine as 'having an itch in its advanced stages' (Carlton Admission records, 21131/SC/CAH/A, BRO). These two admission cases were both girls who had been removed from disorderly homes, reflecting local concerns to 'rescue' these girls from potential abuse and neglect. There was an overlap in the objectives of the Amendment Act 1880, in that it sought to curtail prostitution within working-class communities (Walkowitz, 1980), whilst simultaneously offering protection to girls who were deemed vulnerable (Moore, 2008).

On entry into the school, as well as the medical checks, each of the schools describe a sanitation process by which the girl's clothes were burnt; the girls were then cleaned thoroughly and given clean clothes. The admission records would often describe the condition of the girls on arrival. Ada Holldsworth, admitted in 1875, aged seven was described as: 'a bright looking child but in a terribly dirty state, her head swarming with vermin and several sores which necessitates it being shaved. She also has some glandular fever on her neck' (Carlton Admission records, 21131/SC/CAH/A, BRO). Similarly, the admission notes recorded details of Margaret Smith, admitted in 1879:

> She was in a most disgusting condition; her head, which was wrapped up in an old shawl, was one mass of sores and vermin. It took the greater part of an hour to shave her head. She was shaved and undressed; the rags and filth were burnt. The skin was not really clean until she had had three baths.
>
> (Carlton Admission records, 21131/SC/CAH/A, BRO)

The girls were deemed to have come from polluted environments. Dirt and disease were associated with the urban slums and squalor of the streets. Poovey (1995), in *Making a Social Body*, analysed this period and maintained that: 'The "diseased" (unproductive, criminal, plague-ridden) members, the poor were considered inimical to the health of the body politic' (1995: 7). Thus, the entry process reflected this 'ideology' that the working-class girls needed to be cleansed of their impurities. The checking of their bodies for disease and the process of sanitation represented purity and cleansing the girls of the squalor of their past lives. The burning of their clothes and new identical uniforms represented a new identity and new start.

As well as removing the girls' old clothes, the institutions also encouraged the girls to forget about their past lives: 'Every girl on entering the school is to begin with a new character. She must as far as possible forget the evil of her past life' (Red Lodge Rules and Regulations, BRO 12693/3). All the rules and regulations were read out to the girls on their arrival, including the fact that they were to be isolated for a short period. It was stated:

> When any girl is newly admitted, she must for a time sleep apart from others, and be under the especial care of the teacher; nor must she be allowed to mix freely with other girls, until it appears that she can do so without injury.
>
> (Red Lodge Rules and Regulations, 12693/3, BRO)

As well as isolation within the institutions, the girls were also forbidden from seeing their family for three months after their arrival. All letters to and from the family were read and checked by the superintendents. Visitors were 'particularly requested to abstain from any allusion to the past condition of the girls'. Also, the staff were told that they 'must never converse with the girls respecting their past history' (Red Lodge Rules and Regulations, 12693/3: 7–8, BRO). The girls were not permitted to leave the premises except to attend church, supervised by a matron (Regulation for Management of Carlton House Industrial School, 21131/SC/CAH, BRO).

The entry process into the institutions, involving sanitation, cleansing and removing their old identities, was intended to represent a new start in a 'respectable' life, away from the dirt, disease and squalor of the streets. The girls were expected to look identical with no individual clothing or identity. The institutions provided a uniform and apron for each of the girls. Carpenter stated, 'the clothing of the girls will be a uniform, simple and neat, such as would be suitable for any girl in the labouring classes of society' (Red Lodge Rules and Regulations, 12693/3, BRO). This act of detaching of their old, past life was designed to prepare the girl for their reform and training. Foucault argued that these disciplinary systems create malleable and controllable 'docile bodies' (Foucault, 1977: 138). The institutions promoted industrious feminine habits not only to curb idleness but also to train the girls for their future remunerative employment in the hope that they would obtain a position of respectability and usefulness in the community after leaving the institutions. These gendered identities were regulated and normalized through strict, regimented timetables, which I now explore.

Institutional regimes, daily routines

The institutions for females had a fundamental agenda of teaching females' domestication and their expected place within the private sphere. The 'everyday' drills, training and feminine activities sought to replicate the middle-class home. Cox states that 'the idea that wayward girls needed to be domesticated firmly underpinned the philosophy and practice of girls' reform for the century between the 1850s–1950s' (2013: 87). The strict timetables became integral in the normalizing of these roles every day. A surviving timetable from Manchester Sale highlights a typical day for the girls living in the institutions.

As the timetable shows, the structure of the day from 6.00 am until 8.00 pm was organized around schoolwork, industrial work, meal times and worship, during which the girls were under surveillance and observation by the matrons.

Timetable – for Girls at Manchester Sale (Annual Report of Manchester Industrial School 1879, M369/4/37/1, MRO)

6.00 am – Rise
6.30–8.00 am – Industrial work
8.00–9.00 am – Inspection, breakfast and family worship
9.30–12.00 pm – School and industrial work
12.00–2.00 pm – Dinner and play
2.00–5.00 pm – School and industrial work
5.00–6.30 pm – Tea and Play
6.30–7.30 pm – Classes
7.30–8.00 pm – Family worship
8.00 pm – Retire

The regimented regimes were largely similar across all three institutions. This can be partly attributed to the reformatory and industrial schools' regulations and the introduction of the education policy but mainly the gender-specific discourses and 'ideology' through which the female institutions sought to reform the girls. The girls would receive educational tutelage in the morning and industrial training in the afternoon, which was deemed essential to prepare them for their future life in domestic service.

The education consisted of reading, writing and arithmetic. However, the education within each institution varied, from rudimentary subjects to what the managers of the schools advocated. Carpenter maintained that, in addition to reading, writing and simple arithmetic, 'knowledge of Geography should be given as will enable the girls to read with intelligence ordinary books of an interesting and instructive character' (Rules, Principles and Workings, 12693/12: 5, BRO). It is important to bear in mind that the educational legislation and provision had been evolving since the Education Act 1870, which established compulsory education up to the age of fourteen. Access to education for working-class girls was often constrained due to their responsibilities within the home – within the admission records for Carlton, there were girls sent for section 12, truanting from school to look after their younger siblings. In some instances, when the school board visited the homes, the mothers hid the child as in the case of Keziah Moore. Carlton admissions recorded: 'the stepmother was in the habit of hiding her when the school board officer called' (Carlton Admissions records 21131/SC/CAH/A, BRO).

The education provided by the institutions provided regular schooling for working-class girls during this period (Moore, 2008). However, while it is difficult to measure the education provided by each of the schools, it is possible to gain some insight into the girls' levels of literacy on admission. Crone's (2010) work on 'Reappraising Victorian literacy through Prison Records' maintains that prison registers on literacy data are a valuable source for social historians in that they offer evidence of the labouring poor. The admission records for Carlton detail whether each girl could read or write on admission. Of the 164 admissions for whom this was measured, 98 girls could neither read nor write, 44 could read/ write a little, and 22 could read/write well (Carlton Admission records, 21131/ SC/CAH/A, BRO). The Manchester Sale annual records also highlighted literacy in its admissions. Regarding their education on entry to the school in 1878, of the thirty-three admissions, twenty-nine could neither read nor write, two could read or write a little, and two could read and write well (Manchester Sale Annual Report Book, M369/4/31/1, MRO). The first examination held at Red Lodge in 1856 recorded that of the twenty-seven girls in the school were able to read and write on admission (Rules, Principles and Workings, BRO 12693/12: 19). The admissions records demonstrate that the majority of girls who entered the schools had no or very little ability to read and write.

Worship and religion were also central to the organization of their daily routines. Mahood states that the inmates were reformed through 'a strict regime of mild, wholesome, paternalistic Christian discipline' (1990: 78). The fears and anxiety articulated about working-class life and irreligion remained prevalent throughout the nineteenth century (Briggs, 1963). It is important to note that the similarity of the three institutions chosen in this study is that they admitted girls identified as being Protestant, or affiliated to other Protestant groups, such as Methodists, Presbyterians or Unitarians. All three institutions scheduled worship as the first thing in the morning and the last thing at the end of the day. Family worship was a daily event also, as well as on Sundays, when they spent a lot of the day engaged in worship and attending services. Similarly, Carlton institution recorded within the logbooks that the girls attended church every Sunday morning and evening (Carlton Log Book, 21131/SC/CAH/L, BRO). Moral reform was believed to be achieved through religious doctrine. Carpenter maintained that Reformation of the soul and spiritual awakening was important for the girls to 'feel spiritual affections toward the heavenly father' (Carpenter, 1851: 75). Carpenter stated: 'it will be attempted to make religion a daily influencing motive; whether they eat or drink, whatever they do, to do to the glory of God' (Carpenter, 12693/12, BRO: 5). Religious training was considered the very basis of the reforming process (Jackson, 2000).

As well as collective worship, mealtimes were regulated into the timetable; all of the girls ate the same food at set times. A surviving dietary timetable for Manchester Sale highlights the food that was given on a daily basis to the girls.

Diet and nutrition within the institutions was important, so that the girls would be healthy and strong and so able to undertake industrial training to enhance their future development. Gear (1999) maintains that the need to improve the diet of working-class children was embedded in the reformatory provision. The Red Lodge rules stated: 'the food will be wholesome and sufficient, but perfectly simple' (Rules, Principles and Workings, 12693/12: 6, BRO). The rules stipulated that meals should be eaten in silence, carefully planned, controlled and supervised. However, within the journals, there is frequent mention of children stealing food, such as 'Harvey had been climbing over the pantry window and stealing bread', 'Ackroyd stole the gardener's dinner' and 'Reach on Saturday stole out of the oven ... Yesterday the oven was attacked by one of the older girls' (Red Lodge Journals, 12693/1). This suggests that the girls were hungry, or resisting the arbitrary set times at which they were allowed to eat.

Dietary table (Manchester Sale Reports, M369/4/37/1, MRO)

	Breakfast	**Dinner**	**Tea**
Sunday	6-oz bread and treacle, ½ pint of coffee	1 pint of Hash made with meat and vegetables, 4- to 6-oz bread	6-oz bread and butter, ½ tea
Monday	¾ oatmeal porridge, 4-oz bread	1 pint of rice, milk, fruit when in season and bread	6-oz bread and treacle, ½ pint of coffee
Tuesday	Do.	12-oz meat, pudding, potatoes or either vegetables, bread	6-oz bread and dripping, ½ pint cocoa
Wednesday	Do.	1 pint of barley soup, vegetables and bread	6-oz bread and treacle, ½ pint of cocoa
Thursday	Do.	1 pint of rice with milk, bread, sugar or treacle	6-oz bread, butter, ½ pint of cocoa
Friday	Do.	12-oz Suet pudding, plums and bread	6-oz bread and treacle, ½ pint of cocoa
Saturday	Do.	Meat, vegetables and bread	6-oz bread and dripping, ½ pint of cocoa

The Red Lodge journals indicate that the girls were weighed regularly, which would suggest that there was monitoring and attempts to regulate their bodies at acceptable sizes (Red Lodge Journals, 12693/1, BRO). The female body as disciplinary power is explored by Bartky (1990) where she argues that femininity is socially constructed through the female body. She maintains that exercise and diet regimes, aimed at achieving an 'ideal' body size, aimed to 'produce a body which in gesture and appearance is recognisably feminine' and reinforce a 'disciplinary project of bodily perfection' (1988: 64). Exercise in the form of drill and activities such as walking and swimming are mentioned in the logbooks for the institutions. However, this varied between the three institutions. In the records for Red Lodge, there was very little mention of outdoor exercise, besides walks and play in the garden, particularly in the period when Mary Carpenter was superintendent. There was mention of a walk to Clifton Downs in which six girls ran away (7 March 1857, Red Lodge Journals, 12693/1, BRO). This may explain why leaving the institution was not a daily occurrence at Red Lodge, particularly in the period 1854–77. However, there were changes occurring towards the end of the nineteenth century. The 1896 Departmental Committee maintained that the children at industrial schools particularly needed physical stimulation (*Reformatory and Industrial Schools Committee Report*, 1896: 23). The records for Manchester Sale 1896 noted that walks were taken twice a week as well as physical drill with dumb-bells and parallel bars was taken weekly (Manchester Sale Reports, M369/4/37/2). Carlton logbook recorded that the girls enjoyed a weekly walk as well as the girls going to the swimming baths which gradually became a weekly activity after 1900 (School logbook, 21131/SC/CAH/L/1/1, BRO).

As well as the introduction of exercise and outdoor activities, towards the end of the nineteenth century, the institutions began to take the girls on annual excursions to the seaside or summer camps. Red Lodge's minute book for July 1890 states 'a summer outing was discussed and it was settled that the school be taken to the New Passage for a week'. It continues 'it was decided that Fanny Defler had behaved badly of late that she must forfeit the pleasure of a holiday' (Red Lodge Minute Book July 2nd 1890 12693/8, BRO). This suggests that holidays were a 'privilege that could be used to encourage and reward good behaviour and discourage and punish bad behaviour' (Gear, 1999: 151). The changes with regard to physical health that occurred within the institutions in the period 1880–1914 reflected 'a prolonged and unprecedented public discussion of the physical and mental condition of school children' (Sutherland, 1984: 6 cited in

Hendrick, 1997: 45). Nevertheless, despite the changes that occurred throughout this period, within all of the institutions, it was the girls' industrial training in sewing and laundry that took up the majority of their time.

Industrial training – ideals of domesticity

The daily performance of laundry as industrial training not only generated a profit for the school, but emphasis was also placed on the symbolism regarding cleanliness, purity and unpaid reproductive work within the private sphere, emphasizing domesticity as connected to their feminine code of conduct. Industrial training in laundry service, designed to prepare the girls for domestic service, was their main occupation. Carpenter stated that 'regular industrial occupation will fit the girls for domestic service and prepare them for any situation in life in which they may probably be placed' (Red Lodge Reformatory, Its History, Principles and Working, 1875, 12693/12: 4, BRO).

The timetable highlights that industrial work took up several hours of each day. The laundry work was on an industrial scale, receiving laundry from neighbouring boys' schools, hotels and private customers. It was unpaid labour that required little training. Calebach, in his examination of reformatory and industrial schools, *Caring for Children in Trouble* (1970), describes the Victorian view was that work was a virtue in itself and that habits of work had to be established in children. He maintains that this view that regularity of work habits was a necessary qualification for becoming a respectable citizen of the lower class led to the excessive use of labour in many institutions (Carlebach, 1970: 69).

Moreover, it is important to bear in mind that the conditions in the laundry rooms were often dangerous, and the rooms unbearably humid. Rimmer (1986) describes the appalling conditions in the following quote:

> Work in the laundry was like slavery, with limited and defective equipment in appalling conditions … The floor of the laundry was constantly awash, and there were many instances of girls and slipping and breaking limbs. Harsh soap peeled the skin off chilblained hands and the dank, foul atmosphere and searing fumes took a toll on constitutionally weakened lungs … conditions were toasted and withered from the heat of the ironing stove on which the large, heavy, cumbersome irons lined up.
>
> (1986: 52)

Strenuous work, defective equipment and reports of injuries are documented within the archival records. Within the Manchester Sale Medical Report, it was reported that Amelia Clark's right hand was crushed in the washing machine and that Dr Renshaw sent her to the infirmary, where two of her fingers had to be amputated (The Medical Report, 23 May 1884 Annual Report, M369/4/37/1, MRO). As well as the unknown long-term effects of the fumes in inefficiently ventilated rooms, the laundry work was extremely strenuous and hazardous, involving worn-out equipment, which took its toll on the girls. As well as laundry service, girls were expected to clean and perform housework within the institutions. The excessive work on young girls was commented on in 1916 by Charles Russell, Inspector for reformatory and industrial schools in his report:

> As regards the Girls' Schools I fear that there are still too many in which little girls are employed to an excessive extent upon heavy household work such as scrubbing and cleaning floors, work fitted for a strong healthy charwoman, but not at all suitable for the little child for whom the Industrial School is supposed to take the place of home, but for whom I have sometimes a qualm that it becomes the abode of soulless drudgery. Improvement, however, is to be noticed, and I hope that it may not be long before the old unstained wooden floor has disappeared, or at any rate before arrangements have been made for adult labour to perform the utterly unchildlike task of continually scrubbing the boards.
>
> (*59th Report Reformatory and Industrial Schools*, 1916: 20)

The female institutions regulated girls through domesticity and servitude, which would extend into their licence period as low-paid domestic servants (Rafter, 1985a). A refusal to accept the regulations or conform to the feminine ideals imposed by the institutions would result in disciplinary punishment.

The discipline of the girls through punishment

The discipline within the institutions ranged from removing rewards, such as a walk to Clifton Downs being forbidden as a result of girls' 'daring behaviour' (Red Lodge Journals, 12693/1, BRO), to diets of bread and water, solitary confinement, the use of corporal punishment and sending girls to prison. Cox argues that punishment in the reformatory and industrial schools was mostly focused on the removal of privileges, rather than corporal penalties (Cox, 2013, 23–4). However, the absence of the punishment books from all three institutions, or first-hand accounts from the girls themselves, makes it difficult to say with any certainty if this was true. Hide and Bourke (2018) maintain that it is central to explore the culture of harm in institutions of care. The specific way in which females were disciplined, the extent to which this may have veered into abuse, who sanctioned it and for what behaviour, is difficult to determine quantifiably for each institution, due to the missing archives. The 1866 Industrial Schools Amendment Act stipulated that corporal punishment must be recorded in a punishment book and must only be carried out by the superintendent of the school. However, the punishment books for both Red Lodge and Carlton are missing from the archives. A punishment book for Manchester Sale is present in the archives but only from 1900 (Manchester Sale Punishment Book, M369/4/27, MRO). The missing archives not only raise many questions regarding why they were removed or destroyed, but also make it difficult to make generalizations about the frequency and degree of the punishments administered. However, the minute books for all three schools contain some details of the punishments administered, as well as the journals of Mary Carpenter, which reveal detailed evidence of corporal punishment (Red Lodge Journals,12693/1, BRO).

Carpenter did not condone corporal punishment when setting out to establish reformatory schools, maintaining that no degrading or revengeful measures should ever be taken against the children, since they only 'served to excite a vindictive spirit and harden children ... crushing a child's spirit when the reformatory schools aim was that of elevating and reforming children' (Carpenter, 1851: 87). However, despite these comments made prior to the opening of Red Lodge reformatory, Carpenter's journals reveal evidence of corporal punishment, in which she ordered a girl to have her shoulders bared to be caned:

> On Saturday Apr 17 Mary Clayton when reproved by me acted with such insolent and daring defiance that I at once summoned Miss S. to cane her and being doubtful how far she would do this effectually, I determined to be present, taking with me Annie Davis who had been a witness of her daring. Miss S merely struck her clothes in a manner which could not really hurt her, so I ordered her shoulders bared, and I held her hands. Several sharp strokes were given, and she was really hurt and thoroughly humbled. I did not ask her if she was sorry, feeling that at such a moment, bodily pain must predominate, but I warned her that similar consequences would ensue whenever I witnessed such insolent rebellion in her or anyone else.
>
> (17 April 1858, Red Lodge Journals, 12693/2, BRO)

Carpenter maintained that, if girls were still insolent or absconded from the school, they should be placed in solitary confinement. Within Red Lodge, the punishment cell was located in the cellars, and there are frequent references within the journals of girls being placed in solitary confinement. This is demonstrated in the case of Eliza Collins, who absconded, was brought back from Cardiff, and placed in the solitary confinement cell. The journals revealed that Eliza smashed the windows of the cell and broke the lock, shouting that 'she would rather be in a hovel with the man she loved than anywhere else' (26 November 1855, Red Lodge Journals, 12693/1, BRO). This behaviour was seen as injurious and Collins was sent to the Bridewell for a month. However, it is difficult to know exactly how frequently and for how long the girls were placed in the solitary cell. There is no mention of solitary confinement in the Manchester Sale or Carlton records, although they do record that some girls were sent to Reformatory Schools, as in the case of Fanny Jones, who was believed to be the ringleader of a group of girls who absconded. Jones was sent to prison for twenty-one days and a reformatory for five years (Manchester Minutes, M369/4/1/1, 25 April 1878, MRO).

The institutions not only punished incidents of absconding and insubordination but behaviour such as 'imprudence, wilfulness, immodest talk to little girls, incorrigible, dirty habits, indecency, filthy talk' (Manchester Sale Punishment Book, M369/4/27, MRO). Corporal punishment in these instances was used to regulate every aspect of their character. Rafter (1985a) argues that middle-class reformers had little understanding of the realities of the lives of these girls and subjected them to impossible behavioural standards. Evans (2017) maintains that, within female penal institutions, the standardized ideal of a 'woman' is imposed upon the inhabitants through petty rules and regulations which limit their self-expression and deny them the power to be different (Evans, 2017: 37).

Girls who continually broke the rules were deemed a bad influence and permanently removed to avoid influencing others, as in the case of Ackroyd at Red Lodge who was 'constantly thieving and prying into every part of the house' (Red Lodge Journal, 12693/1, BRO). Carpenter described her as a 'terrible thief' and invited Dr King to conduct a Phrenological examination of Ackroyd, who concluded that she had 'large secretiveness, acquisitiveness, little reverence' (Red Lodge Journal, 12693/1, BRO). After a year of punishment, which included being put on a diet of bread and water and being sent to the cell, for numerous thefts, which included stealing the dormitory keys and burying them in the garden, Carpenter concluded that she suffered from 'absolute mania' and was injurious to the other girls in the school. Ackroyd and her family emigrated to Australia in 1857 (Carpenter's Journals, 12693/1, BRO). Ferguson (2007) has shown how the constitution of the institutionalized child, as both victim and threat, as 'moral dirt' with the potential to pollute the surrounding environment, justified the harsh discipline that too often veered into abuse in institutions.

The scale of abuse occurring within the institutions is difficult to examine in depth without evidence from documents or oral testimony (Humphries, 1981). However, oral testimony did find its way within the public domain through allegations reported in historical newspapers. The local Bristol Newspaper reported allegations of abuse at Red Lodge Reformatory. Three girls, Sarah Berry, Harriet Powell and Jane Crawford, absconded from the reformatory before being arrested and brought before the magistrates. In their defence, the girls claimed that the teachers had beaten them (*Bristol Mercury*, 7 November 1857). Moreover, the revelations of abuse in the Glasgow Girls Industrial School scandal in 1881 were made public in local newspapers, detailing the punishment of Mary Jane Park, aged fourteen, who was laid naked across a bed and flogged by the matron of the school, Miss Wallace (*East and South Devon Advertiser*, 26 November 1881). A sub-committee was appointed to inquire into the management of the school. The investigation revealed that the punishment inflicted on the girl had not been entered into the Punishment book, because it did not form part of the ordinary discipline of the school. Other evidence was collected from former girls, and the punishments mentioned 'bread' 'salt' 'sponge' and 'tongue', although these were not elaborated on and the evidence was less direct and non-definitive. However, some evidence was clear in respect to the flogging of Mary Park and two other girls, so it was resolved to accept the resignation of Miss Wallace and continue the investigation (*Dundee Weekly News*, 10 December 1881). This scandal brought into sharp focus the punishments inflicted on the girls, the flogging of the girls and the baring of their bodies. Gibson (1979), in *The English Vice*, maintains that opponents of corporal punishment for girls, particularly the baring of their bodies, argued that this could be sexually stimulating for both the flogger and the flogged (Cale, 1993). Indeed, the Glasgow Girls Industrial School scandal brought into question the use of corporal punishments for girls. Cox argues that, particularly by the start of the First World War, physical punishments for girls were only recommended for the most 'extreme offences' (Cox, 2013: 96). Extreme offences within the female institutions were associated mainly with sexual 'immorality', which resulted in a swift removal and was part of the sexual regulation of females, which I now explore.

Regulation of sexuality: ideals of chastity and marriage

The regulation and control of female sexuality was an important aspect of the institutions that disciplined and reformed working-class girls. Jeffery Weeks' prominent work, *Sex, Politics and Society: The Regulation of Sexuality since 1800*, maintains that there was 'obsessive concern with the sexuality of the working class' (Weeks, 2018). Prostitution, illegitimacy and infanticide were considered the wretchedness of 'immoral' girls, leading to the spread of disease and undermining the respectability of all classes. The institutions maintained that removing girls from the streets would remove any immoral knowledge and provide moral care and protection, preventing their fall into 'immorality'. Carpenter claimed that, unless girls were saved from an 'immoral' street life, they 'will be the teachers of vice to the next generation' (Carpenter, 1851: 35). The ideals of femininity prescribed that female sexuality should be aimed solely at procreation within marriage. Controlling sexuality, argues Foucault (1979), becomes a key element in the governance of the population and is incorporated into the fields of medicine, psychiatry and criminal justice. Foucault argues how the eighteenth-and nineteenth-century public discourses' emphasis on heterosexual monogamy and the scrutiny of 'unnatural' forms of behaviour (masturbation, homosexuality, perversity) led to the 'policing' and regulation of sex: 'Repression has indeed been the fundamental link between power, knowledge and sexuality' (Foucault, 1979: 5). Barton maintains that 'dangerous sexualities' were controlled through the mobilization of discourses that served to label and categorize women as 'immoral', thus bestowing on them an 'outcast' status (2005: 15).

The institutions sought to regulate female sexuality and impose the ideals of chastity in a number of ways. First, the medical checks carried out on arrival for disease/penitentiary cases; the distinguishing between 'normal' and 'abnormal' bodies was part of the regulation process. There was the regulation of female sexuality, whereby Levine argues that male sexuality was considered constant and natural whereas female sexuality 'had to be grown into, protected and hedged around with constraints and regulations' (Levine, 2007: 17). Deviant sexual behaviour was categorized, defined and prohibited. Girls who rejected the feminine ideals of chastity and passivity were seen as injurious to the institutions and would be removed or punished severely. Mahood and Littlewood maintain that sexual awareness was deemed 'contagious and irreversible' (1994: 568).

Sexual encounter between the girls in residential settings which spatially offered no privacy was also a fear but less of a significant concern compared to relations with men. Within the archival records, there are some indications of sexual encounters between the girls. Lesbianism was hinted at within the records by the phrase 'immoral' behaviour. Within the minutes of Manchester Sale, it is recorded 'A Shoebottom and L Ekersely have been given of immoral conduct. It was so bad it seemed necessary to punish them so severely as to the only way to save them' (Manchester Minutes, M369/4/1/1, MRO).

Similar is the case of Annie Woolham, who was sent to America. The reason for this is unclear. Carpenter wrote that Annie 'became audacious and injurious to others, Mrs Peters thought it necessary to confine her upstairs and this so exasperated her that she revenged herself by talking of gross wickedness to Mrs P's little girl, who unwisely permitted her to sit with her' (Red Lodge Journal, 12693/1: BRO). The details of this improper behaviour, defined as 'gross wickedness', are unclear but appear sufficiently serious for her to have been removed permanently from Red Lodge. This minimal mention in the records would suggest that there was no overwhelming fear of this behaviour in the female institutions, as identified in the boys' institutions (Smaal, 2013). However, any sexual behaviour between the girls was seen as a catalyst leading to heterosexual sexual feelings and desires outside marriage, which might lead to prostitution, which was deemed more dangerous (Cale, 1993). Cale argues that any sexual behaviour within the female reformatories and industrial schools was believed to lead 'to an awakened appetite for heterosexual activity which was immoral and unfeminine' (1993: 216). Chastity and purity until marriage were promoted as the respectable ideal.

Illicit heterosexual activity outside marriage, resulting in the pregnancy of an inmate of an institution, would represent a serious failing and scandal for the school, as in the case of Sarah Berry, who became pregnant. Although there were no official details documenting the case within the school minutes, letter books, or Home Office Reformatory Report for that year, the incident was detailed in Carpenter's journal, involving the governor of the Bridewell and Berry, who had been sent there with Powell and Crawford for absconding in 1857. The specific diary entries for February 1858 revealed that a letter was discovered written by Berry to a former inmate disclosing that the governor had gone to her cell when she was alone and indicated that she was pregnant. The discovery of the letter prompted Carpenter to summon the doctor, who confirmed the pregnancy. Powell was questioned and gave evidence supporting Berry's account. However, Sydney Turner, reformatory school's Inspector, who was summoned by Carpenter, questioned Berry. Whether due to threats or intimidation, Berry then changed her story and said that, the night she absconded, she had slept with several men. The seriousness of the case warranted that a private petty session be held in the school in which Berry was sentenced to six months hard labour, and the other two girls to three months hard labour. Sexual knowledge was deemed contamination, even if the girl were a victim of abuse. Jackson (2000) maintains that victims of abuse were seen as tainted by sexual knowledge. Although Berry was removed, the influence and awareness of the incident among the other girls was deemed to have caused them great harm. According to Carpenter, many girls wanted to be sent to the Bridewell, as it sounded like 'an agreeable visit' (Red Lodge Journals, 12693/2: BRO).

Pregnancy within the institution was not only a failure for the institution, but their whole tenet of reform of working-class girls along with the 'ideology' of respectable femininity, in which marriage and motherhood were now deemed inseparable. The institutions regulated sexuality within the institutions by simultaneously condoning behaviour that was deemed 'immoral', whilst also promoting chastity and marriage. The institutions would invite 'respectable' ladies to the schools to give talks to the girls (Carlton Log Book, 21131/SC/CAH/L, BRO). The schools would give gifts, a silver watch or £5, for those who married (Manchester particulars of discharge, M369/4/19/3, MRO). The institutions all mention an annual tea at New Year, when their former inmates would visit. They would, on this day, celebrate the number of girls who had married, or remained long-term in service. At the annual tea at Carlton, recorded in 1890, '30 from the old girls were present, three married' (Carlton School Journal, 21131/SC/CAH/L/1/1, BRO). Girls who were former inmates who had married and were doing well were mentioned as frequently visiting Red Lodge and seen as a positive influence (Miss Sullivan's Discharge Reports: 5137/1–2, BRO). Davidoff and Hall maintain that, in the nineteenth century, 'marriage became both symbol and institution of women's containment' (1987: 451). Thus, the institutions regulated sexuality within them by simultaneously condoning behaviour deemed 'immoral' whilst also promoting marriage, to which the girls were encouraged to aspire.

This chapter so far has examined how the intersection of gender and class was central in the 'everyday' regulations and discipline of working-class girls in the reformatory and industrial schools of the nineteenth century. However, Feminist theorist such as McNay maintains that a 'fundamental aim of the feminist project to rediscover and re-evaluate the experiences of women' (McNay, 1992: 4). Fraser (1989) and Hartstock (1990) argue examining female agency and resistance is central to building a feminist theory that seeks to subvert and challenge power within the institutions and also challenge the 'institutionalised sexism within criminological theory, policy and practise'. Evidence of resistance through absconding, rioting and a refusal to obey rules enhances our understanding of female experiences, their voices and sense of agency within the institution. I now examine the examples of resistance detailed within the archival data in more depth. The evidence allows us to see the distinctive ways in which the girls articulated their resistance as well as their sense of self and identity.

Modes of resistance

To date, there has been little written on female resistance within female reformatory and industrial schools (Cale, 1993). Examining modes of resistance is central to understanding how the young working-class girls within the reformatory and industrial schools were not simply malleable, but sought to maintain a sense of self (Zedner, 1991b). How females negotiated and resisted the ideals of femininity being imposed on them is essential to understanding and contributing to feminist criminology. Bosworth, in *Engendering Resistance, Agency and Power in Women's Prisons* (1999), argues that the specificity of female experiences in penal institutions has been neglected. Bosworth maintains:

> Despite their seeming passivity and the notorious absence of large-scale disturbances in female prisons, women constantly engage in strategies to reduce the pains of imprisonment.
>
> (1999: 7)

The absence of the inmates' original accounts, voices and narratives necessitates examination of the actions of the girls as recorded within the daily records, minute books and Carpenter's journal. In all three institutions, there is evidence of the girls absconding from the school in groups, rebelling against work and engaging in full-scale riots. These actions demonstrate their agency and encapsulate the voice of the girls through their actions, which reveal that the girls were not docile, but displayed a wilfulness to reject the feminine ideals being imposed upon them. A distinctive subculture and identity were evident among the girls through their methods of resistance, most notably from the fact that the girls absconded in groups. This highlights that the girls had a distinctive inmate subculture, rejecting the institutions' values and seeking to return to their own community. The Red Lodge Minutes and journals document several occasions on which groups of girls absconded. Regarding the example of Crawford, Berry and Powell, this was made public in the local newspaper, as detailed below:

Absconding from Red Lodge

Three girls Sarah Berry, Harriet Powell, Jane Crawford absconded from Red Lodge Reformatory, and they were further charged with having disobeyed the school rules and regulations of that establishment. Miss Carpenter, Superintendent of the institution, was present and was accommodated with a seat on the bench. Mrs Sophia Ann Stewart, the matron of the reformatory, deposed that the prisoners were all inmates, having been committed under orders of various quarter sessions, they have been guilty of disorderly conduct and had absconded twice in the last fortnight. They last absconded on Saturday when as one of the girls appointed for the purpose of cleaning out the vestibule, they took the opportunity of forcing their way by her and rushing out of the door. In about two hours afterwards, they were all brought back by the police, after which they behaved in the most outrageous manner, cursing and swearing, making use of threats, and resisting all attempts to induce them to be quiet. During the whole of the night from Saturday until Sunday morning, there were only two quiet intervals from their noise. Owing to their riotous behaviour, it was found necessary to put them into confinement, but they succeeded in forcing their way out, breaking two strong bolts by which they had been bolted in. Crawford had also picked the lock of the schoolmistresses's desk, the others being cognisant of her so doing, but they did not succeed in getting any money.

(*Bristol Mercury*, 7 November 1857)

The institutional records for Manchester Sale also highlight occasions on which girls absconded, usually in groups: 'Ellen Stockton and Ellen Hughes absconded, they were returned the following day' (Manchester Minutes, M369/4/1/1, 25 April 1878, MRO). Also listed within the same minutes were details of four other girls who absconded: Elizabeth Mayo, Rosanna Syers, Selina Hall and Fanny Jones. The latter, believed to be the ringleader, was sent to prison for twenty-one days and a reformatory for five years (Manchester Minutes, M369/4/1/1, 25 April 1878, MRO).

As well as evidence of girls absconding together, girls also resorted to riotous behaviour, as in the case of the riot at Red Lodge in 1870, which was described in the local newspaper. The riot involved five girls who had barricaded themselves into the laundry, smashing the windows, furniture and crockery. Three girls, the ring leaders, were sentenced to three months' hard labour in prison. Another girl was placed in a punishment cell at the lodge and 'threatened to smash the attendant's head open'. The newspaper report on the riot at Red Lodge read as follows:

Rebellion at Red Lodge

*Five girls barricaded themselves into the laundry and smashed the windows
and plates to damage of £1. Louisa Maddox 17, Emily Britton 16, Eliza Burton
14, Ann Lewis 15, Elizabeth Morton 16. Three were removed to Clifton Police
station 'ringleaders' and one Morton, placed in cell who then threatened to
'spilt the attendants head open' she was removed also to police station. They
were all sent to gaol – ringleaders Burton, Maddox and Lewis got three months
and other two Brittain and Morton got six weeks.*

(Bristol Police Court, *Western Daily Press*, 5 March 1870)

There was also a similar outbreak of insubordination and threats of violence
made against the staff, as recorded in Manchester Sale Minute Book. The
four ringleaders were brought before a magistrate with a view to having
them sent to a reformatory. The matron, Letitia James, testified to riotous
behaviour, during which they threatened that 'they would do murder for
her'. All the girls were guilty of misconduct, with one of them spitting in
the matron's face. (Manchester Sale Minutes, M369/4/1/1, 9 February 1881,
MRO). In another incident, four girls were brought before the magistrates
for threatening to blow up the laundry room. Laura Clarke, Sarah Cavanagh,
Annie Payne and Sarah Jones had threatened to blow up the school using the
steamer in the laundry room. The witness stated: 'it was the superintendent
of the school she threatened to blow up'. The girls were committed to prison
for twenty-one days and then to a reformatory for two years (Manchester
Sale Minutes, M369/4/1/1, MRO). This insubordination at Manchester sale
in 1881 was also documented by Inspector Inglis in the annual report of the
school:

> The record of misconduct and punishment showed that there had been a great
> deal of disorder and unruly and improper conduct during the past 12 months;
> much violence of temper had been exhibited, and many cases of impudence
> and insubordination. There had been several attempts to abscond, discipline had
> been at a low ebb, and the difficulties had been increased by the presence of
> workmen in the house during the alterations. A change of superintendence took
> place in the beginning of May. The school was going on more hopefully, but the
> girls were still in an indifferent frame of mind, and the condition of affairs was
> by no means satisfactory.
>
> (*26th Report of Reformatory and Industrial Schools, 1883*)

The specific details around the number of girls involved are not mentioned in the
annual report, thus making it difficult to know the scale of resistance within the

female institutions. Nevertheless, the reports highlight the modes of resistance that the girls utilized to defy the rules and order being imposed upon them. The site of resistance within the laundry room, the place where the girls spent time together, expected to work, is also significant. Not only did the girls withdraw their labour but they also felt agency in this space. Hamlet posits that 'inmates often used space in their own way, or rooms brought people together in ways unintended by the authorities' (2015: 10).

As well as the riotous behaviour, there were criminal damage and incidents of arson, which caused damage to the institutions. In 1855, Ackroyd had attempted to set fire to the school in the belief that, by doing so, she would be securing the return home of all of the inmates (Carpenter's Journals, 12693/1: BRO). In another instance of attempted arson, three inmates, Mary Ann Martin, Charlotte Shelton and Mary Mathias, lit two fires at the school. They were prosecuted for causing malicious damage to the house. Martin and Shelton were sentenced to two months' hard labour in prison, while Mathias was sentenced to a year in prison followed by two years in a reformatory (Red Lodge Minutes 12693, 21 September 1882, BRO).

However, in examining the modes of resistance within the institutions, it is important to note that not all of the girls responded to their institutionalization by resisting it. We must engage with the view that compliance could have been for these working-class girls a form of agency to navigate the institutions. Bosworth (1999) argues that inmates may choose to adhere to and accept feminine roles in order to develop a sense of agency and identity:

> Femininity plays a crucial, albeit paradoxical, role in their resistance: while it represents the goal and form of their imprisonment, it also represents the means by which they achieve their own ends.
>
> (1999: 7)

Thus, compliance in the form of adhering to the rules of the school and adopting the values of femininity may have offered them a chance to survive the institutions, gain a release on licence and acquire some independence (albeit marginal, whilst still under supervision for three years). Barton agrees, maintaining that embracing the conventional aspects of femininity could be utilized to their 'own ends' as a source of power (2005: 27). Realistically, in the nineteenth century, the only real status that working-class girls could achieve was that of a respectable working-class woman and the route was through regulation and conformity to the standards of femininity. Marshment (1993) agrees, arguing that women may accept the conventional images of femininity and self-regulate themselves because the patriarchal 'ideology' has achieved a general hegemony within society and so acceptance has (short-term) advantages as opposed to the stigmatization associated with an 'outcast' status. Thus, it is imperative to engage with the view presented by Bosworth (1999) and Barton (2005) that the girls may have conformed to the feminine ideals as a form of agency to enable them to survive the institutions and nineteenth-century society. Working-class girls had limited options available to them, so by conforming to the feminine ideal, it gave them a 'respectable' status to obtain employment in domestic service and even a suitable marriage. The reform and socialization within the institutions was central to the regulation of working-class girls along the ideal of femininity and domesticity.

Conclusion

Within this chapter, I have highlighted how the institutions sought to regulate and reform the girls based on multiple overlapping concerns and anxieties around 'immorality', vice, crime, prostitution and protection in urban working-class communities. I explored the 'ideology' and specific institutional regimes in the female reformatory and industrial schools of the nineteenth century. The formal teaching and training constituted an integral aspect of the reform of the girls, but it was the 'ideology' of the home, the ordering of space and the gendered governance which was utilized to regulate females to accept that their place lay within the private sphere, performing domestic duties. Gender-specific discipline, ideals of domesticity were used to regulate the behaviour of 'disorderly' girls, far beyond the walls of the institutions. The constructions of gender, the ideal feminine behaviour around the middle-class ideals, became regulated, resulting in the production of stereotypical forms of 'feminine' identity.

The institutions regulated every aspect of the girls' characters, cultural values and expectations in life. Their clothes were burnt and they were cleansed physically and expected never to discuss their previous life. The timetable, routine and industrial training were gendered, focusing on domesticity and servitude. Sexuality was regulated around discourses related to normal and abnormal bodies. 'Immoral' behaviour was punished, and the perpetrators were removed from the institutions to prevent the spread of sexual knowledge and contamination and promote chastity and marriage.

The female institutions regulated girls in domesticity and servitude, which would extend into their licence period as low-paid domestic servants. In the reformatories, as in other Victorian institutions, it became part of a 'spatial strategy in the production of useful individuals' – 'useful' being defined by middle-class notions of a governable society (Polszajska, 1994: 426). The regulation of juvenile girls was intended to normalize the gendered technologies of social control as self-regulation, which continued even beyond the reformatory and industrial schools' walls.

Within this chapter, the evidence illustrates that the girls developed modes of resistance. These acts of resistance may have been small-scale, but demonstrate that the girls utilized the methods of resistance that were available to them in their constricted environments. The resistance demonstrated by the females within the institutions provides evidence of subcultures and agency. However, overwhelmingly, there also seemed to be compliance with the ideals imposed upon them. This compliance might have represented, for these working-class girls, a form of agency to navigate both the institutions and their licence period. Accepting and adopting the expected feminine ideals afforded them a 'respectable' working-class status to avoid acquiring an outcast status. However, as is evident in the next chapter, the 'ideology' of the home as a 'refuge' was often not the reality for working-class girls in the nineteenth century (Ross, 1993; Clark, 1995; Roberts, 1996; Frost, 2008).

6

Life after the institutions

This chapter explores the aftercare and destinations of juvenile girls after they left reformatory and industrial schools in the nineteenth and early twentieth centuries. Utilizing the discharge records, which traced these girls for a period of three years after their departure (or, in some cases longer), I assembled, coded and analysed the data to explore the lives of these working-class females, their employment routes and family life. This is of central importance for understanding their transition back into society and whether they had been 'reformed' by their time in the institution and successfully reintegrated back into society. As the lives of working-class girls who entered such institutions have thus far not been explored within the literature, the uniqueness and originality of this research complements and builds upon existing research on working-class boys who attended similar institutions (Godfrey et al., 2017). In the context of girls, gendered differences have not been examined to explore how dominant hegemonic discourses of respectability, domesticity and motherhood were used to regulate female behaviour within the institutions. Such discourses were not only imposed on girls as essential if they were ever to be part of 'respectable society', but also mechanisms for their social control after they left the institutions.

This chapter analyses the dynamics and intersection of both class and gender, interrogating how the gendered ideology, which played a significant part in the reform and discipline of working-class female within the institutions, continued to be significant even after they left. The study of class in Thompson's (1963) *The Making of the Working-Class* demonstrated that the members of the working-class were not simply the passive victims of impersonal historical processes, but active agents who had participated, however incompletely, in shaping their world. However, feminist historian Joan Scott's critique of Thompson was that females figure only marginally within this seminal work (Scott, 1988). Feminist historiography by Ross (1993), Clark (1995) and Rose (1993) all seek to address the role of gender and the working-class. However, there remains a lacuna in the literature around class, gender and deviance. William's *Wayward Women* (2016) and *Criminal Women* (Godfrey and Williams, 2018) focused on criminal women, but working-class girls and their experiences at the point of leaving the juvenile institutions in the nineteenth century have not been examined. This has been neglected in the research mainly due to the nature of the sources and the difficulties associated with tracing females, and so these histories have become unknown or marginalized. Marginalized histories are always about what has survived and the history that has not been recorded, or written down, is the history that we need to hear. Gallagher et al., (2013) highlight how women have been excluded, silenced and misrepresented in stories of the past, as well as distorted or simplified in the conventional historical accounts (2013: 5). This study addresses the research gap by examining the licencing practices of the juvenile institutions and enhancing our understanding of girls' transitions within nineteenth-century society.

Utilizing primary historical sources, this chapter highlights the licence experiences of juvenile girls in the nineteenth and early twentieth centuries, by presenting empirical data to address how gender and class intersected in their licence period as well as examining the licences practices and conditions placed on the girls. This chapter will map out how the ideals of respectability, domesticity and motherhood were central to the development of 'ideal' femininity and the lives of working-class girls. However, owing to the nature of the female archival sources, it is impossible to trace females throughout their life course, mainly owing to the inconsistent and fragmentary nature of the sources. D'Cruze and Jackson (2009:1) maintain that 'the process of "Counting" is riddled with difficulties'. Barr (2019) argues that, even within the current criminological research, there exist methodological difficulties related to gaining a viable sample of women, who are poorly represented within the criminal justice system. These difficulties have been well-documented (Maruna, 2001; Barry, 2006; Healy and O'Donnell, 2006). As Gallagher et al., (2001) argue, 'reinterpreting the experiences of women in the past should take place in terms of that experience; that is to say feminist historians accept that it is not possible to interpret lived realities with the tools and approaches offered by any one discipline alone' (2001: 8). Cain posits that, in order for the 'criminological gaze' to truly 'see and speak gender', it must start outside the discipline of criminology, with an interrogation of the social construction of gender, in order to explore the 'total lives' of its subjects (Cain, 1990: 10–11).

Essentially, it is by starting from the 'outside', through understanding female lives outside incarceration and outside penal spaces, that we can begin to build up and understand how the construction of gendered identities intersected with class in the regulation of working-class girls (Carlen, 2002). Skeggs (1997), in *Formations of Class and Gender: Becoming Respectable*, argues that class and gender must be fused together to produce an accurate representation of the power relations within society. Heidensohn (1985) maintains that an understanding of women's offending will only be gained through the study of society as a whole and, in particular, the nature of the controls employed to persuade all women to modify their behaviour to suit the normative discourses of femininity (Heidensohn quoted in Evans and Jamieson, 2008: 249). This chapter will examine the licencing period, highlighting how gendered feminine routes deemed 'respectable' by the institutions continued to be mechanisms of regulation and social control beyond the institutions. I begin by examining the licencing system, including the age and conditions at and under which the girls were licenced by the institutions.

Licencing age and conditions

The licence system was similar for both the reformatory and industrial schools as the girls could be sent out on licence with a 'trusty and respectable person' after serving eighteen months of their term until they reached the age of sixteen years (Gear, 1999). A suitable work placement for girls was domestic service, which also provided accommodation. Any misconduct or unsatisfactory behaviour would result in the revoking of the girl's licence and her returning to the school. The institutions recorded details of the girls' lives for between three and five years after their release. The licence/aftercare supervision provided a period of transition and a network of contact for the girls transitioning back into society. Hartley (1986) maintains that 'the scheme was more popular in the 1890s than it had been thirty years earlier; in 1867, 453 boys and 130 girls had been licenced out whereas by 1894, 1082 boys and 196 girls had been placed on licence' (1986: 258). In 1894, the Industrial Schools Amendment Act extended the period for which the girls became liable for continued supervision by their school until they reached the age of eighteen years. The decision to send the girls out on licence was at the discretion of the managers of the institutions. However, Cale argues that the power to licence was not used as frequently as it might have been, suggesting 'that this was because older girls could take on more lucrative industrial work than their younger counterparts' (Cale, 1993: 278). Cale also points to the criticism made by the Departmental Committee on Reformatory and Industrial Schools, in its report of 1896, that there was a 'tendency of the superintendents of both reformatory and industrial girls' schools to keep the inmates inside the school to the very last day of their period of detention' (1993; 278). However, Gear (1999) maintains that some school boards also believed that licensing was good for children and wanted to encourage it. One such board was the Manchester School Board, which provided an incentive in the form of a monetary premium for every child licensed before the age of sixteen years (1999: 189).

The ages of the girls who were sent out on licence from the institutions were not always discernible from the sources available; for instance, Red Lodge discharge book failed to record the girls' ages when they were sent out on licence. However, the data that are available offer an indication of the typical ages of the girls who were sent out on licence.

Figure 3 highlights that the majority of the girls who were sent out on licence were aged fifteen years and that they were sent out for three years, finally being discharged at the age of eighteen years. Some girls were licenced as young as fourteen years and in some instances thirteen years by both schools. However, it is important in each case to consider the duration of their detention. As shown in Chapter 4, some girls entered the institutions at a very early age, as young as seven years, and then remained in the institution for over five years, as in

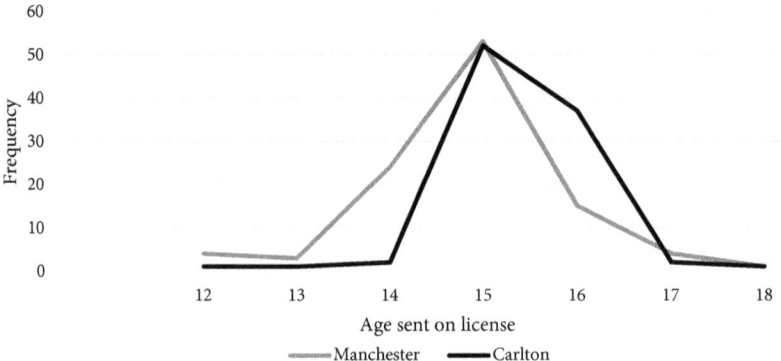

Figure 3 Age of girls sent out on licence from Manchester Sale and Carlton.

Source: Manchester Sale Licences, M369/23; Carlton Discharge books 21131/SC/CAH/A/2.

A total of 103 Manchester licences and 97 Carlton licences based on those admitted 1875–1900.

*The ages for the girls leaving Red Lodge are not given in the discharge books.

the case of Eliza Harris who entered the industrial school in 1887 aged seven and was released on licence seven years later, in 1894. In one instance, Annie Williams who entered Carlton in 1879, aged eight, under section 15, remained in Carlton as an assistant to the matron during her licence period and continued in employment until 1898, spending almost twenty years within the institution (Carlton Discharge books 21131/SC/CAH/A/2, BRO).

The decision to release the girls depended on whether they were deemed ready and suitable for this. Although the discharge records for Red Lodge do not contain any details on the girls' ages when they were sent out on licence, a hint can be gleaned from the superintendent of Red Lodge, Miss Langabeer, in her response to questions posed by the *Departmental Committee on Reformatory and Industrial Schools* in 1896. Below is a short section of the interview (with the questions posed by the committee shown in bold):

What is your rule as to licensing them?
We have no hard and fast rule.

What are the considerations which govern you?
Whenever there is a suitable situation, and we feel the girl is suitable for the place, she goes out.

The situation comes first, and the girl next?
If we have a girl ready there is no difficulty in getting a situation; there is no difficulty about that. We have far more applications for girls than we have girls to send out.

You do, as a matter of fact, keep them three and a half years. If you say there is no dearth of situations, I suppose the situation might come at the end often second year? – Why do you not allow them to go?
We do if we have a girl suitable. We have a girl whose time is just up, and she has been in a situation 2½ years.

You do not often do that?
Not often. Unless a girl is very suitable we do not let her go.
(*Report, Department Committee on Reformatory and Industrial Schools*, Minutes of evidence, 1896, 197.)

Superintendent Langabeer seems to suggest that the licencing of the girls from Red Lodge was in large part related to the girl's suitability and preparedness to transition. This suggests that the managers wished to ensure that they were ready to be successful during their licence period and beyond.

For each of the girls released on licence, an individual licence/discharge record was kept for three years, and in some instances longer. The institutions also had to produce annual reports that gave an overall evaluation of the girls who had left the institutions. The Red Lodge Return for Discharges for the years 1893–5 reveals that, of the forty-five girls discharged, thirty were identified as 'doing well', five as 'doubtful', two had been convicted of a crime, seven were 'unknown' and one was 'since dead', with a total of 68 per cent 'doing well'. Five were later 'reconvicted' (*40th Report for Reformatory and Industrial Schools*, 1897: 484). Miss Langabeer was probed further about these classifications during the examination by the *Department Committee on Reformatory and Industrial Schools* in 1896:

> **With regard to classification into 'good,' 'doubtful,' and so on, do you include the idea of prosperity in 'doing well,' or do you look upon it simply as a term referring to their moral life?**
> I look upon it as referring to their moral life.
>
> (1896, vol. 2: 199)

Thus, the classification of 'doing well' for girls mainly rested upon the girl's moral life. Cox maintains that 'a girl could be considered to be a certified school success if she kept clear of the courts, became a self-supporting servant and ultimately, made a respectable marriage' (Cox, 2013: 86). Thus, through the individual licence records, we can examine the girls' pathways out of the institutions and whether they were deemed to have been successfully 'reformed', which, according to the criteria of the institutions, meant that they obeyed the law, were in stable employment and eventually married. Girls leading an 'immoral life', offending or turning to vice were deemed a failure for the institutions and as exceeding the bounds of 'ideal femininity'. Thus, using these criteria, I will examine the girls' pathways, first based on whether or not the girls came into further contact with the law.

Offending and re-institutionalization

The institutions defined the successful reform of girls as being based on whether or not they went on to lead a respectable life which was free from criminality, entailing stable employment in domestic service and, ultimately, marriage. Girls who were convicted after leaving the institutions were deemed a failure for the schools, as this indicated that the whole tenet of the 'reform' had not worked. It is important to note that, although the Home Office Reformatory and Industrial School Reports refer to further contact with the law as 'reconvictions', the vast majority of the girls who entered the industrial institutions, Carlton and Manchester Sale, had not committed any crime. Also, although the majority of the girls who entered Red Lodge had been convicted of a crime, as shown in Chapter 4, largely for petty larceny, in some instances the girls were admitted for vagrancy. From a feminist standpoint, it is difficult to adhere to the historical criterion of 're-conviction' since, for the majority of the girls who were convicted during their licence period, this represented their first conviction. Below is a table of the 'convictions' for each institution, as recorded in the licence records.

Table 7 shows that nearly nine out of ten girls of the sample did not commit any offences. In total, from all three institutions, there were thirty occasional crimes (which meant fewer than five offences) and four persistent offenders (which meant over five offences). These categories of 'occasional' and 'persistent' criminality were utilized by Godfrey et al., (2017) *Young Criminal Lives*. As well as using the discharge records, I also checked the names, as far as they were traceable, against the online prison databases catalogued on *Find My Past* and *Ancestry*. The data show that the conviction rates across all three institutions were less than 5 per cent.

Table 8 highlights a larger sample examined for the period 1880–1920. The number of convictions appears similar in these results, again the conviction rate for females was below 5 per cent. Most schools claimed a very high level of success based on this criterion. However, Cale (1993) has questioned the reliability of figures which were collected by the managers of the schools, who were obviously keen to present their schools favourably. Notwithstanding this,

Table 7 Convictions-Core sample in the licence period (1854–1900).

	Non-offenders (per cent)		Occasional (per cent)		Persistent (per cent)		Total
Red Lodge	92	(84)	15	(14)	3	(3)	110
Manchester	132	(92)	10	(7)	1	(1)	143
Carlton	207	(98)	5	(2)	0	(0)	212

Source: Discharge licences: Miss Sullivan's Discharge book, 5137/1; M369/23 Licences; Carlton Discharge books 21131/SC/CAH/A/2.

*The percentages in these columns do not total 100 due to rounding.

Table 8 Convictions Red Lodge and Carlton (1880–1920).

	Non-offenders (per cent)		Convictions (per cent)		Occasional (per cent)		Persistent (per cent)		Total
Red Lodge	359	(86)	30	(7)	22	(5)	8	(2)	420
Carlton	392	(94)	14	(3)	14	(3)	0	(0)	420

Source: Miss Sullivan's Discharge book, 5137/1; Carlton Discharge books 21131/SC/CAH/A/2.

*The percentages in these columns do not total 100 due to rounding.

the results for the three institutions in this study bear similarity with juvenile boys who attended similar institutions as outlined in *Young Criminal Lives* (2017) who found that convictions for boys after leaving the institutions were 22 per cent over their whole lives and only 2 per cent more than one crime after release. Bearing in mind the historical definitions of conviction/re-conviction alluded to earlier, comparing the data on offending during that period in context with contemporaneous figures, the *Youth Justice Statistics for England and Wales* (2019/2020) revealed that the re-offending rate for males was 40.3 per cent compared to 28.7 per cent for females (Ministry of Justice, 2021: 65). The re-offending rate within the first two years was considerably high, so exploring why some may have (re-)offended during this initial probationary/licence period while others discontinued is critical within the criminal justice policy and practice discourse and debates. The quantitative data indicates that the number of convictions was lower for females than males during the nineteenth century after they left the institutions. However, it is necessary to explore this further in order to identify the factors related to female convictions during this period and what, if anything, this tells us about the intersection between gender and class transitioning out of the institutions.

Gendered offending – re-institutionalization

The data presented in Tables 7 and 8 indicate that there was a low conviction rate amongst the girls once they left the institutions, so it is necessary to explore the reasons for this as well as why some girls offended and a minority persisted in doing so during their licence period. Within the data, from each school, around five to fifteen girls offended (according to the schools' records) within the three-year period. Steffensmeier (1996) contends that macro-social factors are important for understanding female and male pathways into crime. The types of crimes that the females were committing point to their economic marginality as a factor in their offending. Similarly, in the case of persistent offending (more than five offences), the crimes were also property offences: larceny and theft. The macrosocial conditions that females faced during this period and continue to face in patriarchal societies, particularly the 'feminization of poverty', mean that the concentration of poverty among women drives females to engage in economically based crimes (Steffensmeier and Allan, 1996). Sharpe (2011) contends that girls' relationship with consumer culture plays an explanatory role in their criminal behaviour: 'Consumption is embodied' for young women in a way that it is not for their male counterparts (Sharpe, 2011: 95). Sharpe argues consumer culture around fashion and beauty, is central to expectations of femininity and female motivation to commit crime. However, Daly (1989) argues that poverty and economic marginalization are central factors in female crime. Daly maintains that the division of labour is linked to poverty in one of two ways: First, household work may prevent women from being employed and, second, employment is generally confined to and similar to the work performed at home and low paid. In the nineteenth and early twentieth century, female employment options were limited. The gendered divisions of labour and construction of a gendered ideology around domestic servitude placed females in marginal positions. Duckworth (2002) maintains that young servant girls, who were poorly paid and surrounded by the trappings of wealth, would steal from their household. Examining individual cases of girls who were convicted during their licence period and the types of crimes they committed helps us to understand how gender and class intersected during this period. The case of Ruth Williams, which I highlight below, provides details on her offending and re-institutionalization in prison and an inebriate reformatory.

Ruth Williams, who entered Red Lodge for stealing a cape in 1893, was sent out on licence on the 12 February 1896. While in her first job, she frequently stayed out all night and, by the end of the year, was residing at a Salvation Army Home. Within eighteen months of leaving the institution, Ruth was arrested for stealing a cape, the same offence that had her sent to Red Lodge previously, in 1893. The discharge book states: 'she seems to have gone altogether wrong now' (Miss Sullivan's Discharge book, 5137/1: 223, BRO). On her release, the Prisoner's Aid Society took charge of Ruth, but was unable to control her, so she was then sent to a home of refuge as an inmate in January 1899. Ruth was sent into service but failed to sustain employment and in 1901, was sent to Prison for three months for stealing from a visitor whilst employed as a domestic servant. In 1906, under the alias May Johns, she was again sent to prison to serve three terms concurrently for three separate occasions of theft (Metropolitan Police: Criminal Record Office: Habitual Criminals Registers and Miscellaneous Papers 1906). Williams did not settle in employment (domestic service), but persisted in criminality, using several different aliases. The final admission available is a record within the Habitual Criminals register that shows in 1907 she was convicted of stealing. Ruth was admitted to an inebriate reformatory for three years. Inebriate reformatories were established under the Inebriates Act 1898 for those convicted of drunkenness but also included criminal inebriates. The final record in the discharge books was dated 1910: 'In St Mary's Home,

Wantage – I do hope they will keep her – perhaps it may do her good. It is sad for such a young woman to live such a life of crime' (Miss Sullivan's Discharge book, 5137/: 223–4, BRO). Below are the details of the crimes committed by Ruth Williams in the Habitual Criminal Register. Ruth used several alias names which are identified in her record.

Ruth Williams (Alias Alice Long) Habitual
Criminal Record 1893–1907

Fourteen days and three years, Reformatory, Rhymney Petty Session, 27 June 1893 (stealing capes) as Ruth Williams.

Twenty-one days, Bristol Petty Sessions, 7 April 1898 (stealing a cape), as Ruth Williams.

Three months, Marylebone Police Ct., 30 September 1901 (stealing money, & c), as Ruth Williams.

Six weeks, Marylebone Police Ct., 15 December 1905 (stealing money) as Mary Johns.

Eighteen months, eighteen months and eighteen months (concurrent), Middlesex sessions, 26 May 1906 (stealing a purse, money and jewellery), as Ruth Roberts.

Three years, P.S., East Kent Sessions, 31 December 1907 (stealing jewellery), as Ruth Roberts.

Source: England & Wales, Crime, Prisons & Punishment, 1770–1935: M0140: 314.

The case of Ruth Williams highlights that all of her crimes were related to stealing and economic marginality. Ruth, by this time, was in her thirties and had spent most of her young and adult life going in and out of institutions. Her case is typical of the girls in the dataset who offended, whilst out on licence. Being formally charged and sent to prison or Borstal would have made it difficult for an individual with a criminal background to find employment, resulting in further criminality. As in the case of both Julia Jane Bridget Morris and Rose Davies, which are very similar, they both offended during their licence period and were sent to Borstal, and later prison. Borstal Institutions were established in 1902 for offenders under the age of twenty-one years. Borstal sentences were between two and three years, with the possibility of early release on licence for good progress. Similar to the female reformatories, the emphasis was on moral reform.

In the case of Julia Jane Bridget Morris, she was sent to Red Lodge Reformatory aged fourteen years for stealing. Julia remained at Red Lodge for two years before being licenced to her father in Peckham, London, on 21 December 1918. However, the discharge book recorded that, on 21 February 1919, her father sent a letter stating that 'Julia had gone away from home quite suddenly and he feared has taken £8–10–0 from a box in his landlady's room. Her father had put the matter to Peckham Police' (Miss Sullivan's Discharge book, 5137/2:197, BRO). Julia was found, brought back to Red Lodge and then transferred to Warwickshire Training home, Kenilworth, when Red Lodge closed in March 1919. It is unclear when she left Kenilworth; however, when the census was taken in June 1921, Julia was registered at a Refuge for Girls Edgbaston, Smethwick Worcestershire, under the management of Elizabeth Norton.

In November 1921, Julia, by then aged nineteen years, came before Birmingham Petty sessions, convicted of stealing a currency note for £1 belonging to Adeline Mildred Sims. Julia was detained under penal discipline in a Borstal institution for three years (Calendar of Prisoners 1868–1929, HO140). On her release from Borstal, during her licence period, Julia again re-offended. The newspaper report below described the incident in great detail, revealing also that she had a child, who was in the care of the Salvation Army. It is unclear from the records exactly when she became pregnant or gave birth, nor what happened to her child when she was sent to prison. However, it is clear that her re-offending while out on licence from both the reformatory and borstal as both a female and now a mother had broken the 'ideals of femininity'. The judgement of the magistrate, as reported in the article below, was that Julia was an 'incorrigible thief'; he told her 'you have abused every chance that has been held out to you to earn an honest living' (*West London Observer*, 18 September 1925).

Children left in West Kensington flat

Julia Jane Bridget Morris, 23 domestic servant, no home, was charged, on remand, with stealing jewellery and clothing to the value £75, belong to James Erbetta, restaurant manager of Purnell mansions, Queens Club Gardens, West Kensington, she pleaded guilty. Det-Sergeant starling stated in 1916 the prisoner was sent to a Reformatory for stealing money, in 1921 she was sent to a Borstal Institution for theft and she was now on licence. There were also two other convictions for theft. She had been in the care of the Salvation Army, who were now looking after her baby of 14 months old. The Salvation Army obtained this situation at Queen Clubs Gardens for her, where she received a weekly wage of 18s. On August 31st she was left in charge of the flat and had her mistress's two little children to look after. Mrs Erbetta, who was out that evening, chanced to telephone to the flat and receiving no reply hurried home, when she discovered that the prisoner had abandoned with the clothing and jewellery leaving the children alone in the flat. Mr Cousins observed that she seemed one of those persons who could not be helped: 'You have abused every chance that has been held out to you to earn an honest living' said the magistrate, 'and you have shown the honest ingratitude towards those who have sought to befriend you. I am afraid you are incorrigible thief.' His worship passed sentence of Six months hard labour.

(*West London Observer,* 18 September 1925)

On release from her six months' sentence of hard labour in prison, in around February 1926, the records indicate that Julia was then sent to prison again for the same offence: stealing clothing. Several other charges were brought against Julia during the period 1926–31, which are detailed below. The complete records for Julia are within the public domain on Ancestry.com and she is deceased, which prompted my decision in this instance to extend this research beyond 1920 and not anonymize this case. Julia's offences recorded between 1916 and 1928 are listed below.

Morris, Julia Jane Bridget, 26, Servant,
Criminal Record 1916–28

Previous convictions: –

Reformatory, Tower Bridge P.C., 8 December 1916 (stealing money).

Three months, Great Malvern P.C., 26 January 21 (stealing money, etc.) as Julia Morris.

Three years, Borstal Institution, Birmingham Sessions, 23 November 1921 (stealing jewellery) as Julia Morris.

Three months and licence revoked, Enfield P.S., 3 December 1923 (stealing jewellery) as Julia Morris.

Six months, West London P.C., 11 September 1925 (stealing clothing, etc.).

Six months, Lambeth P.C., 22 March 1926 (stealing clothing), as Julia Morris.

Six months, Marylebone P.C., 3 November 1926 (stealing clothing) as Julia Morris.

Committed from North London, by Basil Watson, Esq., K.C., 30 April 1928, received in prison, 23 April 1828.

Offence – 1st *Charge* – Stealing the sum of £10 15s. and six pairs of stockings, the property of Leah Wacholder, her employer.

2nd *Charge* – Receiving.

3rd *Charge* – Stealing one wristlet watch, one diamond clasp and other articles, together of the value of £57 3s.4d., the property of Pearl Wacholder, in the dwelling house of Leah Wacholder.

4th *Charge* – Receiving.

Tried before Sir Robert Wallace, Kt., K.C., 9 May 1928.

Plea – Guilty to charge 3 to the value of £44 3s.4d., except the wristlet watch and diamond clasp. Other charges not proceeded with.

Previous convictions – Marylebone P.C., 3 November, as Julia Morris.

Sentence – Nine months, Holloway Prison.

Source: UK, Calendar of Prisoners, 1868–1929: HO 140.

In 1931, there was a further criminal record for Julia, under the alias 'Mrs Bamsey', although there is no marriage record for this period, indicating she may have been cohabiting with a Mr Bamsey and took his name (MEPO6/63). The records indicate that Julia married and had four children during the period 1930–40. There are no further criminal records for Julia after 1931 under the names Julia Morris or Bamsey. Six months after Mr Bamsey died, Julia remarried in 1946 and again in 1963. She died in 1972. Marriage may have provided economic stability in her life and contributed to ceasing offending.

A similar case of a reformatory girl who was committed to borstal and later prison was that of Rose Davis, who was sent to Red Lodge in 1912, aged thirteen years, for 'housebreaking' and two charges of larceny. Rose was licenced in 1916 to her father. Mr Stanley Davies, who lived in Bristol, and she found employment in munitions. However, she left her factory job because she 'found working hours long'. The record entry for 6 January 1917 states:

We are getting a very poor account of Rose she has been stealing everywhere or rather getting things in my name collecting for wounded soldiers and the Red Cross. Was in Eastville Workhouse in December – ran away from there and has been doing this sort of thing since. I hope the police will find her. Mother gave a poor account of her – since then all the things have come out.

(Miss Sullivan's Discharge book, 5137/2: 109, BRO)

The licence record then proceeded to list her offences at Bristol Police Court, from where she was sent to Horfield Prison on four charges of stealing for three months in each case. The record then states 'This may be a lesson to her' (Miss Sullivan's Discharge book, 5137/2: 109, BRO). A list of charges was recorded in the discharge book's entry for 22 January 1917 as follows:

1.   A basket of soiled laundry – sold some torn up for rags, rest recovered.
2.   Stopped an old almshouse woman posing as Red Cross keeper – took watch and chain.
3.   From a person at Bedminster, two night frocks and a broach.
4.   From a young person stole a purse and 11/-.
5.   From Mrs Turnbull, another almshouse called for her bit of laundry, also took ½ full milk's jug of another.

The discharge book continues:

> Ran away from Salvation Army with their clothes, called at Miss Wreford Brown children's home and said she was collecting for Red Cross. Went to Mrs Dawich had 5lb Apples, 2/-eggs – Mrs Geary 2lbs of Bacon and Groceries. Went on to ordering a whole outfit, when they said they would send to Red Lodge – she disappeared. Took several children's coats and Hats from the cloakroom of St Georges Canal school pawned and sold some.
>
> (Miss Sullivan's Discharge book, 5137/2: 109–10, BRO)

Miss Langabeer, the superintendent, recorded in the discharge book that she visited Horfield prison on three occasions to see Rose, in May, July and September 1917. The final entry in the discharge book, for 17 January 1918, notes that: 'Miss Holmes Gov told me Rose had been sent to Borstal Aylesbury for three years' (Miss Sullivan's Discharge book, 5137/2: 109–10, BRO). The newspaper article below describes Rose being sent to Borstal in 1918:

A case for Borstal 1918 newspaper
Rose Florence Davies (19), a factory hand was brought up for sentence, she having been convicted at Lawford's gate of stealing a mackintosh. The case was submitted to the Quarter Sessions, the magistrate considering the case for borstal treatment – P.C. Turner proved the conviction and said she was the associate of bad characters – P.C. Bradley, who had known the girl for 16 years said she had a good father and mother, but she always given them trouble, being guilty of pilfering from an early age. A warrant charging prisoner with

theft of a pair of boots was also taken into consideration – she was sent to Borstal for three years.

(*Gloucester Journal*, 5 January 1918)

In 1921, shortly after her release from her three-year sentence in Borstal, Rose was sent to prison for twelve months. The record below details four aliases that Rose adopted and four separate crimes.

Rose Davies, aliases Clara Whatmore, Clara Jane Whatmore, Mary Mason and Madge Mason – Sentenced 8 December 1921 to twelve months imprisonment for larceny.

i) During the night, entered a house where she had recently been employed as a servant and stole articles of value.

ii) Called at a house and asked for a fictitious person, when left alone stole a watch and decamped.

iii) With aid of false references, entered the service of a doctor as a housemaid and after a few days absconded with articles of clothing, the property of a fellow servant.

iv) In the company with a confederate, called on various people in answer to advertisements for maids and cooks, and when left alone in the house stole any article to value in the house.

Source: Registers of Habitual Criminals and Police Gazettes, 1834–1934 (Ancestry).

There are no further records for Rose Davies in the criminal registers after 1924, and it is difficult to trace her from this point onwards. She may have used another alias and gone undetected, adopted another man's surname during cohabitation, or ceased offending.

Within the licence records is also the case of Rose Groves, who completed her three-year licence period without coming into any further contact with the law; however, before her final discharge, she was sent to prison, which resulted in further offending on her release. Rose was sent to Red Lodge Reformatory in 1903 for obtaining under false pretences. She was sent out on licence as a parlour maid in 1906; however, she did not remain in stable employment and frequently moved location. However, Rose kept in contact with Red Lodge, sending a photograph and returning to visit it in 1909, which was recorded in the discharge book with a later entry:

April 1909 – 'Rose came to the school with a long story – Matron got her a situation, but she was found to have told such a tissue of falsehood that she left it quite unexpectedly'.

September 1909 – Rose went to a fresh place, 'sent a very pretty view of the house – has a good chance now to do herself some good and stop roaming – did so well for some time'.

(Miss Sullivan's Discharge book, 5137/1: 469–70, BRO)

Despite the hopes that the matron had for Rose, at the end of her licence period she was sent to prison for twelve months for obtaining goods under false pretences (four counts) and stealing a lady's diamond ring. Obtaining goods under false pretences was the original pathway of Rose Groves into the institution in 1903. Having spent three years in Red Lodge, and almost four years after leaving the institution, Rose was re-convicted. A newspaper article was attached to the discharge record, which stated 'it is such a pity a girl as promising should do this' (Miss Sullivan's Discharge book, 5137/1: 469–70, BRO).

Girls depredations

Rose Groves was charged, on remand, with obtaining goods by false pretences (4 counts) and further with stealing a lady's Diamond ring, Value £7, the property of Mrs Clarke, wife of Mr Clarke of Fremington, Devon.

Detective-sergeant Wood said on the 24th he arrested the prisoner on other charges in Stoke Croft. At 35, Brooklyn Street, Ashley Vale, where prisoner had been lodging, he found the pawn-ticket produced for a lady's diamond ring pledged for £3. He asked her how she became the possessor of the ring. She said she was in service at the Imperial Hotel, Lynton, where she lent some money to a barmaid, who gave her the ring in the lieu of returning the money. Inquiries were made, and the story was found to be incorrect.

Thomas Crocker, assistant to Graham and Co. Pawnbrokers of Cumberland Street, Bristol, deposed to the pawning of lady's ring (produced). It was pledged for £3 by prisoner who gave her own name. Edward John Clark said the prisoner was in his wife's service as cook, but was inefficient. Since she had left, his wife had missed the ring. It was worth about £7. The Magistrate consulted with the clerk, and the Chairman announced that the prisoner would be sent to prison for three months on each charge, making 12 months in all, and the Governor would be asked to deal with her in a reformatory manner. Prisoner had previously been convicted (Bristol Police Court, 1911).

Rose went on to re-offend after leaving prison but appears to have evaded the law until 1919, when she was charged with a spate of robberies and sent to prison. The following newspaper record suggests that there was a series of planned robberies.

> Following a series of daring robberies at local hotels and boarding houses at Weston-Super – Mare, which has baffled the local police. Rose Groves, employed at a Weston-Super-Mare hotel, was arrested, and was on Wednesday committed for trial on a charge of stealing property, including a costly diamond broaches and cigarette cases. Accused, who admitted her guilt, is stated to have made a systematic itinerary of hotels and boarding houses and one occasion when challenged, allayed suspicion by carrying a bunch of Flowers and claiming acquaintance with a lady staying at the hotel.
>
> (*Central Somerset Gazette*, 27 June 1919)

Rose was sent to prison in 1919 and, shortly after her release, re-offended and was sent back to prison for stealing. Rose persisted in her offending, and the crimes for which she was apprehended are listed in the habitual register below:

Groves, Rose, 38, Nurse

Previous Convictions

Reformatory Cardiff P.C., 18 November 1903 (false pretences).

Three months and three months (concurrent) and three months and three months (consecutive) Bristol P.C., 1911 (stealing ring and false pretences) – four cases.

Twelve months, twelve months and twelve months (concurrent), Somerset sessions, 2 July 1919 (stealing jewellery, etc. – three cases).

Four months, Bristol P.C., 27 July 1920 (stealing coat).

Six months, Marlborough Street P.C., 18 October 1921 (stealing coat).

Six months, three months and three months (consecutive), Hove P.S., 16 November 1921 (stealing Jewellery, etc. – three cases).

Six months, three months and three months (consecutive), Ipswich P.S., 12 February 1923 (stealing jewellery, etc. – three cases) as Rose Lilian Groves.

Three months, three months, three months and three months (consecutive), Norwich City Sessions, 14 January 1924 (stealing necklet, etc. – four cases), as Rose Lilian Groves.

Six months, Marylebone P.C., 22 April 1925 (stealing jumper).

Three months, Lambeth P.C., 24 October 1925 (stealing gloves, etc.).

Committed from Westminster, by A. E. Gill. Esq., 29 January 1926.

Received in prison, 29 January 1926.

Offence – 1st charge – stealing seventy-two handkerchiefs and one waterproof coat, (the property of Harrods).

  – 2nd Charge – Receiving.

   Averment of previous conviction

Tried before Sir Robert Wallace, Kt., K.C., 4 February 1926.

Plea – Guilty to Charge 1.

Previous conviction – Lambeth P.C., 24 October 1925.

Sentence – fifteen months – Holloway Prison.

Source: UK Calendar of Prisons, 1868–1929 for Rose Groves 1926. London: Central Criminal Court (Old Bailey).

The 1921 Census listed Rose as a chambermaid at Hotel Sillwood Hotel in Brighton, despite her previous convictions. It appears that Rose moved to different cities to gain employment and commit crimes. The register listed her convictions for obtaining under false pretences and larceny in Cardiff, Bristol, Hove, Ipswich and Weston-Super-Mare. The habitual register noted in the description 'A Criminal who obtains situations as a chambermaid and then steals articles of value from the various bedrooms: she is also a persistent shoplifter' (*Metropolitan Police: criminal record office, habitual criminals' registers and miscellaneous papers* MEPO6). The subsequent history of Rose listed a further crime committed on 29 May 1937 in Bristol. There are no further records, so it is unclear what happened to Rose after 1937. There are no marriage records for her nor any children listed. Rose died in 1956 aged sixty-nine, and is buried in St. Mary Redcliffe Cemetery.

The cases of 're-offending' represent 'incorrigible' girls who failed to be 'reformed' by the institutions. Although the number of girls offending and being re-institutionalized represented a small minority of the dataset, they highlight the individual factors and experiences of working-girls who were navigating society during this period. Their options were limited if they did not remain in employment. Finding employment with a criminal conviction would have been

Table 9 Types of work undertaken on licence (1880–1900).

	Service (per cent)		Factory/Mills (per cent)		Laundress (per cent)		Hospital (per cent)		Shop (per cent)		Total
Carlton	136	(81)	20	(12)	8	(5)	3	(2)	1	(1)	168
Manchester	74	(72)	14	(14)	7	(7)	3	(3)	5	(5)	103
Red Lodge	119	(85)	8	(6)	13	(9)	0	(0)	0	(0)	140

Source: Carlton Discharge books 21131/SC/CAH/A/2; Manchester Sale Licences, M369/23, MRO; Miss Sullivan's Discharge book, 5137/1, BRO.

more difficult, and in these cases may have also been a significant contributing factor to their reoffending. However, as illustrated in Tables 8 and 9, the majority of the girls did comply with their licensing conditions, remained in employment, did not come into any further contact with law and were eventually discharged. In part two of life after the institutions, we will examine employment for the girls while out on licence.

Employment on licence

The reformatory and industrial schools maintained that stable employment in domestic service was an essential condition of their licencing and stable transitioning back into society. Employment in domestic service was not only central for ensuring probationary surveillance over the girls, but also reaffirmed the gender and class order. Ideal femininity was constructed around the 'cult of domesticity' and domestic servitude. Skeggs (1997) argues that the 'cult of domesticity' was central to middle-class consolidation, the self-defining of the middle-classes and the maintenance of the ideas of an imperialist nation (1997: 12). A short period of domestic service was regarded as good preparation for keeping one's own home. However, the implications of this for working-class girls who made up the servant class, coming from reformatory and industrial schools, are largely neglected in the literature. I will now discuss the girls' employment routes within the dataset, highlighting how gender and class intersected to place working-class girls in domestic servitude and under close surveillance.

Employment of female's post-institution

Within the discharge books, what emerges as significant are the details about their employment destinations after leaving the institutions. Domestic service was considered ideal because it simultaneously provided employment and accommodation. It was deemed the most appropriate type of work, for young females, placing them in a supervised occupation in the private sphere away from corrupt influences that existed in factory work. Mahood and Littlewood maintain: 'As a servant, a young woman laboured in private, she was a dependent in someone's home; she was not in competition with men; she was subjected to close personal control by a supervisor; and engaged in appropriate "women's work"' (1994: 562). Using this information, I was able to compile data on the girls' employment destinations during the licence period. I further examined the employment destinations up until 1920 to understand how the changes over time may have affected employment for females, particularly during the onset of the First World War when women were encouraged into munitions factories, due to shell and labour shortages (Woollacott, 1994; Noakes, 2007; Braybon and Summerfield, 2012).

The licence records highlight that girls mainly went into domestic service, despite the demand for factory work in Bristol and in the spinning mills of Manchester. Further analysis of the licence records for both Red Lodge and Carlton up until 1920 in Table 10 shows the employment routes during and post-First World War period.

Table 10 demonstrates that there was a slight increase in factory work, owing to National Service and girls going into munitions. The discharge books' attitude towards girls working in the factories seems positive in these instances, as in the case of Annie Bently, who 'sent a photo in munitions uniform, getting on very well' (Miss Sullivan's Discharge book, 5137/2, BRO: 119). Although there was no picture within the discharge book, the matron seemed proud of their contribution to the war effort. This is also evident in the case of Lillian Bland, who joined the Women's Army Auxiliary Corps (WAAC) which was set up to assist with non-combatant tasks during the war. Lillian went to France towards the end of the war, in 1918, and wrote asking for crochet. In 1919, Lillian was not demobilized and the final record for her dated 22 April 1919 recorded 'still in France, sent photos' (Miss Sullivan's Discharge book, 5137/2, 111: BRO). The case of Lillian is unique in the records and highlights how the war allowed these

Table 10 Discharge Carlton and Red Lodge employment (1880–1920).

	Service (per cent)		Factory (per cent)		Laundress (per cent)		Hospital (per cent)		Shop (per cent)		Total
Carlton	253	(78)	46	(14)	14	(4)	6	(2)	6	(2)	325
Red Lodge	274	(83)	32	(10)	21	(6)	2	(1)	2	(1)	331

Source: Miss Sullivan's Discharge book, 5137/1/2, BRO; Carlton Discharge books, 21131/SC/CAH/A/2, BRO.

girls to take routes that differed from those that the institutions expected of them. Further research is certainly warranted on how this happened in other institutions across England during the war period. However, despite some of these changes that occurred during wartime, domestic service remained the main route of employment for girls leaving the institutions in both Bristol and Manchester both before and after the war.

However, it should be noted that there was variation in the types of domestic service. The licence records for the institutions in this study did not specify which types of work within domestic service the girls went into. However, in 1897 the inspectors asked the managers to provide more detailed information on specific employment in their reports of girls. The Home Office Reformatory and Industrial Schools discharge reports from 1897 provide information for schools across England, which provides more scope to examine employment destinations and mobility. Tables 11 and 12 are the licence records for girls across England, presenting what was happening on a larger scale.

This table suggests that 'general servant' was the main job of the girls leaving the reformatory and industrial schools, although there is some variation within

Table 11 Licence for females from reformatory and industrial schools across England for 1897.

Occupation	
General servants	1,143
Housemaids	259
Laundry-maids	216
Kitchen-maids	74
Nurse-maids	59
Cooks	28
Dairymaids	9
Factories/Mills	256
Regular employment	326
Casual employment	318
Emigrated	34
Convicted	75
Dead	88
Unknown	351
Total	3,236

Source: *Forty-First Report of the Inspector of Reformatory and Industrial Schools 1897* (1897: 47). (First year, the schools provided more detailed reports as requested by the Home Office.)

Table 12 Licence for females from reformatory and industrial schools across England for 1912.

Occupations	End of 1912		
General servants	1,071	Clerks, typists	4
Cooks	39	Teachers	4
Housemaids	209	Scholars	25
Kitchen-maids	113	Shop assistants	29
Ladies-maids	5	Waitresses	27
Laundry-maids		Casual – including charing	181
– Private	118		
– Public	60	Others in regular employment	18
Dressmakers	56	Marriage	85
Factories or mills	262	Convicted	46
Assisting parents in housework	116	Dead	39
Nurse-maids	74	Unknown	133
		Total	2,750

Source: *Fifty-Sixth Report of the Inspector of Reformatory and Industrial Schools* (1912: 23).

the service, with some listed as housemaids, kitchen-maids and laundry-maids. Domestic service, in some form or other, was, in 1897, the main destination for the girls leaving the institutions. However, by 1912, as shown in Table 12 below, we begin to see some changes and mobility into other types of employment.

Table 12 highlights that there was some girls discharged into employment other than domestic service jobs. In particular routes of employment in 1912, such as clerks, scholars, teachers and shop assistants (see *Shopgirls*, Cox and Hobley, 2014), were not included in 1897. This would suggest there was some mobility for working-class girls who left the reformatory and industrial schools. However, this was around 1 per cent of the total discharged in 1912 so not significant mobility but demonstrates that there were employment options taking place into the twentieth century. One example of this is the case of Constance May Bendall, who was licenced in 1915 and went into service as a parlour maid but moved to Stroud Hospital as the head housemaid. However, she left her position to nurse her mother in 1917. The discharge book entry for 30 July 1917 reads: 'Trying to get into Shirley Isolation Hospital always had a desire for nursing' (Miss Sullivan's Discharge Book, 5137/2:57). The Final admission within the discharge book in 1918 recorded 'Still at nursing'. Constance trained as a nurse and was certified by Birmingham Union, Selly Oak Hospital in 1921–4 and registered in 1925. Constance was still registered as a nurse in the 1934 register for nurses. Constance continued to live in Birmingham, never married or had children, and died in 1977, at the age of eighty. Constance achieved her desire to become a nurse, achieving an independent life far away from her pathway into Red Lodge Reformatory in 1912 for obtaining groceries under false pretences from Stroud Co-operative Society (*Gloucester Citizen*, 22 March 1912). Nursing as a profession increased particularly when the war and its aftermath opened up opportunities for women. Although the number of girls out on licence who went into nursing is small, it highlights the obstacles that Mary Bendell encountered particularly with her early start in life. The employment of girls from the reformatories and industrial schools is certainly an area that demands further research, and the licence records provide an avenue for social and economic historians to examine working-class employment and mobility in the nineteenth and early twentieth centuries.

Both the licence records from the institutions in this study and those in the Home Office Reports highlight that overwhelmingly the major route of employment during their licence period for girls was into domestic service. Managers of the institutions sought to place girls in domestic service even if this meant relocation to other cities or rural locations. Manchester Sale relocated a total of forty-three girls from the urban environment to domestic service in Carmarthen, Wales. Red lodge relocated fifty-six girls from Bristol to service in other parts of England, namely London, Hull, Birmingham and Wales. Both Bristol and Manchester were deemed unsuitable locations for young, unsupervised females. Removal from criminal urban locations was believed to be a crucial factor in preventing the girls from coming into contact with criminal associations, as in the case of Charlotte Howell, who left Red Lodge in 1860, returned to her previous environment pre-Red Lodge and was arrested for stealing. Charlotte has a PCOM record (Home Office and Prison Commission: Female Licences, licence 2443) which details her criminal offences from her admission into Red Lodge in 1857 until 1866. The record shows that she entered penal institutions repeatedly. In 1862, after three previous convictions, Charlotte was sent to prison for four years: 'The recorder considered all attempts to reform the prisoner had been without effect, sentenced her to four years' (*Bath Chronicle*, 10 July 1862).

Similarly, Martha Dyson was discharged from Manchester Sale, committed theft against her employer whilst in domestic service, returned to Manchester and was sent to prison. The newspaper report below sensationalized the story, describing theft as her 'career':

Extraordinary career of a girl

A remarkable career on the part of Martha Dyson, of Denton, was illustrated at the Manchester County Police Court on Monday, the girl being charged with theft from a house of her employer at Eccles. In 1887, the girl was sent to an industrial school for dishonesty and two years later was allowed out on licence. In 1893 she was arrested by Manchester City Police for an offence and discharged on the condition she went to a home. She did go, but at once made her escape. Next, she was heard of Stockport, where she contracted for lodgings on the strength of a statement that she had been engaged as a member of a theatrical company. The following day she disappeared.

(*Lancaster Guardian*, 24 February 1894)

Martha Dyson was admitted into Manchester Witherington Workhouse on 4 July 1893 which explains where she was before her arrest (Manchester Workhouse Registers 1800–1911, M327/2/2/15). Martha's return to Manchester, to a familiar environment and associates known prior to her being sent to Manchester Sale, was seen as contributing factor to her offending.

As well as the institutions relocating the girls into service in other cities, they also relocated them abroad, for instance to Canada. The relocation of the girls is evident from the dataset. In total, ninety-one girls were sent to Canada from Red Lodge and Carlton. Child/youth emigration during this period was not uncommon. Maria Rye, the social philanthropist, began taking children, mostly girls, to settle in Canada as early as 1867 and was described 'the most successful of the priestesses of emigration' (*Times,* 29 October 1869). However, research on juvenile institutions removing children to Canada by Parker (2010) and Parr (1994) highlights the severe failings regarding the protection of girls sent to Canada, including the case of a girl sent from Manchester Sale in 1887, in which the girl was 'ruined'. Parker maintains 'the files contain considerable correspondence on the case, partly as a result of endeavours to establish just when and where the girl was "ruined"' (NAC, RG 17/572/64465. Lyons to Fyles, 22.3.88, cited in Parker, 2010: 229–30). This incident, in 1887, may explain why no further girls were sent to Canada from Manchester Sale. The Doyle Report (1875), an inquiry conducted by Local Government Board Inspector Andrew Doyle, was initiated after reports of mistreatment and limited supervision in improper placements in Canada. Doyle interviewed 400 children and expressed concern relating to their aftercare and welfare in the report published in 1875 (Parker, 2010).

Despite these concerns, the managers deemed domestic service the ideal employment for females, removed from criminal environments and work within the factories. However, Weeks (2012) maintains that this did not necessarily offer them security, but placed them in a vulnerable position and exposed them to sexual exploitation (2012: 80). Within the Carlton discharge records, it was recorded that Agnes Harman, who entered domestic service in New Brunswick, Canada, was returned to Bristol pregnant (Carlton Discharge Books, 21131/ SC/CAH/A/2: BRO). The licence records do not go into any details about the pregnancy, except to note that Agnes was returned from Canada. It is difficult to locate sexual abuse within the licence records examined in this study, but that is not to say that it was not occurring (Jackson, 2000).

However, within the discharge sample, the case study of Ellen Louise Cook (Nelly) licenced in 1912 demonstrates mistreatment by her mistress, who constantly humiliated her. Her employer also played a part in the girl being sent to prison as she was blamed for attempting to take her own life. Nelly, while in service at Brock Holme Farm (service on farms was physically demanding), attempted to drown herself, telling sergeant Richardson 'I am tired of life and I fully intended drowning myself' (Miss Sullivan's Discharge book, 5137/1: 568). In a letter sent from Hull Prison to Miss Langabeer, the matron of Red Lodge, Nelly wrote: 'Mistress kept throwing up the reformatory' (Miss Sullivan's Discharge book, 5137/1: 568). Nelly's previous reformatory life and abuse by her employer had a negative impact on her progress and stability. Nelly was sent from Hull prison to Aylesbury Borstal for twelve months, where the magistrate stated 'she would be taught to start again' (Miss Sullivan's Discharge book, 5137/1: 568).

Moreover, domestic service was not only difficult work for the girls but in one situation led to the loss of life. Eva Witty was licenced in 1913 to Clifton as a general servant and, in 1914, her apron caught fire and she was burned so severely that she later died of her injuries. Eva's licence record reported:

> 11th May 1914 – oh! Such a sad, sad thing, poor Eva, caught herself on fire first thing this morning – Mistress got her by motor ambulance to infirmary. It was 6 pm before we knew the situation. Miss Sullivan went to infirmary at 8.00 only to learn that Eva passed away at 3 am. I went to infirmary to identify Eva, poor child it must have been awful time for her – so badly burned. I attended inquest with mistress in the afternoon.
>
> (Miss Sullivan's Discharge book, 5137/2: 5/6)

Although the superintendent displayed sadness and stated that it must have been distressful for former girls to hear the tragic news, there was no reflection on the conditions or safety of domestic service work. The inquest into her death returned a verdict of accidental death, and the newspaper cutting below was attached to the licence record of Eva Witty, with no further comments.

Bristol inquests – fatal burns

Mr A. E. Burns, the city coroner, held an inquiry yesterday respecting, the death of Eva Witty, 19, a domestic servant, employed at 14 Bayswter Avenue, Redland, who died as the result of burns received when her clothes caught on fire, on Saturday last. Evidence of Identification was given by the matron of Red Lodge where the deceased had lived previous to going into service. Ernest Graham Murray, a little boy, said that on Saturday morning Miss Witty's apron caught fire while she was in the breakfast room. She was standing by the fire at the time. Witness called his mother. Mrs Edith Murray, of 14 Bayswater Avenue, said that deceased was in the employ as a general servant. On Saturday morning her little boy called her to the breakfast room, and outside the door she found Miss Witty enveloped in flames. Witness wrapped a hearthrug around her, and then put out the flames with water. She was taken to the infirmary in the ambulance. Witness did not think that any of the deceased clothes were of Flannelette. Her little boy told her that the corner of the deceased's apron caught on fire. The medical evidence was to the effect that the death was due to shock, following burns. A verdict of 'accidental death' was returned.

(*Western Daily* Press, 13 May 1914)

Despite these incidents that were recorded within the licence records, domestic service continued to be promoted as the ideal employment route for the girls when released on licence. It was regarded as respectable and the ideal preparation for marriage, when the girls would run their own home (Mahood, 1995). The institutions placed significant emphasis on marriage as a criterion for success in their lives. Once married, the discharge books follow the girls less closely. Marriage was also expected to put an end to employment, as married females were expected to carry out their duties in the private sphere, as 'unpaid domestics'. Although, for working-class girls, marriage and the ideal of a 'male-saviour' to provide for them was not in line with the middle-class ideal presented. Part III explores marriage within the dataset and determines its significance amongst working-class girls during the nineteenth century.

Marriage and motherhood

During the nineteenth century, marriage was promoted by middle-class reformers and the institutions as the ideal pathway for females to follow. However, marriage for working-class girls during the nineteenth century did not afford them the same privileges as middle-class marriage. In working-class communities, the work available to working-class men was uncertain, periodic, seasonal or poorly paid, so females would have to work to maintain the family. Frequently, working-class females could not reside in the household, as the middle-class ideal promoted, but had to continue working to subsidize the family income. Moreover, it is important to understand that due to economic marginality and poverty, the members of the working-class were often not in a position to marry formally, so often cohabited. Holmes (2017) argues that it is important to understand the complexity of marriage among the working-classes. Holmes argues that in this 'era of mandatory marriage' (a phrase coined by Gillis 1985), because couples were often not immediately in a position to afford a marriage ceremony, legal marriages among the Victorian working-class were preceded by a short period of cohabitation (2017: 2). Frost (2008) maintains that cohabitation, however, placed working-class women in a contested terrain, as these females, together with any (illegitimate) children they bore, were subject to violence, particularly if her cohabitee could not control her finances.

The dataset shows that the majority of the girls did not marry within the licence period, bearing in mind that most girls left the institutions on licence when they were around 15 and marriage tended to happen around the age of 22–4. This could also reflect the fact that the girls were not economically in a position to marry and cohabit with partners.

The data in Table 13 highlights which girls married within the licence period. From Manchester Sale, only 20 of the total of 143 girls married during the licence

Table 13 Marriage of the girls that left the institutions within licence period.

	Married (per cent)		Unmarried (per cent)		Total
Manchester	20	(14)	123	(86)	143
Carlton	37	(17)	175	(83)	212
Red Lodge	79	(41)	116	(59)	195

Source: Miss Sullivan's Discharge book, 5137/1/2, BRO; Carlton Discharge books, 21131/SC/CAH/A/2, BRO; Manchester Sale Licences, M369/23, MRO.

period, or shortly after. However, this contrasts with the number of marriages of former inmates from Bristol. Although Red Lodge's girls licensed before 1880 are not included in the table, between 1880 and 1900, 79 out of the total of 195 girls were recorded as married in the discharge book. Both Red Lodge and Carlton had slightly more girls marrying than Manchester, which is significant, as this may have reflected the different social and economic circumstances in the two locations. Gomersall (1997) argues that in Industrial Lancashire, the changes in the organization of labour in textile production, which led to employing women as independent workers, 'flouted the cultural norms of women's social position' (1997:4). This is certainly an area that demands closer scrutiny in relation to working-class marriage practices in the north and south of England in the nineteenth century. However, my dataset focuses on the immediate discharge and details contained within the licence records, which highlights a slightly higher rate of marriage in Bristol compared with Manchester.

Marriage was promoted as a 'domestic ideal' for the girls in the institutions, as is particularly evident in the Red Lodge discharge records. A comfortable marriage, as in the case of Elizabeth Lewis, who married Mr Eldred and became a friend of Red Lodge, was deemed a success by the institution. Elizabeth (also referred to as 'Betsy' in the records) was admitted to Red Lodge on a charge of larceny in 1881. She was discharged and left for Canada to engage in domestic service in 1886, where she married Mr Eldred in 1896. Elizabeth came a long way in life, from her admission to the school in 1881. She relocated, married, had four children and went on to support other Red Lodge Girls. The discharge book records that, in 1904, Elizabeth came to stay at the school. It states:

> 18 years since Betsy went to Canada; she is a very nice little woman, married very well. Has four children, 2 boys and 2 girls. Did our girls in school very much good to have her here.
>
> (Miss Sullivan's Discharge book, BRO, 5137/1: 331)

Elizabeth wrote frequently to the school, according to the records, and returned there in 1906 for 'three months bringing Annie and baby Jack' (Miss Sullivan's Discharge book, BRO, 5137/1: 331). The school had a close personal relationship with Betsy which is interesting and points to the recent research by Soares (2023) '*A Home from Home*', which examines how family-type relationships were sustained following the girls' discharge from the institutions. The case of Elizabeth Eldred certainly points to a close, sustained relationship decades after she left Red Lodge.

According to the discharge book, twenty-three girls went out to Canada and she is mentioned repeatedly throughout: 'Betsy and her husband visit and befriend all Red Lodge girls in Montreal' (Miss Sullivan's Discharge book, 5137/1: 331). In many of the discharge records, the girls in Canada mention Mrs Eldred's assistance and friendship. They state: 'Mrs Eldred she mothers them all' in reference to her care of the girls who went on licence to Canada (Miss Sullivan's Discharge book, 5137/1: 463). Elizabeth Lewis left her former life of crime behind, married well and even gained 'respectability' through her adoption of middle-class values. To the reformatory, she was a success and when she visited it with her children, the matron wrote: 'it did our girls in the school very much good to have her here' (Miss Sullivan's Discharge book, 5137/1: 331). The reformatory's tone in the records indicates a close personal relationship with Elizabeth, involving respect and pride. She was deemed successful because she represented what the institution sought to achieve for the girls; a respectable life, a comfortable marriage with children and fulfilling moral work for the school, ensuring that other girls led respectable lives in Canada. However, a comfortable marriage was often unattainable in working-class communities during the nineteenth century. Marriage was often less about a romantic match, than a means of practical convenience and financial survival for females during this period (Godfrey et al., 2017). This was evident in the case of Jane Avery who, at the end of her licence period at Manchester Sale, married a man twenty-four years her senior (M369/23 Licences No. 374).

An examination of the effect of marriage in the dataset suggests that some girls who had come into further contact with the law after leaving the institution engaged in no further criminal activity once married. This was exemplified in the case of Sarah Parker who left Red Lodge for domestic service in Canada in 1890 and was sent to prison within a year for stealing. Sarah married and remained so according to the discharge book records in 1904, with no further records of criminality (Miss Sullivan's Discharge book, 5137/1: 22). Similarly, Rose Hughes, who left Red Lodge on licence in October 1893, was convicted and sent to prison in 1895 for stealing a watch. Rose married Mr Evans the following year and moved to Pontypridd. There is no record of any further criminal activity and Red Lodge kept in contact with her until 1906 (Miss Sullivan's Discharge book, 5137/1:129). In addition, there is the case of Marion Kenyon, who was licenced in 1906 to her grandmother in Manchester. Marion kept in contact with the matron by writing to her during her licence period and telling her that she was doing well. However, Marion led a dishonest life for some time before she was finally caught.

THE FALLEN STAR
Bradford Girl's Amazing Audacity

A remarkable case of fraud by a young woman came before the magistrate today. The prisoner was Mirian Kenyon (23) of no settled abode, and she was charged with obtaining lodgings and food by false pretences at two houses in Cheetham Hill district. In one case the prosecutrix was Mrs. Lucas, Dalimer-street, and in the other the charge was preferred by Mrs Charlotte Linsey, Smedley Road.

The evidence was that the prisoner told Mrs Lucas she was a student at Owens College, that she had an income of £2 a week from her father, a retired admiral living in Lord Byron's House at Bristol. This story was accepted as correct by Mrs. Lucas. One day the prisoner received a printed envelope and told Mrs Lucas it was a cheque for £3 from her father; but after the girl had left it was found that it actually the copy of an advertisement from Longton. On August 29th the girl left the house wearing two dresses and two blouses, and Mrs Lucas did not see her again until yesterday. To Mrs. Kinsley the prisoner was alleged to have represented she was writing a play for Miss Horniman. She produced an exercise book in which she was writing the play, and from this Mrs Kinsley gathered that the title was 'The Fallen Star.' As in the previous case, the prisoner said she was the daughter of a retired admiral … Detective Warwick said the prisoner had told him her father was a canal boatman living in Bradford. The accused admitted the false representation but denied that she intended to defraud. It was stated that when a girl she was in a reformatory for several years. She was now sent to gaol for two months.

(*Newcastle Journal*, 10 September 1910)

It is unknown for exactly how long Marion perpetrated these fraudulent pretences, and the witnesses in court accounted for the fraud twelve months before 1910. It appears that she carried out these pretences in order to obtain lodgings. The entries in the licence record suggest that Marion lacked stable employment during her probationary period. The final record for October 1909 reads: 'Lady wrote for character reference for assistant in Children's Home' (Miss Sullivan's Discharge book, 5137/1: 464, BRO). This suggests that she sought to gain employment at a children's home. Carlen (1988) posits that there is a link between women, crime and poverty, in which theft and fraud are most the common offences among women living in poverty, which results in a cycle of further poverty and crime. However, for Marion Kenyon, there was no further crimes detailed within the discharge book or criminal registers. The 1911 census indicates that she was living with her mother and married, in 1916, a certain Frank Hobson, a military sergeant. The 1921 census listed no children and both Marion and her husband were in employment. Thus, a stable marriage during this period afforded the girls financial stability and security which may have been the stabilizing factor that prevented any further offending in their lives.

However, the dataset contains examples of a husband with a criminal past and, rather than marriage promoting stability and respectability, we see both husband and wife being sent to prison, as in the case of Elizabeth Ann Smith, who left Red Lodge in April 1909. Within a year of leaving the institution, she was stealing and was sent to prison in 1910. The discharge book recorded: 'Father wrote a sad-sad letter. Lizzie has been up to her old tricks again – a thief will always be a thief she always will be, I suppose, poor girl' (Miss Sullivan's Discharge book, 5137/1: 523). Elizabeth was sent to prison for six weeks. Within three months of being convicted for stealing, she was back in prison in June of that same year. Elizabeth married within that year Mr Whiston. The matron was relieved and thought that this might end her criminal activity, writing in the discharge book:

> 31st December 1910 'Is actually married. What a relief to me – Mrs Whiston, 10 Brook Street Swansea. Sister Walker says "He is such a steady young fellow and knows all about Lizzie". Truly love is a wonderful thing.
>
> (Miss Sullivan's Discharge book 5137/1: 523)

Elizabeth went on to have a child, Alice Gwendoline Maud Whiston, who was born in Swansea in 1911. In 1912, the police informed the Red Lodge that the husband was in prison and, in 1913, Elizabeth was committed to trial for stealing (Miss Sullivan's Discharge book, 5137/1: 523). Below are details of her pilfering and the decision of the judge to give her another chance.

A pilferers career

Elizabeth Ann Whiston (23) laundress pleaded guilty to stealing a mourning ring, value of £4, the property of David Thomas … also to stealing a broach value of £2.2s … The recorder said that the prisoner had been given several chances. She started pilfering when she was 12 years of age. She was bound over. Two years later she stole some clothes and was sent to a reformatory school for five years. No sooner did she come home than she began pilfering clothes again, and in 1910, before she was married, she was sentenced to six

months at Swansea Petty sessions. At the time prisoners committed these last
two offences, she was married, but her husband was not with her, and her baby
was in the workhouse. He would give her another chance and deal leniently
with her, but he warned her that if she was brought up again before him or any
judge, she would probably be sent to penal servitude.

(*Cumbrian Daily Leader*, 4 April 1913)

A year later, the discharge book records further criminality, stating on the 9 March 1914: the 'Governor of Swansea prison sent a notice that she had been taken up again and sentenced to three months hard labour' (Miss Sullivan's Discharge book, 5137/1: 524). Elizabeth was again sent to prison for three months for obtaining by false pretences.

At the 'CO-OP' Swansea woman sent to prison for false pretences
Elizabeth Ann Whiston (24), married woman, was charged … with obtaining
goods under false pretences from Mary Andrews, at 50, Norfolk-street, on
November 24th, and on a second charge with obtaining a quantity of groceries,
value £2 1s 6½ d., by false pretences from Cwnbwrla Co-operative store, on
November 30th. In regard to the first charge, the evidence showed that the
woman went to Mrs Andrews' shop and represented that she had been sent
to purchase the goods by Mrs Marian Harris, wife of the landlord of the
Mountain Dew Hotel. Prisoner pleaded guilty to this and the other charge,
which was not gone into, and eight previous convictions were proved for till
robbery and various thefts. She was sent to Prison for three months.

(*Cumbrian Daily Leader*, 2 December 1914)

Elizabeth's marriage did not promote stability and respectability in her life. Thus, the ideal promoted by the institutions that marriage was the goal and measure of success and stability did not necessarily apply to working-class girls. Marriage within working-class communities did not always provide females with the 'male saviour' that the middle-class 'ideal' promoted. As the data demonstrates, criminal spouses and abusive relationships lead to instability as well as further contact with the law, as in case of Alice Rosina Balson, who was murdered by the man with whom she was cohabiting. Alice was discharged on licence in December 1902 to St Clements Vicarage, but did not settle in her employment. In 1906, the discharge book reported that Alice was sent to prison:

September 1906 was arrested for bad conduct in street at night. 7 days at Horfield – matron thinks she is kept by a gentleman – she will not go to a home.

(Miss Sullivan's Discharge book, 5137/1: 375)

Alice, it was believed, cohabited with Maurice Cecil Alabaster, a married man, in a flat for many years but, when she attempted to leave him, he strangled her. In court, it was heard that in the period preceding her death, they had stolen from a tobacconists' shop in Green Street, Leicester square. However, as Alice was dead she could not testify or defend herself. Maurice implied they both had committed the crime in order to make a fresh start. It is now difficult to verify whether Alice was coerced into committing this crime, or acted as an accomplice. Maurice Cecil Alabaster was deemed a respectable, educated man who came from a good family and received only nine months' imprisonment in the second division for murdering Alice, where he pleaded guilty to manslaughter. In stark contrast, Alice was seen as 'unrespectable' and 'immoral' due to cohabiting and being kept by a married man.

Sentence at the Old Bailey

At the Old Bailey today Maurice Cecil Alabaster, 23, Clerk, indicted for murdering Alice Rosina Balson at a Flat in Marylebone on February 28th, pleaded guilty to manslaughter, and was sentenced to nine months' imprisonment in the second division. Counsel stated that the accused, who was of good education and parentage had deserted his wife and lived with Balson, upon whose earnings prisoner depended.

(*Nottingham Evening Post*, 14 June 1912)

Marriage was not the safe haven that the Victorian ideal suggested it was for working-class females, who were often subjected to abuse and coercive control, which frequently resulted in further criminality and even serious violence. In the same way as femininity was the ideal for women, 'manliness' was articulated as an ideal for men. As Connell (1987) maintains to understand femininity, it is also necessary to understand masculinity. According to Shani D'Cruze (1998), Victorian men wished to be 'masters in their own house' and would use violence to obtain this mastery (D'Cruze, 1998: 68). Clark argues, for example, that the Victorian 'domestic ideal' of the male breadwinner and the domesticated wife 'could excuse violence against those wives who their husbands perceived as failing to fulfil their domestic responsibilities' such as not having their dinner on the table (Clark, 1995: 261). Thus, the Victorian ideal of marriage that the institutions promoted was not the ideal for these girls. Working-class marriages were sites of social control, in which females were subject to abuse and violence (Tomes, 1978; Tosh, 1999; Wiener, 2004).

Marriage for working-class females in the nineteenth century did not necessarily provide the stability that the middle-class ideal promoted (Ross, 1993; Clark, 1995). Carlen (2002) argues that marriage and a family for women is a major ideological site of social control. Indeed, we must nuance the link between marriage and further criminality for females. As well as criminal partners, females were subject to mistreatment and violence. Within the dataset, there is evidence of mistreatment mentioned within the records, as in the case of Ethel Goldspunk. Ethel left Red Lodge in 1908 and entered domestic service in Hull, close to her family and had been satisfactory. In 1912, Ethel married Mr Wright. In 1913, she was in the workhouse, and the discharge book records: 'her husband treated her badly, left her – baby born six weeks ago in the workhouse' (Miss Sullivan's Discharge book, 5137/1: 515). Roberts (2014) argues that mistreatment and abusive relationships can see women initially become involved in crime but can also contribute to them revolving in and out of the criminal justice system (Barr, 2019). The Corston Report (2007) highlighted domestic violence, abusive and coercive relationships, and the desire to escape violence within the home are central factors leading to criminality among females. The statistics highlight that over 60 per cent of women in prison, or under community service, are the victims of domestic violence, and that domestic violence was a trigger to their offending. Thus, marriage for working-class girls who were also navigating the social stigma of their past lives, did not always prove advantageous. It is important that the intersection of gender and class is re-nuanced when understanding post-supervision and probationary practices in the past and even within contemporary practice.

As well as marriage, motherhood was presented as the natural feminine role and ideal by the institutions. However, the impact of motherhood on working-class girls who left the reformatory and industrial schools in the nineteenth century has not been examined. Motherhood for working-class girls, similar to marriage, did not promote stability in their life but, in fact, did quite the opposite, placing them in insecure, unstable positions, particularly regarding children born outside marriage, which was deemed outside the bounds of respectability.

Motherhood

In Victorian society, motherhood, like marriage and domesticity, has been constructed as central to 'ideal femininity'. However, Motherhood, for the females in the dataset, especially when children were born outside formal marriage contracts, increased the burdens and pressure to provide for their children and survive in their already economically margined positions. In the nineteenth century, pregnancy before marriage for girls whilst still on licence was not deemed 'respectable' behaviour by the gendered standards of the day. The new Poor Law from 1834 stipulated that women with 'illegitimate' children were not entitled to 'outdoor relief' and thus had no choice but to reside in a workhouse. The very use of the term, 'illegitimate' or 'fatherless' had a negative connotation that females had stepped outside the bounds of 'ideal femininity'. Thus, a pregnancy during a licence period for unmarried girls was seen as a failure of the institution, just as much as a conviction. Within the data, children are mentioned in the licence records with regard to those unsuccessful cases of girls who 'got themselves into trouble' by having children outside of wedlock.

Within the dataset, in the period 1855–1920, for all three institutions, there were twenty-eight girls who had children before marriage whilst on licence, and forty-four after marriage, recorded within the discharge books. The girls with children recorded in the discharge records and also those born outside wedlock, almost all ended up in a union or workhouse. Motherhood, outside marriage, lay outside the bounds of respectable femininity, particularly if the girls broke the law, as in the cases outlined above of Julia Bridget and Elizabeth Smith. There was disapproval of females who were convicted after having children, as in the case of Ada Cope, who had come before the magistrates on charges of house burglary. During her trial, the magistrates did not consider the fact that Ada Cope was pregnant as a cause for leniency but stated: 'Even though she is with child she must serve 12 months imprisonment' (*Sheffield Daily Telegraph*, 25 May 1911). Zedner argues that females who broke the law were treated more harshly because they were deemed 'doubly deviant'; 'as not only flouted the criminal law but, more heinously still, had contravened the norms of femininity' (1991a: 82). The case of Ada Cope was detailed in the discharge book and the institution included the newspaper report entitled 'Girls Life of Crime', which contained an extended description of her personal life, abandoning her children and cohabiting with a man, while posing as his wife. Both jointly plotted and carried out house burglaries involving large sums of money, jewellery and artefacts. The character of Ada was described by the court as follows:

Girl's life of crime

In April, 1901, when 12 was charged with robbing her father, and was sent to Bristol for four years. On leaving she had various situations, and in September, 1907, a child was born. She remained in a home for some time and in February 1909 she was sentenced to six weeks' imprisonment for thefts as a servant. Later she worked as a waitress in the city, and then as a servant, until in February, 1910, another child was born in Lambeth infirmary. She remained until September, and subsequently went to live with a foreigner in the West End. On December 31st last, however, she accused him of assault and of living on her earnings, and for a former offence he was ordered one month's imprisonment. A month later Cope abandoned her second child at a board school in Poplar. She also took a situation at the Savoy Hotel, strand, but was discharged for dishonesty. Previously to committing the present offences, prisoners had lived together at Vauxhall Bridge Road, where they stole a lodger's clothing, Cope, who had also arranged with Mrs Riley, daughter of Hon. Mrs Riley, to as a nurse in France, next took a situation in Sutton. She arrived on a Saturday night, and on Sunday, while the family was at church, she absconded with property value £50. This situation she obtained by false character … Mr Wallace said the girl had lived a life of crime and irregularity, and though she was to become the mother of another child, she must undergo 12 months imprisonment.

(*Sheffield Daily Telegraph*, 25 May 1911)

Ada's character was seen as more depraved than that of William Baker, as reflected in the headline and the lengthy description of her. Ada was seen as an 'immoral mother', who broke the codes of respectability and femininity (Johnston, 2019). During the trial, there was an altercation between the two in court and the details of what was said were recorded in the newspaper; 'what did you do with the man you had before me?' (*Manchester Courier and Lancashire General Advertiser*, 25 May 1911). It was believed that Ada's previous partner was sent to prison for physically assaulting her, indicating Ada was a victim of physical abuse, which could have played a part in her offending. However, a further record from 1912 shows that Ada had taken Laudanum and sought to end her life (*Nottingham Journal*, 20 August 1912) resulting in further criminalization.

The case of Ada Cope highlights that motherhood did not necessarily promote stability for working-class girls, particularly if they had children outside marriage, which is believed to have marginalized females and exposed them to even greater poverty and criminality (Moffitt, 1993). Similar is the case of Susannah Williams, who continued to offend despite marriage and motherhood. Susannah (also known as Susan) Williams was admitted to Red Lodge Reformatory at the age of thirteen years for pickpocketing in 1893, and remained there until 1895 when she was transferred from Red Lodge to the East Chapel Reformatory, Bearsden, Glasgow. The reformatory, similar to Red Lodge, was certified in 1854 and relocated from Rottenrow to Bearsden (a rural location). The rural setting was considered a healthier surrounding, away from the urban city.

Transfering Susannah from Red Lodge Reformatory to another reformatory was deemed the best solution to prevent her corrupting other girls. Susan's frequent insubordination was recorded in the school minutes. It was stated:

> Susan was at present time in the cell to which she had been sent the previous evening because she stopped the girls in her dormitory from sleeping by her rude behavior and noisy singing. It was resolved that for her to go to another reformatory.
>
> (Red Lodge Minute Book No. 2. 1889–1900, 12693/8: BRO)

Image 7 East Chapel Reformatory, Bearsden, Glasgow (Source: Peter Higginbotham, www.childrenshomes.org.uk).

However, according to the discharge books, after only two days at East Chapel Reformatory, Susannah was returned home to her family and friends in Swansea (Miss Sullivan's Discharge book, 5137/2: 191, BRO). Without employment and having been returned to her friends, she soon came into contact with the law on separate charges of drunkenness, theft and assault, in 1898. In each case, Susannah evaded prison. She also associated, and was later brought before the bench, with Bridget Thomas for stealing.

Very lucky

Bridget Thomas and Susanna Williams, two showily dressed young women, were brought up in custody on the charge of stealing two sovereigns from the person of Wm. Thomas on Saturday night. The Prosecutor did not appear, and the defendants were accordingly discharged. They left the dock smiling.

(*South Wales Daily Post*, 1 May 1899)

However, Susannah did not keep out of trouble, despite being 'very lucky' to be given a second chance. Instead, she gained a reputation for 'ill-repute' and was sent to prison later that year, in August 1899. The newspaper stated that: 'Bridget Thomas and Susannah Williams, two young women of ill-repute, were sent to prison for a month for drunken and disorderly conduct' (*Cumbrian*, 4 August 1899). On their release, both girls were brought back before the bench for 'Alleged robbery' in regard to stealing £3 in gold and silver from a seafaring man named Charles Francis Butler in February 1900; however, a verdict of 'not guilty' was returned (*South Wales Daily Post*, 10 February 1900). Shortly after this verdict, Susannah was sent to prison in April 1900 for assault. The newspaper article below detailed the incident of Susannah and two other girls:

Bridget Thomas, Susannah Williams, and Mary Elizabeth Williams, three young women who appeared in the dock attired in gorgeous coloured costumes, were charged with assaulting another young woman, named Philips ... from evidence ... defendants were charged at the Borough Quarter Sessions and acquitted ... Philips had given evidence against them, and meeting her on Saturday night they knocked her on the ground and kicked her in a savage manner. In defence they strongly denied the allegations, but the magistrates were convinced that an assault had been committed, and committed them to prison for 14 days, [hard labour] and taken below, uttering all manner of threats against Philips.

(*South Wales Daily Post*, 9 April 1900)

After her release, according to the Census records, Susannah gave birth to a child in 1901, William Williams, and in the same year married Edward Waldermarsden, a sailor, whom she lived with at 10 Union Court, Swansea, Glamorganshire, Wales. Yet, despite her marriage and motherhood, the records indicate that Susannah was sent to prison four times between 1902 and 1904 for being drunk and disorderly and assaulting a man, David Llewellyn (Swansea Gaol records, 1877–1922). However, it is important to bear in mind that the working-class occupations for men during this period were low-paid. Accordingly, Edward Waldermarsden, who was a sailor, was not only low-paid but could also be away at sea for long periods, during which he presumably left Susannah to support herself. Birth and death records indicate that Susannah and her husband lived together and had two sons, Henry in 1905 and Edward in 1906 (Ancestry). Susannah does not appear to have engaged in any criminal activity between 1905 and 1908. However, both of her children died; Henry at the age of around five months and Edward at the age of around fifteen months. It was shortly after the death of her second son that Susannah was sent to prison for six weeks for stealing. Below is a list of the further convictions of Susannah in the habitual register, which recorded twelve summary convictions between 1897 and 1909.

Susannah Waldermarsden, 28

B.O., Swansea Borough Petty sessions 7 November 1892 (stealing a shilling), as Susannah Williams.

Ten days and four years, Reformatory, Swansea Borough Petty Session, 12 June 1893 (Reputed thief), as Susannah Williams.

Six weeks., Swansea Borough Petty Session, 17 November 1908 (stealing money, person).

Three months, Swansea Borough Petty Session, 29 April 1909 (stealing money, person).

Twelve summary convictions: drunkenness, assault, &c., 1897–1909.

Source: England & Wales, Crime, Prisons & Punishment, 1770–1935 (Ancestry).

Susannah went on to give birth to a another son, Richard, in March 1909. However, shortly after his birth, in April 1909, Susannah was apprehended and sent before the bench for stealing. In court, she made a request for the police court missionary to look after her baby.

'My Little Baby'

Unfortunate Woman's Request to Police Court Missionary

Susannah Waldermarsden (25) and Annie Harvey (30), unfortunates, were brought up at Swansea police court on Thursday on the charge of stealing and receiving £3 3s. 6d from James Thomas in the Rosebury Arms. Waldermarsden and Harvey both pleaded guilty. There were previous convictions against them. Waldermarsden was sent down for three months, and Harvey for two months. Waldermarsden 'Sister Wray kindly look after my baby' Sister Wray said that she would.

(*Cambria Daily Leader*, 29 April, 1909)

Susannah's son was taken to a missionary, but sadly died in August 1909. Shortly after the death of her third son, Susannah was re-convicted in February 1910 for larceny and again in March for stealing money and swallowing it. (A Calendar of Prisoners Tried at the Winter Assizes for the Year 1910.) Susannah was sent to prison for four months and the following year gave birth to another child in 1911, Victor Andrew, who also died less than a month later. The records also indicate that Susannah's husband died at sea in 1911 (Deaths at Sea 1891–1972: Archive Reference, BT 334). Susannah died shortly afterwards, in 1914, at the age of thirty two years. The life of Susannah Williams (Waldermarsden), her life of crime and loss of four children, her husband and her own death at thirty two years, highlights that not all the girls led stable lives following marriage and motherhood. There is no personal testimony that might clarify Susannah's persistent offending, but the trauma of losing four children and being separated from her child when sent to prison may have had a significant impact on her, alongside her economic instability when her husband was away at sea, which may have contributed to her offending. The incarceration of mothers, their feelings of regret and grief at being separated from their children, and the gendered pains of imprisoned women have not been examined in this period and represent an area which could be examined further (Crewe, Hulley and Wright, 2017).

Motherhood for girls on licence, particularly those born outside of marriage, was particularly difficult in this period. In some instances, the girls were not even permitted an opportunity to be a parent, as in the case of Lillian Erskene, who left Manchester Sale in 1895 on licence for Carmarthen. Lillian, in service as a domestic servant, was described as a 'big stout girl capable of any amount of work' who, the following year (1896), was in a workhouse in Carmarthen with an 'illegitimate child' (M369/23 Licences, No. 434, MRO). The child was given to the family in the belief that this would give her a chance in life. Other girls became pregnant as a result of abuse, as in the case of Sarah Brick, aged thirteen years, who also entered Carlton in 1885 under section 14, having been found begging in the streets, pretending to sell sticks. The admission stated 'Sarah is very untruthful, deceitful girl, she looks a bright girl and now been a fortnight here and will not learn her letters. She is too deceitful to settle her thought to think' (Carlton Admission records, 21131/SC/CAH/A, BRO). However, in 1897, Sarah was sent home to her mother, and deemed 'unfit for service' (Carlton Discharge books 21131/CAH/A/2, BRO). The licence records kept track of Sarah even though she had been sent home to her mother. A year later, Sarah returned to the streets to sell sticks, attended the annual tea party and was reported to be 'doing well'. However, in 1890, the matron submitted a disturbing report, which stated, 'Had to attend court to testify S.B imbecile when here … December, still in lunatic asylum, gave birth to a child, her uncle the father of the said child' (Carlton Discharge books 21131/CAH/A/2, BRO). The case was reported in the newspapers, but there was no mention of abuse or incest.

The judge on two years' imprisonment

William Brick, 49, a hawker, was charged with assaulting an imbecile woman, his niece, Sarah Brick, at Bristol. Mr C. Mathews was for the prosecution, and Mr Seton, at the request of the learned judge, undertook the defence. After some evidence had been given, the prisoner, on advice of his counsel, withdrew his plea of not guilty. The prisoner, it was said, had undergone several terms of imprisonment one being 10 years for burglary. His lordship said the only reason why he should not give the accused the full sentence of two years' hard labour was that he was told, and believed with some reason that, such a term was almost more than any man could bear without being driven out of his senses. He would, therefore, be sent for 18 months' hard labour.

(*Bristol Summer Assize*, 8 August 1890)

The leniency of the sentence was due to concern that the accused man who had abused his niece was 'such a term would almost more than any man could bear without being driven out of his senses' (*Bristol Summer Assize*, 8 August 1890). This sentence does not reflect the severity of the crime and abuse committed. This is largely because, in 1890, there were no incest laws, combined with the diminishing of Sarah as a victim by portraying her as an 'imbecile'. Blaming the victim in cases of sexual assault has been researched in the contemporary criminology literature (Eigenberg and Garland, 2008; Gravelin et al., 2019). However, historical empirical evidence of sexual assault cases would support the association between rape and victim blaming (Jackson, 2000). Sarah remained in the asylum for longer than the prison term imposed on the uncle who assaulted her. It is unclear for exactly how long Sarah remained in the asylum. The final record about Sarah in the discharge book reads: '1892 Brick called at the school to see her dear friends as she called us all. Girl talked very sensibly, got a good home in asylum' (Carlton Discharge books, 21131/CAH/A/2, BRO). The 1901 census recorded Sarah as living with her mother, but there was no mention of the child she gave birth to in the asylum either in the census records or the Carlton discharge records.

A further case in the dataset where a girl out on licence became pregnant is that of Hilda Daddy, who entered Red Lodge in 1907, aged fourteen years, for stealing and licenced into service back in Hull, near her family, in 1912. Hilda was reported to be doing well, and in stable employment for the first year, but the matron received a letter from Hilda's aunt in November 1913 that stated: 'sorry Hilda is in trouble' (Miss Sullivan's Discharge book, 5137/1: 571, BRO). Hilda became pregnant a year after leaving the institution. Hilda gave birth to her baby in March 1914, and died on 18 April. The matron wrote: 'I pity the feelings of the young man and what he must think or call himself' (Miss Sullivan's Discharge book, 5137/1: 571, BRO). Hilda was buried in Hull, in the same grave as her mother, and the matron recorded in the discharge notes that she sent flowers. Similar to the case of Sarah Brick, there was no further mention of the child she had and whether she remained with her aunt or was sent to an orphanage.

Thus, motherhood was not even an option for unmarried girls and, rather than bringing them stability, it increased their propensity to commit crime as a means of survival or saw them re-enter the institutions. Thus, the middle-class feminine ideals prescribed by the institutions' domestic service, marriage and motherhood did not always apply to and match the social and economic circumstances of working-class girls' lives. As Rafter maintains, 'reformers hoped to recast offenders in their own image, to have them embrace the values … of the lady' (Rafter, 1985b: 175). As demonstrated in the cases of the girls explored in this chapter, they were stigmatized further if they deviated from the prescribed gender ideals, or when the 'gender contract' has been damaged (Worrall, 1990). Skeggs argues that there is a long history of shaming and humiliating working-class women (2004). The domestic ideals promoted by the institutions during the licence period were believed to transition the girls to lead 'respectable' lives, but these ideals were unrealistic, which placed the girls in marginal, subservient employment and dependent positions. However, some girls did not conform to the ideals of femininity promoted by the institutions and went on to lead independent lives.

Outside the bounds of femininity

The data examined so far has explored females' employment routes, marriage and motherhood and presented the economic marginality, difficulties and structural constraints that they faced in nineteenth – and early twentieth-century society. However, it is important to bear in mind, in the field of feminist criminology, the common pitfalls associated with presenting all females as victims. Assumptions about females' lack of agency, then, are in turn reinforced by the 'hiddenness' of women (Gallagher et al., 2001: 4). Within the dataset are examples of girls who had stable lives outside the bounds of what the institutions prescribed. As in the case of Beatrice Meylor, with whom I opened this book, the discharge records detail her return to criminality after leaving Red Lodge, but also highlight her break from further criminal activity in 1894. Her marriage and employment may have been factors in her stability and move away from further contact with the law, but there is also her own agency to lead an independent life. The final record in the discharge book for Beatrice dates to 1914, twenty-three years after she left the institution:

> 31st December 1914 [Beatrice] has been for some time head of the women's department store at Bristol Hippodrome, getting a good salary. Does not live with her husband anymore – has not for years.
>
> (Miss Sullivan's Discharge Books, 5137/1: 73–4)

One must also consider the economic opportunities for females; the barriers to working and obtaining financial independence made a difference to her pathway. Her means of independence and self-efficacy regarding her own life and choices are important factors in Beatrice's ability to lead a stable, autonomous life, away from crime. The school disapproved of her decision to divorce, as this did not comply with feminine standards of respectability, but Beatrice established that she did not need a husband in order to live. Beatrice stepped beyond the bounds of respectable femininity but had economic autonomy which gave her control and agency over her own life. The structural changes in society from the time when Beatrice entered the institution in 1877 meant that she found herself in very different circumstance in 1914. The discharge records do not detail her husband's name and continued to refer to her as Beatrice, so I was unable to trace her further in the 1921 Census.

Another case was that of Glady Hughes who, following her discharge, went on to become an actress. The discharge book recorded that she sent pictures of herself acting at the Lyric in *Violette* (Miss Sullivan's Discharge Books, 5137/2:43, BRO). Glady Hughes did not enter domestic service but broke the ideal of 'respectable' femininity by placing herself in the public sphere, as an actress on the stage. She resisted the conventional role expected of her and had agency. The case of Glady Hughes brings to mind that of Ella Fitzergerald, an American jazz singer who, according to the public records (New York State Archives: Prison Public Memory Project), was sent to the New York State Reformatory for Girls because she was 'ungovernable'. Ella, according to the records, ran away from the institution and in later life went on to be one of the greatest singers in American history (Prison Public Memory Project). These histories are unmapped in the literature, so the multidimensional aspects of these females' lives, which are valuable, remain hidden and unappreciated. We need to capture both the female agency and constraints in women's lives and 'foreground differences among women as well as between women and men' (Gallagher et al., 2001: 16). However, the focus cannot be solely on the individual lives without acknowledging the broader context and social and economic structures at play. The girls leaving the institutions in the nineteenth and early twentieth centuries were navigating patriarchal structural systems, histories of abuse, victimization and marginalization. Within this chapter, the data show how the girls sought to navigate from these marginal positions and how limited their options were, especially if they strayed from the path of respectability and ideal femininity. workhouses, inebriate reformatories, asylums, borstals and prisons were mentioned as further destinations for the girls who failed to re-integrate into society.

Conclusion

This chapter highlighted females' lives beyond the institutions on licence and when transitioning back into society. Examining the intersection between gender and class has shown the impact of this on working-class girls' lives. The close surveillance of their lives after they left the institutions meant that females were constantly watched, by their employers, the local police and the managers of the schools. Successful reform was defined as girls attaining and living according to the ideals of respectable femininity which were often unattainable by working-class girls during the nineteenth century. The chapter shows that females were in economically marginal positions, limited in the occupations they could attain and subject to surveillance, control and even abuse while in employment. Domestic service work reinforced the inequality and servitude of working-class girls. The data also highlight that the feminine ideals of marriage and motherhood did not always lead to stability and, in some cases, even placed girls in a vulnerable position, resulting in abuse and further contact with the law. The blurred boundaries between victimization, marginalization and criminalization, identified in their pathways into the institutions, were also significant during their licence period.

What is evident throughout the chapter is that the patriarchal culture and dominant discourses of 'respectability, domesticity and motherhood' were mechanisms for social control and the desire to forge socially approved identities during their licence period and beyond. This chapter highlights working-class females' experiences while out on licence and the continued mechanisms of gendered regulation related to their transition back into society. Whilst this research examined the experience of working-class girls' transition into early adulthood in the nineteenth and early twentieth centuries, key issues remain significant for female juveniles within the current criminology and youth policy. The gendered ideology around respectability and femininity, which shaped the criminalization of females during the Victorian period, continues to be embedded and demonstrated in the paternalistic nature of the criminal justice system today. A recent report by the Howard League, *Reset: Rethinking Remand for Women* (2020), notes, 'under a law redolent of Victorian values, too many women are remanded to prison for their own protection' (2020: 1). Thus, the data in this chapter are important when considering the wider discussion today around gender, probation and youth policy for females (Goodfellow, 2019; Fitzpatrick et al., 2022). The criminal justice system practice and policy in relation to juvenile girls and females who come into contact with the law, or whom are deemed 'at risk', need to reflect the broader factors mentioned in this chapter, around the social constructions of gender, class, female victimization, as well as the economic constraints and social inequalities existing in the wider society, in order to transfer lessons from history to future policy.

7

Conclusion

This book has been built upon research that explored the lives of juveniles before, during and beyond institutional care (Shore, 2002; Godfrey et al., 2017; Watkins, 2020), focusing here on juvenile females. This study has been foregrounded on gender and class analysis, exploring incarceration and the regulation of juvenile girls in Victorian juvenile institutions. I explored three primary questions: what was the nature of juvenile crime and 'at risk' behaviour that led to girl's incarceration in reformatory and industrial schools; what strategies were used to reform and regulate the girls; and, last, explore the destinations and how they transitioned back into society during the licence period and slightly beyond. This concluding chapter surmises the main aims and draws together the major arguments and themes of this book. In so doing, I outline the contribution this research makes to the field of crime history and feminist criminology.

This book has examined the pathways into the institutions by first scrutinizing the reform discourse and the gendered representations of delinquent girls as 'wayward' and 'prostitutes' stepping outside the bounds of ideal femininity and respectability (Cale, 1993; King, 2009; Pasko, 2010). The gendered 'ideology' and the ideals of 'femininity' and 'respectability' not only resulted in the criminalization of girls who failed to conform to these ideals, but also conditioned the regulation and reform of working-class girls in the nineteenth century. The urban public sphere became associated with 'immorality', vice and promiscuity. Young girls on the streets who had committed minor offences, or were deemed to be wandering or loitering, were deemed as being 'at risk' and in need of 'saving'. The reform 'ideology' was as much about restoring the gendered order, as the class order.

The investigation of the pathways in Chapter 4 revealed that girls were overwhelmingly admitted to Manchester Sale and Carlton Industrial School for status offences, such as wandering, loitering, truancy and being in 'want of proper guardianship'. The majority of those admitted to Red Lodge Reformatory had committed property crimes, such as theft and petty larceny, usually related to items of relatively small value. There was no admission of females for prostitution, as presented in the reform 'ideology', nor for committing assault, or serious violence in the pathways of the 420 girls into any of the three institutions. This data correlates with current data that shows that girls are being arrested for less serious offences than their male counterparts (Goodfellow, 2019). This highlights the possibility, as Cook maintains, that justice for women has 'more to do with who they are than what they have done' (Cook, 2006, 82).

The interrogation of the admission records and details of the cases recounted in historical newspapers allowed me to examine the girls' lives and examine the factors associated with the onset of their law-breaking, or behaviour, that was identified by the authorities as placing the girls 'at risk'. The data revealed evidence of victimization, both sexual and violent in nature, which precipitated the girls to run away or be on the streets, as in the cases of Jane Crawford, Bertha Wright and Clara Jones discussed in Chapter 4. Victimization, both sexual and violent in nature, was highly correlated with female pathways into the reformatory and industrial schools in the nineteenth century. Feminist criminologists have cautioned that it is likely that the vast majority of juvenile girls who end up on the streets, running away, or committing petty crime, who then come into contact with the criminal justice system, have experienced childhood abuse, particularly sexual abuse (Belknap et al., 2011; Pasko and Chesney-Lind, 2013; Goodfellow, 2019). Sharp (2015) would agree, maintaining that:

> [O]ne of the most consistent findings of feminist pathways research is that justice system-involved young women have experienced extremely high violent and sexual victimisation rates. However, this relationship between victimisation and criminal behaviour remains under-theorised.
>
> (2015: 12)

The dataset also highlights that other 'risk' factors, such as family background, particularly having parents with a criminal or 'immoral' background, were identified among the admissions. Working-class families during this period were denigrated and often seen as exerting a corrupting influence on children, leading to their criminal behaviour. Young girls who were associated with criminal, or 'immoral' families were at risk of falling into corruption and depravation. In particular, girls with single mothers whose character was categorized as 'drunk' were overwhelmingly admitted under section 14 (the want of proper guardianship) but, when the father's character was associated with drinking, this fact alone was not considered a sufficient reason for a girl to be admitted to an industrial school. Walkowitz (1980) argues that the removal of children from 'immoral' mothers was a radical effort to refashion working-class culture, in which 'control of children was the key to this radical transformation' (1980: 251). Within the admissions, it is evident that the intersection of class and gender was a factor in the criminalization of girls and their families. This corresponds with current pathways of girls, Sharp argues that 'policing and court practices involve judgements about the respectability, riskiness, and reformability of girls – and, importantly, their families (Donzelot, 1979) – which are cross-cut by "race" and class, and which ultimately over-determine working-class and minority girls' entry into the justice system' (2015: 9).

Examining the pathways of working-class girls highlights the Victorian construction that they were 'at risk' of engaging in actions that would increase the likelihood of their pathways into juvenile institutions. The welfare needs of the girls led them to being categorized as 'at risk'. Shore (2011) argues that the juvenile reform system is problematic; although harsh, 'it is also a system that has rescued them from abusive adults, educated them, trained them in occupational skills, given them a chance of a new start in life' (Shore, 2011: 130). However, Cox and Godfrey (2020) maintain that 'these protective effects came at a substantial and questionable cost. They were rooted in draconian practices of child removal and were enacted within institutions that, taken as a whole, had a poor or hidden record of child maltreatment' (2020: 278). The need to 'rescue' girls and prevent 'immorality' led to the blurring of the division between the penalization and welfare established for juvenile girls. Chesney-Lind and Sheldon (2014) maintain that the blurring of the division between the penalization and protection of juvenile girls has become embedded in the juvenile institutions for girls today.

This book has highlighted how the Victorian gendered 'ideology' and ideal of 'respectable femininity' conditioned the criminal justice responses of the first carceral juvenile estate established for girls. It developed a system of admission based on behaviour that was considered to place them 'at risk', which was constructed around gendered stereotypes and female victimization. Thus, if juvenile girls are to receive a form of justice that does not revolve around their gendered construction of 'risk' and adherence to, or deviation from, the dominant gendered stereotypes, then we must deconstruct, both theoretically and practically, the gendered discourses and stereotypes that are associated with institutions for girls.

As well as the pathways into the institutions, this study examined the female experience within the institutions by examining the institutional networks and cultures within the reformatory and industrial schools. Chapter 3 explored the internal and external networks of the three institutions within their local communities. This chapter highlighted various groups in society (politicians, educationalists, businesspeople, child savers, reformers, faith groups and philanthropists) who shared an overlapping interest in developing the youth institutions in the nineteenth century (Godfrey et al., 2017; Case and Smith, 2020). However, the general goal concerning juvenile girls was to reform them and train them for domestic service. The evidence highlighted that the female institutions explored in this study were situated in urban locations, where there was a 'perceived' rise in juvenile delinquency in particular, as girls in urban spaces were categorized as being 'at risk' of sexual delinquency. This coincided with a substantial growth in the number of factories and mills in Manchester and Bristol. However, the reformatory and industrial Schools in Manchester and Bristol sought to place girls in domestic service, even if this meant relocating them to other cities and further afield to Canada. This also reflected both the moral objectives to place girls in domestic servitude as well as the intention of the institutions to place them far away from their 'corruptive' families and any criminal associations they may have had prior to entering the institution. A return to their family and previous life was deemed a failure for the institution (Mahood, 1990).

The domestic ideal was reflected in the 'reforming' of the girls in their daily life within the institutions. Chapter 5 examined the institutional culture in terms of how the institutions sought to re-moralize and re-socialize working-class girls. The governance within all three institutions reflected the micro-politics of the domestic home. The institutions for females sought to replicate the gendered structure and responsibilities of the home. Gendered identities were intensely regulated and normalized through strict, regimented timetables, in which daily worship and industrial service constituted a central part of the girls' daily routine. The institutions' gendered 'ideology' of the home and private sphere was central to its structure and governance, normalizing gendered identities (Barton, 2005; Cox, 2013). Within the institutions, the daily engagement in laundry not only generated profits for the school, but emphasis was also placed on its symbolism regarding cleanliness and purity, linked to the ideals of femininity. Reproductive, unpaid work within the private sphere emphasized domesticity as symbolically connected to the girls' feminine role and what was expected of them. The regulation and control of female sexuality was an essential aspect of the institutions that disciplined and reformed working-class girls. Deviant sexual behaviour was categorized, defined and prohibited. Girls who rejected the feminine ideals of chastity and passivity were seen as injurious to the institutions and would be removed or punished severely.

The specific way in which females were disciplined, their punishment and institutional abuse are challenging to determine quantifiably for each institution, due to the incomplete archives. There is evidence of punishment cells and girls being placed in solitary confinement, the use of the cane, the cutting of hair and the withholding of food documented in the archives. Cunningham argues that these institutions were not family-like institutions at all, but places of terror, and argues that the brutality within these institutions was far worse than the treatment they suffered at the hands of their parents (Cunningham, 1991: 152). The extent to which punishment veered into abuse within the institutions is difficult to determine, particularly in the absence of punishment books for each institution and first-hand accounts by the girls themselves. However, recent studies of historical institutional abuse (Bingham et al., 2016) and the reports on institutional abuse within Magdalene reformatories in Ireland (Ryan Report, 2009; McAleese Report, 2013) highlight that cross-institutional studies are needed across other female institutions in the nineteenth and twentieth centuries to uncover these histories.

Chapter 6 explored the pathways of the girls who left the institutions, during their licence period and in some instances beyond, examining whether or not they were deemed to be 'doing-well' and had transitioned successfully. The institutions defined the successful reform of girls as their ability to go on to lead a respectable life that was free from criminality, involving stable employment in domestic service and, ultimately, marriage. Girls who offended during their licence period were deemed a failure for the schools, as this indicated that the whole tenet of 'reform' had not worked. The discharge and licence records indicate that the offending rate during the licence period was marginally low. The records indicate that, for all three schools, the conviction rate was less than 5 per cent, which correlates with the national records for all female industrial and reformatory schools (*56th Report of Reformatory and Industrial Schools, 1914*). The results are similar to those for juvenile boys who attended similar institutions, as outlined in *Young Criminal Lives* (2017), which found the offending rate among boys during their licence period to be less than 22 per cent. They argue that the low conviction rate during the licence period is likely to point to the pattern in youth offending more broadly, rather than reflecting the reformative 'success' of this particular system (Godfrey et al., 2017). Moreover, it is not the aim of this book to suggest a return to the practices of the past, based on low conviction rates, but rather to highlight the gendered disciplining of girls both within and beyond the institutions. The lower rate of convictions for females during this period highlights that there exist gendered differences within the pathways and re-integration into society post-incarceration, which demand closer scrutiny in future research and probationary practice.

Chapter 6 examined the cases of girls who broke the law and were re-institutionalized during their licence period. Overwhelmingly, in every case, their offence was stealing (property offences). The cases of Ruth Williams, Martha Dyson and Elizabeth Ann Whiston were all convicted of stealing whilst employed in domestic service. Duckworth (2002) maintains that young servant girls, who were poorly paid and surrounded by the trappings of wealth, would steal from their household. Domestic service was low-paid, marginal work, highlighting the structural inequalities for females during this period, particularly for working-class girls who were out on licence, which meant that their employment options were limited, particularly if they offended. Steffensmeier (1996) argues that the concentration of poverty among women drives females to engage in economically based crimes (Steffensmeier and Allan, 1996). Identifying the reasons why some girls offended and were re-institutionalized during their licence period is critical to inform the *Beyond Youth Justice* policy and practice.

Chapter 6 also explored the employment destinations of the girls on licence. Employment in domestic service was seen as a central factor in ensuring that close surveillance was extended over the girls and was deemed the ideal life cycle job to prepare them to become a wife and mother in their own household. As Higgs (1983) maintains, women in the nineteenth century, whether as wives or servants, were supposed to be the embodiment of the feminine ideal, that ideal included the performance of gender-defined work. The records indicate overwhelmingly that the girls on licence were placed in domestic service, despite the demand for factory work in Bristol and in the spinning mills of Manchester. Although employment in service was deemed a successful transition and fulfilling, a feminine ideal for working-class girls was difficult, menial work which also resulted in abuse, as in the case of Nelly Cook, who attempted to drown herself (Miss Sullivan's Discharge book, 5137/1: 568, BRO) and also the tragic case of Eva Witty, who died from severe burns while in domestic service (Miss Sullivan's Discharge book, 5137/2: 5/6, BRO). However, the institutions deemed employment in domestic service as respectable and 'doing well', regardless of the conditions or how difficult this work was for the girls. Rafter (1985a) suggests that middle-class reformers had little understanding of the reality of the lives of these girls and subjected them to impossible behavioural standards. The domestic ideal and the promotion of marriage marked the end of their discharge record, signifying that this was the ultimate goal of the institutions.

The institutions placed significant emphasis on marriage as a criterion for success in the girls' later life. Marriage was seen as the ultimate measure of success for the girls and was encouraged by the matrons through offering them financial incentives if they could provide a marriage certificate at the annual reunion, which they were encouraged to attend every New Year's Day. Older and more recently licenced girls would attend to celebrate their success with regard to employment and marriage. The school would welcome former inmates, such as Betsy Lewis, who married well and they were proud when she visited the school. An examination of the effect of marriage in the dataset suggests that some girls, who were convicted after leaving the institution, engaged in no further criminal activity once they married. However, there were also instances where marriage failed to have a protective effect in terms of supporting their stability. As in the cases of Elizabeth Whiston and Susannah Walmarsden who persisted in criminality beyond marriage, demonstrating marriage did not provide them with stability that the institutions hoped it would. As well as criminal partners, females were subject to mistreatment and violence within marriage (Tomes, 1978; Tosh, 1999; Wiener, 2004). Thus marriage, which was promoted by the institutions, did not necessarily provide stability, and could also result in mistreatment and further criminality (Heidensohn, 1996; Corston, 2007; Barr, 2019).

This study has sought to capture working-class females' lived experiences on their entry to the institutions and also while out on licence, not only to address a gap in the literature but also to contribute to the current policy related to girls and youth custody. The individual micro-histories within the dataset highlight the complexity of the issues and overlapping factors of inequality in society that the girls had to navigate. The dataset also highlights that the blurred boundaries between victimization, criminalization and inequality within the patriarchal and capitalist society of the nineteenth century remain significant today and have been identified as factors contributing to female contact with the criminal justice system. The micro- and macro-factors, taken together, highlight the importance of reformulating the feminist frameworks that consider the intersection of gender, class, as well as age within the pathways in and out of juvenile institutions.

It is also important to state that it is not the intention of this book to present females as passive, to whom things simply happen. Throughout the book, in each chapter, I highlight, by offering micro-examples of the girls' agency, their modes of resistance and defiance. They were marginalized economically, socially and culturally, yet we still obtain glimpses of their modes of resistance both inside and outside the institutions. Also, it is vital to remember that displaying compliance to the gendered ideals of domesticity and marriage, to survive the harsh circumstances of nineteenth-century life, could also have signified the girls' agency to choose to navigate life the best they could with the resources available to them (Marshment, 1993; Bosworth, 1999). Feminist theorists, such as McNay, maintain that a 'fundamental aim of the feminist project is to rediscover and re-evaluate the experiences of women' (1992: 4). Fraser (1989) and Hartstock (1990) argue that examining female agency is central to building a feminist theory. The case of Beatrice Meylor, with which I opened this book, highlights how she navigated into and out of Red Lodge Reformatory. Meylor managed to gain economic autonomy and lead an independent life, despite her early beginning. However, it is difficult, without having access to life-course evidence about all of the females included in this study, to determine how unique or representative her life was among the total body of girls who left the institutions. Nevertheless, the accounts of females outlined in this study highlight how much we can learn by weaving together the data that do exist.

The uncovering of the lives of the girls in this research has been a challenging undertaking. Researchers examining girls and young women based on the archives must contend with the difficulties related to this undertaking. The incomplete, fragmentary and missing archives require one, in many ways, to 'read against the grain' in order to tease out the hidden stories or highlight phenomena that seem ordinary in the archives. Gallagher et al., (2013) argue that a critical component of re-presenting the past is to pay particular attention to interpreting the sources, 'to use the double-consciousness so often ascribed to feminist working within the academy (as insider/outsider) to read between the lines' (2003: 8). I employed this double-consciousness to 'see' female lives in the historical data. The difficulties associated with conducting archival research on females have been documented by Williams (2014, 2018), who has written extensively on female offenders and cites some of the associated problems:

> Female offenders can be amongst the hardest characters of all to find. Not only were they, like male offenders, keen to escape the eye of the authorities, but by virtue of being women, their identities were more changeable, and their lives were less consistently recorded.

(Williams and Godfrey, 2018: 2)

The difficulties associated with tracing females are more problematic when researching juvenile girls. If they married or changed their name, it becomes impossible to trace them unless there exists a marriage certificate containing their maiden name. I also encountered a further difficulty which was the complete absence of letters or diaries written by the girls themselves, so we do not have their voices or know how they felt about their time within and after leaving the institutions. As a result of the challenges related to locating and tracing females in the archival sources and documentation, female working-class history has been neglected in the literature, so these histories become unknown, or marginalized. It is these marginalized histories, that have neither been recorded nor written down, that we need to hear (Gallagher et al., 2001). Digital data has opened up the possibility of uncovering the history of ordinary people in unique ways; for example, recent research has measured social mobility by examining details on marriage certificates (Todd, 2014, 2021). The digitization of the 1921 Census, which is now available to the public, provides an opportunity for historians and researchers to uncover a wealth of information to trace the micro-histories of individuals and families in this period. As Godfrey states, 'the availability of digital data on the internet offers a hyper-extension of criminology's reach towards uncovering and recovering the lives of the disposed and powerless' (Godfrey, 2017: 140). This research has highlighted numerous possibilities for future work in examining marginal voices that have not thus far been researched, thereby linking the past with present.

Epilogue

This book has focused on juvenile delinquency and the criminal justice system's treatment of female offenders historically, which is central to the present. However, it would be remiss to conclude this book without making some mention of the future. The plight of young girls who end up in the youth justice system today is still primarily motivated by a desire to protect them from the 'moral danger' of prostitution and/or pregnancy (Worrall, 1999: 41). The inquiry on girls in *From Custody to Court* stated that 'girls are still being treated more harshly by magistrates if their behaviour contradicts gender stereotypes' (Girls; from courts to custody, APPG Inquiry, 2012).

More recently the report entitled *Disrupting the Routes between Care and Custody for Girls and Women* (2022) has highlighted the numerous challenges that care-experienced girls and women in conflict with the law face, as they are often 'disadvantaged by negative gendered judgements' (Fitzpatrick et al., 2022: iii). Thus, it remains clear that the underlying factors which cause girls to come into contact with the criminal justice system and their treatment both within the institutions and beyond youth custody need to inform the related planning and policy. It is also important to consider girls from minority groups, who do not figure in the dataset of historical institutions in this research, although recent reports, such as the *Lammy Report* 2017, posit that the BAME proportion of youth prisoners had risen from 25 to 41 per cent during the period 2006–16 (2017: 4). The recent report entitled 'We've not given up: Young women surviving the criminal justice system' (2022) focuses on young women, aged seventeen to twenty-five years, particularly the experience of Black, Asian and minoritized young women, who come into contact with the criminal justice system and are overlooked in the policy. This is an area that needs further research both historically and in the future.

On a final note, it is important to discuss the state of female youth custody today and the implications for the future. The report entitled *Outnumbered,*

Locked up and Overlooked? The Use of Penal Custody for Girls in England &
Wales (2019) highlights that the very small population of girls currently in
custody should be seen as presenting a timely opportunity to develop more
innovative and appropriate responses to their needs (2019: 54). The report calls
for a 'commitment to the application of deprivation of liberty as an absolute last
resort' as well as offering many other recommendations 'to end the imprisonment
of girls in all penal detention facilities' as well as the 'commitment to deliver
holistic, individualized and gender-sensitive support, that addresses the root
causes of girls' problems, minimizes the damage caused by custody and prepares
them for a positive future' (2019: 55). Policy in the future must begin with these
recommendations and those of the United Nations to 'develop and implement a
national strategy aimed at replacing the detention of children in penal facilities
with non-custodial solutions based upon broad consultation with experts, civil
society and children themselves' (United Nations, 2019: 336 cited in Goldson,
2020: 330). As Cox and Godfrey maintain:

> [S]ince the early 19th Century, subsequent generations of reformers have tried
> and failed to improve conventional juvenile justice institutions. We argue that
> it is time to stop believing that we can do this, and time to start thinking more
> creatively about real alternatives to youth incarceration.

(2020: 280–1)

The historical insights and experiences of the girls investigated in this research
provide ample evidence to inform the current debates, advocate for change
and gender responsive alternatives, rather than a recycling of the custodial
institutions of the past that marginalize girls even further but to re-imagine
alternatives in future policy and practice.

Bibliography

Primary sources

Manchester Sale Industrial School, Manchester Record Office

Certified Industrial Schools Girls Branch Sale Reports, 1876–86: M369/4/37/1
Admission Registers, 1883–1932: M369/4/18/2/3
Particulars of Discharge, 1890–1921: M369/4/19/3/4
Punishment Book, 1900–40: M369/4/27
Minute Books, 1877–1924: M369/4/1/1/3/4
Medical Officers Report Book, 1877–1936: M369/4/15
Manchester Constabulary and Police Statistical Returns (GB127.M117, MRO)

Red Lodge Reformatory, Bristol Record Office

Red Lodge Journals, 1857–60: 12693/1/2
Rules and Regulations, 12693/3
Rules, Principles and Workings, 1875: 12693/12
Minute Book No 1., 1878–89: 12693/7
Minute Book No 2., 1889–1900: 12693/8
Miss Sullivan's Reports on Future History and Conducts of Girls Who Attended the Red
    Lodge Reformatory Volume 1, 1887–1912: 5137/1; Volume 2, 1912–21: 5137/2
Picture Box: A collection of Images (PicBox/8/Ex/1-8)
Bristol School Board, 1867–1914: 21131/BSB
Bristol Magistrates Records (Bristol Archives J/MAG/J/1/1)
Watch Committee Reports (Bristol Archives M/BBC/WAT/2/6)

Carlton Industrial School Bristol Record Office

Admission Records, 4 volumes, 1875–1927: 21131/SC/CAH/A
Discharge Books, 4 volumes, 1878–1924: 21131/CAH/A/2
School Logbook: 21131/SC/CAH/L/1/1
Regulation for Management of Carlton House Industrial School: 21131/SC/CAH
Visiting Committee Books, 3 volumes, 1875–1924: 21131/SC/CAH/V
Correspondence, 4 volumes, 1879–1927: 21131/SC/CAH/CO/1

Liverpool Record Office

Records of the Liverpool Juvenile Reformatory Association, Liverpool Archives (Liverpool Record Office, 364 CAT).

Parliamentary papers

1857 Industrial Schools Bill [amended in committee on re-commitment and on consideration of bill as amended] provision for the care and education of vagrant, destitute, and disorderly children – for the extension of industrial schools. House of Commons Sessional Papers, available https://parlipapers-proquest-com.liverpool.idm.oclc.org/parlipapers/docview/t70.

Report of the Select Committee on Contagious Diseases Acts, together with the proceedings of the committee, minutes of evidence, and appendix, 1882. http://parlipapers.chadwick.co.uk.ezproxy.liv.ac.uk/home.do.

Select Committee of House of Lords to inquire into State of Law relating to protection of young girls from artifices to induce them to lead corrupt life: Report proceedings, minutes of evidence, House of Commons 1882, paper number: 344.

Select Committee on Administration and Operation of Contagious Diseases Act: Report proceedings, minutes of evidence, House of Commons Papers, Reports of Committees Parliament: 1882, paper number: 340.

Reformatory and Industrial Inspector Reports

3rd Report of Reformatory and Industrial Schools, 1860, Report of Inspector, paper number: C.2688

6th Report of Reformatory and Industrial Schools, 1863, Report of Inspector, paper number: C.3193

14th Report of Reformatory and Industrial Schools, 1871, Report of Inspector, paper number: C.373

18th Report of Reformatory and Industrial Schools, 1875, Report of Inspector, paper number: C.1311

21st Report of Reformatory and Industrial Schools, 1878, Report of Inspector, paper number: C.2117

26th Report of Reformatory and Industrial Schools, 1883, Report of Inspector, paper number: C.3716

38th Report of Reformatory and Industrial Schools, 1895, Report of Inspector, paper number: C.7820

40th Report of Reformatory and Industrial Schools, 1897, Report of the Inspector, paper number: C.8566

41th Report of Reformatory and Industrial Schools, 1898, Report of Inspector, paper number: C.8996

42nd Report of Reformatory and Industrial School, 1899, Report of Inspector, paper
    number: C.9450

56th Report of Reformatory and Industrial Schools, 1914, Report of Inspector, paper
    number: C.7196

59th Report of Reformatory and Industrial Schools, 1916, Report of Inspector, paper
    number: Cd.8367

Reformatory and Industrial Schools Committee Report, 1896, vol. 1 & Appendix Cd.8204

Reformatory and Industrial Schools Committee Report, 1896, vol. 2, Evidence & Index,
    Cd.8290

Newspapers

Liverpool Mercury, 8 November 1869

Liverpool Mercury, 2 February 1880

Bristol Mercury, 7 November 1857

East and South Devon Advertiser, 26 November 1881

Dundee Weekly News, 10 December 1881

Western Daily Press, 5 March 1870

Devizes and Wiltshire Gazette, 10 January 1856

Leamington Spa Courier, 18 January 1862

Manchester Times, 17 July 1875

Manchester Courier and Lancashire General Advertiser, 29 March 1902

Nottingham Evening Post, 14 June 1912

Cumbrian Daily Leader, 4 April 1913

Bath Chronicle, 10 July 1862

Sheffield Daily Telegraph, 25 May 1911

Bristol Mercury, 13 December 1889

Cumbrian Daily Leader, 2 December 1914

The Guardian, 24 May 2000

Western Daily Press, 13 May 1914

West London Observer, 18 September 1925

Gloucester Journal, 5 January 1918

The Western Times Exeter, 29 March 1856

Western Daily Press, 1 June 1882

Contemporary sources

Acton, W. (1857) *Prostitution, Its Moral, Social, and Sanitary Aspects in London and
    Other Large Cities and Garrison Towns,* London, John Churchill & Sons.

Book digitized by Google and uploaded to the Internet Archive 2008, https://archive.
    org/details/prostitutioncon00actogoog

Carpenter, M. (1853) *Juvenile Delinquents Their Condition and Treatment*, London, W. & F.G. Cash.

Carpenter, M. (1857) On the Importance of Statistics to the Reformatory Movement, with Returns from Female Reformatories, and Remarks on them, *Journal of the Statistical Society of London*, vol. 20, No. 1 (March), pp. 33–40.

Carpenter, M. (1868) *Our Convicts*, London, Longman and Green.

Carpenter, M. (2013) *Reformatory Schools, for the Children of the Perishing Classes and Dangerous Classes, and for the Juvenile Offenders*, New York, Cambridge University Press (Digital reprint, originally published 1851).

Doyle, A. (1875) *Emigration of Pauper Children to Canada*, LSE Selected Pamphlets.

Engels, F. (1845) *The Condition of the Working Class in England, 1845*, London, Penguin Classic edn. 2009.

Neale, W. (1840) Juvenile Delinquency in Manchester, Its Causes and History, Its Consequences, and Some Suggestions Concerning Its Cure: JSTOR 01-01-1840. http://jstor.org/stable/10.2307/60229190.

Secondary sources

Alexander, R. (1995) *The 'Girl Problem': Female Sexual Delinquency in New York, 1900–1930*, Ithaca, NY, Cornell University Press.

Alexander, S. (1987) *Women's Work in Nineteenth Century London: A Study of the Years 1820–50*, London, Pluto Press.

Anderson, A. (1993) *Tainted Souls and Painted Faces*, Ithaca, Cornell University Press.

Archer, J. (2011) *The Monster Evil; Policing and Violence in Victorian, Liverpool*, Liverpool, Liverpool University Press.

Arnot, M. and Usborne, C. (2001) *Gender and Crime in Modern Europe*, London, Oxford University Press.

Auerbach, N. (1982) *Woman and the Demon: The Life of a Victorian Myth*, Massachusetts, Harvard University Press.

Bailey, J. (2012) *Parenting in England 1760–1830: Emotion, Identity and Generation*, Oxford, Oxford University Press.

Ballinger, A. (2000) *Dead Woman Walking; Executed Woman in England and Wales*, Oxon, Routledge.

Barr, U. (2019) *Desisting Sisters; Gender, Power and Desistance in the Criminal (in) Justice System*, Switzerland, Palgrave Macmillan.

Barr, U. and Christian, N. (2019) A Qualitative Investigation into the Impact of Domestic Abuse on Women's Desistance, *Probation Journal*, vol. 66, No. 4, pp. 416–33.

Barrett, M. (1980) *Women's Oppression Today: Problems in Marxist Feminist Analysis*, London, New Left Books.

Barry, M. (2006) *Youth Offending in Transition: The Search for Social Recognition*, London, Routledge.

Bartky, S.L. (1990) *Femininity and Domination: Studies in the Phenomenology of Oppression*, London, Routledge.

Bartky, S.L. (1992) 'Foucault, Femininity and the Modernization of Patriarchal Power', in Kourany, J., Sterban, J. and Rosemarie, T. (eds.), *Feminist Philosophies: Problems, Theories, and Applications*, New Jersey, Prentice Hall, pp. 25–45.

Bartley, P. (2000) *Prostitution Prevention and Reform in England, 1860–1914*, London, Routledge.

Barton, A. (2005) *Fragile Moralities and Dangerous Sexualities: Two Centuries of Semi Penal Institutionalisation for Women*, Aldershot, Ashgate.

Barton, A. (2011) A Woman's Place: Uncovering Maternalistic Forms of Governance in the 19th Century Reformation, *Family and Community History*, vol. 14, pp. 89–104.

Batchelor, S.A. (2005) 'Prove Me the Bam!': Victimization and Agency in the Lives of Young Women Who Commit Violent Offences, *Probation Journal*, vol. 52, No. 4, pp. 358–75.

Bates, R. (2009) Building Imperial Youth? Reflections on Labour and the Construction of Working-Class Childhood in Late Victorian England, *Paedagogica Historia*, vol. 45, No. 1–2, pp. 143–56.

Bates, V. (2016) *Sexual Forensics in Victorian and Edwardian England: Age, Crime and Consent in the Courts*, Hampshire, Palgrave Macmillan.

Bates, V. (2017) The Child as Risk: Precocious Girls and Sexual Consent in Late Victorian Britain, *Law, Crime and History*, vol. 1, pp. 126–44.

Bean, P. and Melville, J. (1989) *Lost Children of the Empire*, London, Unwin Hyman.

Begiato, J. (2020) *Manliness in Britain, 1760–1900: Bodies, Emotion, and Material Culture*, Manchester, Manchester University Press.

Behlmer, G.K. (1979) Deadly Motherhood: Infanticide and Medical Opinion in Mid-Victorian England, *Journal of the History of Medicine and Allied Sciences*, vol. 34, pp. 403–27.

Behlmer, G.K. (1982) *Child Abuse and Moral Reform in England: 1870–1908*, California, Stanford University Press.

Belknap, J. (2007) *The Invisible Woman: Gender, Crime and Justice*, Belmont, CA, Thomson Wadsworth.

Belknap, J. and Holsinger, K. (2006) The Gendered Nature of Risk Factors for Delinquency, *Feminist Criminology*, vol. 1, pp. 48–71.

Belknap, J., Gardner, E., Holsinger, K., McDaniels-Wilson, C. and Cady, B. (2011) 'Using Girls Voices and Words to Study Their Problems', in Kerr, M., Stattin, H., Engels, R., Overbeek, G. and Andershed, A. (eds.), *Understanding Girls' Problem Behaviour: How Girl Delinquency Develops in the Context of Maturity and Health, Co-Occurring Problems, and Relationships*, Oxford, Wiley-Blackwell, pp. 95–115.

Berg, B. (2001) *Qualitative Research Methods for the Social Science*, Neeham Heights, Allyn and Bacon.

Besemer, S. and Farrington, D.P. (2012) Intergenerational Transmission of Criminal Behaviour: Conviction Trajectories of Fathers and Their Children, *European Journal of Criminology*, vol. 9, pp. 120–41.

Besemer, S., Farrington, D.P. and Bijleveld, C. (2013) Official Bias in Intergenerational Transmission of Criminal Behaviour, *The British Journal of Criminology*, May 2013, vol. 53, No. 3, pp. 438–55.

Besley, T. (2002) *Counseling Youth: Foucault, Power, and the Ethics of Subjectivity*, Westport, CT, Praeger.

Bingham, A., Delap, L., Jackson, L. and Settle, L. (2016) Historical Child Sexual Abuse in England and Wales: The Role of Historians, *History of Education*, vol. 45, No. 4, pp. 41–29.

Bland, L. (2001) *Banishing the Beast: Feminism, Sex and Morality*, New York, Tauris Park Paperbacks.

Bordo, S. (1988) 'Anorexia Nervosa: Psychopathology as the Crystallization of Culture', in Diamond, I. and Quinby, L. (eds.), *Feminism and Foucault: Reflections on Resistance*, Boston, North-eastern University Press, pp. 87–118.

Bordo, S. and Jaggar, A. (1992) *Gender/Body/Knowledge: Feminist Reconstruction of Being and Knowing*, New Jersey, Reuters University Press.

Bosworth, M. (1999) *Engendering Resistance: Agency and Power in Women's Prisons*, Aldershot, Ashgate.

Bosworth, M. (2000) Confining Femininity: A History of Gender, Power and Imprisonment, *Theoretical Criminology*, August, vol. 3, No. 3, pp. 265–84.

Bosworth, M. (2001) The Past as a Foreign Country? Some Methodological Implications of Doing Historical Criminology, *British Journal of Criminology*, vol. 41, No. 3, pp. 431–42.

Boucher, E. (2014) *Empire's Children: Child Emigration, Welfare and the Decline of the British World 1869–1967*, Cambridge, Cambridge University Press.

Bourke, J. (1993) *Working Class Cultures in Britain, 1890–1960: Gender, Class and Ethnicity*, London, Routledge.

Braithwaite, J. (1989) *Crime, Shame and Reintegration*, Cambridge, Cambridge University Press.

Braybon, G. (2012) *Women Workers in the First World War* (1st edn.), London, Routledge. Available at: https://doi.org/10.4324/9780203104217.

Brenzel, B. (1983) *Daughters of the State: A Social Portrait of the First Reform School for Girls in North America, 1856–1905*, Cambridge, MA, MIT Press.

Brigden, S. (2011) Mary Carpenter: Her Father's Daughter? *Doctoral Thesis*, University of Southampton.

Briggs, A. (1963) *Victorian Cities*, England, Penguin Books.

Bush, E. and Moore, C. (2019) Policing Immorality in a Virginia Girls' Reformatory, *Southern Cultures*, vol. 25, No. 2, pp. 46–61.

Butler, J. (1990) *Gender Trouble*, New York, Routledge.

Cain, M. (1989) 'Introduction: Feminists Transgress Criminology', in Cain, M. (ed.), *Growing Up Good: Policing the Behaviour of Girls in Europe*, London, Sage, pp. 1–8.

Cain, M. (1990) Towards Transgression: New Directions, *Feminist Criminology, International Journal of the Sociology of Law*, vol. 18, pp. 1–8.

Cale, M. (1992) Working for God, Staffing the Victorian Reformatory and Industrial School System, *History of Education 1992*, vol. 21, No. 22, pp. 113–27.

Cale, M. (1993) Girls and the Perception of Sexual Danger in the Victorian Reformatory System, *The Journal of the Historical Association*, vol. 78, pp. 201–17.

Campbell, K. (2004) *Jacques Lacan and Feminist Epistemology*, London, Routledge.

Carlebach, J. (1970) *Caring for Children in Trouble*, London, Routledge and Kegan Paul.

Carlen, P. (1983) *Women and Imprisonment: A study in Social Control*, London, Routledge and Kegan Paul.

Carlen, P. (1988) *Women, Crime and Poverty*, Milton Keynes, Open University Press.

Carlen, P. (2002) *Women and Punishment: The Struggle for Justice*, Cullompton, Willan.

Carlen, P. (2005) *Criminal Women: Autobiographical Accounts (Feminist Perspectives)*, Cambridge, Polity Press.

Carrington, K. and Pereira, M. (2009) *Offending Youth: Sex, Crime and Justice*, Sydney, The Federation Press.

Case, S. and Smith, R. (2020) The Life Course of Delinquency: Reflections on the Meaning of Trajectories, Transitions, and Turning Points in Youth Justice, *International Journal of Comparative Applied Criminal Justice*, vol. 45, No. 4, pp. 1–5.

Chesney-Lind, M. (1977) Judicial Paternalism and the Female Status Offender: Training Women to Know Their Place, *Crime and Delinquency*, vol. 23, pp. 121–30.

Chesney-Lind, M. (1989) Girls' Crime and Woman's Place: Toward a Feminist Model of Female Delinquency, *Crime and Delinquency*, vol. 35, pp. 5–30.

Chesney-Lind, M. (1997) *Female Offender, Girls, Women, and Crime*, Thousand Oaks, CA, Sage.

Chesney-Lind, M. and Pasko, L. (2013) *The Female Offender: Girls, Women and Crime* (3rd edn.), Thousand Oaks, CA, Sage.

Chesney-Lind, M. and Sheldon, R. (2014) *Girls, Delinquency and Juvenile Justice*, UK, Wiley-Blackwell.

Chinn, C. (2006) *They Worked All Their Lives: Women of the Urban Poor*, Lancaster, Carnegie Publishing Ltd.

Chrystal, P. (2022) *Factory Girls; From the Industrial Revolution to 1914*, Yorkshire, Pen and Sword History.

Churchill, D., Yeomans, H. and Channing, I. (2022*) Historical Criminology*, Oxen, Routledge.

Clark, A. (1995) *The Struggle for the Breeches; Gender and the Making of the British Working-Class*, Berkeley, University of California Press.

Clark, J. (1975) 'The Three Rs – Repression, Rescue and Rehabilitation: Ideologies of Control for Working Class Youth', in Munice, J., Hughes, G. and McLaughlin, E. (eds.) (2002) *Youth Justice: Critical Readings,* London, Sage.

Cohen, S. (1985) *Visions of Social Control: Crime, Punishment and Classification,* Cambridge, Polity Press.

Cohen, S. (2011) *Folk Devils and Moral Panics,* London, Routledge.

Collingwood, R. (1946) *The Idea of History,* Oxford, Clarendon Press.

Conley, C. (1991) *The Unwritten Law: Criminal Justice in Victorian Kent,* Oxford, Oxford University Press.

Connell, R.W. (1987). *Gender and Power: Society, the Person and Sexual Politics,* Cambridge, Polity Press.

Connell, R.W. (1995) *Masculinities,* Cambridge, Polity Press.

Connell, R.W. (2000) *The Men and the Boys,* UK: University of California Press.

Connell, R.W. (2013) *The Men and the Boys,* Oxford, Wiley.

Cook, D. (2006) *Criminal and Social Justice,* London, Sage.

Cossins, A. (2015) *Female Criminality: Infanticide, Moral Panics and the Female Body,* New York, Palgrave Macmillan.

Cox, P. (1997) State Sponsored Citizens? Delinquent Girls and Certified Schools Paper American Educational Research Association 'Punitive Pedagogies and Potential Citizens: Girls, Delinquency and Education in Britain, 1900–1933'. Paper presented at the Annual Meeting of the American Educational Research Association in Chicago, IL.

Cox, P. (2003) *Gender, Justice and Welfare: Bad Girls in Britain, 1900–1950,* Basingstoke, Palgrave Macmillan.

Cox, P. (2013) *Bad Girls in Britain, Gender, Justice and Welfare 1900–1950,* Basingstoke, Palgrave Macmillan.

Cox, P. and Godfrey, B. (2020) The 'Great Decarceration': Historical Trends and Future Possibilities, *The Howard Journal of Crime and Justice,* vol. 59, No. 3, pp. 261–85.

Cox, P. and Hobley, A. (2014) *Shopgirls: True Stories of Friendship, Hardship and Triumph from behind the Counter,* London, Hutchinson.

Cox, P. and Shore, H. (2002) *Becoming Delinquent: British and European Youth, 1650–1950,* Dartmouth, Ashgate.

Cox, P., Shore, H., Godfrey, B. and Alker, Z. (2019) Tracking the Gendered Life Courses of Care Leavers in 19th-Century Britain, *Longitudinal and Life Course Studies,* 2019, vol. 9, No. 1, pp. 115–28.

Crewe, B., Hulley, S. and Wright, S. (2017) The Gendered Pains of Imprisonment, *The British Journal of Criminology,* vol. 57, No. 6, pp. 1359–78.

Croll, A. (2000) *Civilising the Urban, Popular Culture and Public Space in Merthyr 1870–1914,* Cardiff, University of Wales Press.

Crone, R. (2007) Crime Reporting, *British Library Newspapers,* Detroit, Gale.

Crone, R. (2010) Reappraising Victorian Literacy through Prison Records, *Journal of Victorian Culture,* vol. 15, No. 1, pp. 3–7.

Cruze, S.D. (1999) Sex, Violence and Local Courts: Working-Class Respectability in a Mid-Nineteenth-Century Lancashire Town, *British Journal of Criminology*, vol. 39, No. 1, pp. 39–55.

Cunningham, H. (1991) *Children of the Poor*, Oxford, Blackwell.

Cunningham, H. (1995) *Children and Childhood in Western Society since 1500* (Studies in Modern History). New York, Longman.

Curtin, G. (2020) 'The Child Condemned': The Imprisonment of Children in Ireland, 1850–1908, *Irish Economic and Social History*, vol. 47, No. 1, pp. 78–96.

Daly, K. (1989) Rethinking Judicial Paternalism: Gender, Work-Family Relations, and Sentencing, *Gender & Society*, vol. 3, No. 1, pp. 9–36. Available at: https://doi.org/10.1177/089124389003001002.

Daly, K. (1992) Women's Pathways to Felony Court: Feminist Theories of Lawbreaking and Problems of Representation, *Review of Law and Women's Studies*, vol. 2, pp. 11–52.

Daly, K. (1994) *Gender, Crime and Punishment,* New Haven, London, Yale University Press.

Daly, K. and Chesney-Lind, M. (1988) Feminism and Criminology, *Justice Quarterly*, vol. 5, No. 4, pp. 101–43.

Davidoff, L. (1999) *The Family Story: Blood, Contract, and Intimacy, 1830–1960*, London, Longman.

Davidoff, L. and Hall, C. (1987) *Family Fortunes: Men and Women of the English Middle Class 1780 – 1850*, Chicago, University of Chicago Press.

Davies, A. (1999) 'These Viragoes Are No Less Cruel than the Lads': Young Women, Gangs and Violence in late Victorian Manchester and Salford, *British Journal of Criminology*, vol. 39, No. 1, pp. 72–89.

Davies, A. (2009) *The Gangs of Manchester: The Story of the Scuttlers, Britain's First Youth Cult*, Wrea Green, Milo Books.

Davies, C. (2017) *Girls and Juvenile Justice: Power, Status and Social Construction of Delinquency*, Palgrave Macmillan.

Davies, G. (1991) *The Irish in Britain: 1815–1914*, Dublin, Gill and Macmillan.

D'Cruze, S. (1998) *Crimes of Outrage: Sex, Violence and Victorian Working Women*, London, Routledge.

D'Cruze, S. and Jackson, L. (2009) *Women, Crime and Justice and England since 1660*, Basingstoke, Palgrave Macmillan.

De Beauvoir, S. (1973) *The Second Sex*, trans. E.M Parshley, New York, Vintage.

Deveaux, M. (1994) Feminism and the Empowerment: A Critical Reading of Foucault, *Feminist Studies*, vol. 20, No. 2, pp. 223–47.

Diamond, I. and Quinby, L. (1988) *Feminism and Foucault: Reflections on Resistance*, Boston, North-eastern University Press.

Dobash, R., Dobash, R. and Gutteridge, S. (1986) *The Imprisonment of Women*, Oxford, Basil, Blackwell.

Donzelot, J. (1979) *The Policing of Families*, New York, Random House.

Dresser, M. (2016). *Slavery Obscured: The Social History of the Slave Trade in an English Provincial Port,* United Kingdom, Bloomsbury.

Dreyfus, H. and Rabinow, P. (1982) *Michel Foucault: Beyond Structuralism and Hermeneutics*, Sussex, The Harvester Press.

Driver, F. (1990) Discipline without Frontiers? Representations of the Mettray Reformatory Colony in Britain, 1840–1880, *Journal of Historical Sociology*, vol. 3, No. 3, pp. 272–93.

Duckworth, J. (2002) *Fagin's Children; Criminal Children in Victorian England*, London, Hambledon and London.

Dyhouse, C. (1981) *Girls Growing up in Late Victorian and Edwardian England*, London, Routledge and Kegan Paul.

Ehrensaft, M., Cohen, P., Brown, J., Smailes, E., Chen, H. and Johnson, J. (2003) Intergenerational Transmission of Partner Violence: A 20-Year Prospective Study, *Journal of Consulting and Clinical Psychology*, vol. 71, No. 4, pp. 741–53.

Eigenberg, H. and Garland, T. (2008) 'Victim Blaming', in Moriarty, L. (ed.), *Controversies in Victimology,* New York, Routledge.

Emmerichs, M. (1993) Trials of Women for Homicide in Nineteenth-Century England, *Women & Criminal Justice*, vol. 5, pp. 99–109.

Emsley, C. (1991) *The English Police: A Political and Social History*, Longman, Harvester Wheatsheaf.

Emsley, C. (1996) *Crime and Society in England 1750–1900*, London, Longman.

Emsley, C. (2005) *Hard Men: Violence in England since 1750*, London, New York, Hambledon and London.

Emsley, C., Dunstall, G. and Godfrey, B. (2003) *Comparative Histories of Crime*, Canada, Willan.

Engels, F. (2004) *The Origin of the Family, Private Property and the State*, Australia, Resistance Books.

Estrada, F. and Nilsson, A. (2012) Does It Cost More to Be a Female Offender? A Life Course Study of Childhood Circumstances, Crime, Drug Abuse, and Living Conditions, *Feminist Criminology*, 2012, vol. 7, No. 3, pp. 196–219.

Evans, K. (2017) *Gender Responsive Justice: A Critical Appraisal* (1st edn.), United Kingdom, Routledge. Available at: https://doi.org/10.4324/9781315231310.

Evans, K. (2018) *Gender Responsive Justice: A Critical Appraisal*, London, Routledge.

Evans, K. and Jamieson, J. (2008) *Gender and Crime: A Reader, McGraw Hill*, New York, Open University Press.

Faith, K. (1993) *Unruly Women: The Politics of Confinement and Resistance*, Vancouver, Press Gang.

Farnie, D.A. and Jeremy, D. (2004) 'The Role of Cotton as a World Power, 1780–1990', in Farnie, D.A. and Jeremy, D. (eds.), *The Fibre That Changed the World: The Cotton Industry in International Perspective, 1600–1900s,* Oxford, Oxford University Press, pp. 3–15.

Farrall, S. (2002) *Rethinking What Works with Offenders*, Cullompton, Willan.

Farrall, S. and Calverley, A. (2006). *Understanding Desistance from Crime* (Crime and Justice Series), London, Open University Press.

Farrington, D.P. and Welsh, B.C. (2007) *Saving Children from a life of Crime: Early Risk Factors and effective interventions*, Oxford, Oxford University Press.

Farrington, D.P. and West, D.J. (1995) 'Effects of Marriage, Separation, and Children on Offending by Adult Males', in Blau Smith, Z. and Hagan, J. (eds.), *Current Perspectives on Aging and the Life Cycle* (4th edn.), Greenwich, CT: JAI Press, pp. 249–81.

Farrington, D.P., Lambert, S. and West, D. (1998) Criminal Careers of Two Generations of Family Members in the Cambridge Study in Delinquent Development, *Studies on Crime and Crime Prevention*, vol. 7, pp. 85–106.

Farrington, D.P., Coid, J.W. and West, D. (2009) The Development of Offending from Age 8 to Age 50: Recent Results from the Cambridge Study in Delinquent Development, *Journal of Criminology and Penal Reform*, vol. 92, pp. 160–73.

Farrington, D.P., Jennings, W.G. and Piquero, A.R. (2013) *Offending from Childhood to Late Middle Age: Recent Results from the Cambridge Study in Delinquent Development*, New York, Springer-Verlag. Available at: https://doi.org/10.1007/978-1-4614-6105-0.

Feeley, M. and Little, D. (1991) The Vanishing Female: The Decline of Women and the Criminal Process, 1687–1912, *Law and Society Review*, vol. 25, pp. 719–58.

Ferguson, H. (2007) Abused and Looked after Children as 'Moral Dirt': Child Abuse and Institutional Care in Historical Perspective, *Journal of Social Policy*, vol. 36, No. 1, pp. 123–39.

Finnegan, F. (1979) *Poverty and Prostitution: A study of Victorian Prostitution in York*, Cambridge, Cambridge University Press.

Foucault, M. (1977) *Discipline and Punish: The Birth of the Prison*, London, Ransom House.

Foucault, M. (1979) *The History of Sexuality*, London, Allen Lane.

Foucault, M. (1980) *Power/knowledge: Selected Interviews and Other Writings 1972-77*, Gordon, C. (ed.), trans. [from the French] Gordon, C., et al., Brighton, Harvester.

Foucault, M. (2001) *Madness and Civilisation*, London, Routledge.

Foucault, M. (2003) *Psychiatric Power: Lectures at the College de France, 1973-1974*, New York, Picador.

Fraser, N. (1989) *Unruly Practices: Power, Discourse and Gender in Contemporary Social Theory*, Cambridge, Polity Press.

Frost, G. (2008) He Could Not Hold His Passions: Domestic Violence and Cohabitation in England (1850–1905), *Crime, Histoire & Sociétés/Crime, History & Societies*, vol. 12, No. 1, pp. 43–63.

Gallagher, A., Lubelska, C. and Ryan, L. (2001) *Re-Presenting the Past: Women and History* (1st edn.), New York, Routledge. Available at: https://doi.org/10.4324/9781315838670.

Garland, D. (1990) *Punishment and Modern Society: A Study in Social Theory*, Chicago, University of Chicago Press.

Garland, D. (2001) *The Culture of Control: Crime and Social Order in Contemporary Society*, Oxford, Oxford University Press.

Gartner, R. and McCarthy, B. (2014) *The Oxford Handbook of Gender, Sex and Crime*, Oxford, Oxford University Press.

Gatrell, V. (1990) 'Crime, Authority, and the Policeman-State', in Thompson, F. (ed.), *Cambridge Social History of Britain 1750-1950*, vol. 3, Cambridge, Cambridge University Press, pp. 243–310.

Gehring, T. and Bowers, F. (2003) Mary Carpenter, English Correctional Education Hero, *Journal of Correctional Education*, vol. 54, pp. 116–22.

Gelsthorpe, L. and Sharpe, G. (2006) 'Girls, Crime and Justice,' in Goldson, B. and Muncie, J. (eds.), *Youth Crime and Justice*, London, Sage, pp. 49–64.

Gelsthorpe, L. and Worrall, A. (2009) Looking for Trouble: A Recent History of Girls, *Young Woman and Youth Justice*, vol. 93, pp. 209–23.

Gelsthorpe, L. and Wright, S. (2015) 'The context: Women as Lawbreakers', in Annison, J., Brayford, J. and Deering, J. (eds.), *Women and the Criminal Justice; From the Corston Report to Transforming Rehabilitation*, Bristol, Bristol University Press, Policy Press, pp. 39–58.

Giallombardo, R. (1974) *The Social World of Imprisoned Girls: A Comparative Study of Institutions for Juvenile Delinquents*, New York, Wiley.

Gibson, I. (1979) *The English Vice: Beating, Sex and Shame in Victorian England and After*, London, Duckworth.

Gillis, J. (1975) The Evolution of the Juvenile Delinquency in England 1890–1914, *Past and Present*, vol. 67, pp. 96–126.

Gillis, J. (1979) Servants, Sexual Relations, and the Risks of Illegitimacy in London, 1801–1900, *Feminist Studies*, vol. 5, No. 1, pp. 142–73.

Giordano, P.C., Cernokovich, S.A. and Rudolph, J.L. (2002) Gender, Crime and Desistance: Toward a Theory of Cognitive Transformation, *American Journal of Sociology*, vol. 107, pp. 990–1064.

Gleadle, K. (2001) *British Women in the Nineteenth Century*, Hampshire, Palgrave Macmillan.

Glueck, S. and Glueck, E. (1930) *Five Hundred Criminal Careers*, New York, Knopf.

Glueck, S. and Glueck, E. (1934) *One Thousand Juvenile Delinquents: Their Treatment by Court and Clinic*, Boston, MA, Harvard University Press.

Glueck, S. and Glueck, E. (1968) *Delinquents and Non-Delinquents in Perspective*, Boston, MA, Harvard University Press.

Godfrey, B. (1999) Law Factory Discipline and 'Theft': The Impact of the Factory on Workplace Appropriation in Mid to Late Nineteenth Century Yorkshire, *British Journal of Criminology*, vol. 39, No. 1, pp. 56–71.

Godfrey, B. and Lawrence, P. (2005) *Crime and Justice, 1750–1950*, Cullompton, Willan.

Godfrey, B., Farrall, S. and Karstedt, S. (2005) Explaining Gendered Sentencing Patterns for Violent Men and Women in the Late-Victorian and Edwardian Period, *British Journal of Criminology*, vol. 45, pp. 696–720.

Godfrey, B., Cox, D. and Farrall, S. (2007) *Criminal Lives, Family, Life, Employment and Offending*, Clarendon Studies in Criminology, Oxford, Oxford University Press.

Godfrey, B., Cox, P., Shore, H. and Alker, Z. (2017) *Young Criminal Lives: Life Courses and Life Chances from 1850*, Oxford, Oxford University Press.

Goldson, B. (1997) '"Childhood": An Introduction to Historical and Theoretical Analyses', in Scraton, P. (ed.), *'Childhood' in Crisis?* London, Routledge, pp. 1–27.

Goldson, B. (2020) Excavating Youth Justice Reform: Historical Mapping and Speculative Prospect, *The Howard Journal*, vol. 59, No. 3, September, pp. 317–34.

Goldson, B. and Muncie, J. (2006) *Youth Crime and Justice*, London, Sage.

Gomersall, M. (1997) *Working Class Girls in Nineteenth Century England: Life, Work and Schooling*, Hampshire, Macmillan.

Goodman, J. (2003) Sex and the City: Educational Initiatives for 'Dangerous' and 'Endangered' Girls in Late Victorian and Early Edwardian Manchester, *Paedagogica Historica*, vol. 39, No. 1/2, pp. 75–86.

Gordon, C., Marshall, L., Mepham, J. and Soper, K. (1980) *Power/Knowledge: Selected Interviews and Other Writings 1972–1979*, New York, Pantheon Books.

Gorham, D. (1978) The 'Maiden Tribute of Modern Babylon' Re-Examined Child Prostitution and the Idea of Child-Hood in the Late-Victorian England, *Victorian Studies*, vol. 21, No. 3, Spring 1978, pp. 353–79.

Gorham, D. (1982) *The Victorian Girl and the Feminine Ideal*, London, Croom Helm.

Gottfredson, M. and Hirschi, T. (1990) *A General Theory of Crime*, Stanford, CA, Stanford University Press.

Gravelin, C., Biernat, M. and Baldwin, M. (2019) The Impact of Power and Powerlessness on Blaming the Victim of Sexual Assault, *Group Process and Intergroup Relations*, vol. 22, No. 1, pp. 98–115.

Gray, D. (2010) *London's Shadows: The Dark Side of the Victorian City*, London, Bloomsbury.

Gray, D. (2016) *Crime, Policing and Punishment in England, 1660–1914*, London, Bloomsbury.

Griffin, E. (2020) *Bread Winner: An Intimate History of the Victorian Economy*, United Kingdom, Yale University Press.

Griffiths, P. (1996) *Youth and Authority: Formative Experiences in England, 1560–1640*, Oxford, Clarendon Press.

Hakim, C. (2000) *Research Design*, London, Routledge.

Hall, C. (1990) 'Private Persons versus Public Someones: Class, Gender and Politics in England, 1780–1850', in Lovell, T. (ed.), *British Feminist Thought, A Reader*, Oxford, Blackwell, pp. 10–33.

Hall, C. (1992). *White, Male and Middle-Class: Explorations in Feminism and History*, UK, Polity Press.

Hamlet, J. (2015) *At Home in the Institution: Material Life in the Asylum, Lodging Houses and Schools in Victorian/Edwardian England*, London, Palgrave Macmillan.

Haney, L. (2010) *Offending Women: Power, Punishment and the Regulation of Desire*, Berkeley, University of California Press.

Hannam and Dresser essays in Dresser, M. and Ollerenshaw, P. (eds.) (1996) *The Making of Modern Bristol*, Bristol, Redcliff Press.

Harding, S. (1987) *Feminism and Methodology*, Milton Keynes, Open University Press.

Hartsock, N. (1987) 'The Feminist Standpoint: Developing the Ground for a Specifically Feminist Historical Materialism', in Harding, S. (ed.), *Feminism and Methodology*, Milton Keynes, Open University Press, pp. 157–80.

Hartsock, N. (1990) 'Foucault on Power: A Theory for Women?' in Nicholson, L. (ed.), *Feminism/Postmodernism*, London, New York, Routledge, pp. 157–75.

Healy, D. and O'Donnell, I. (2006) Criminal Thinking on Probation: A Perspective from Ireland, *Criminal Justice and Behaviour*, vol. 33, pp. 782–802.

Heidensohn, F. (1985) *Women and Crime*, London, Macmillan.

Heidensohn, F. (1996) *Women and Crime* (2nd edn.), Basingstoke, Macmillan.

Heidensohn, F. and Silvestri, M. (2012) 'Gender and Crime', in Maguire, M., Morgan, R. and Reiner, R. (eds.), *The Oxford Handbook of Criminology* (5th edn.), Oxford, Oxford University Press, pp. 336–61.

Helen Thomas, H., Tomlinson, R. and Zutshi, M. (2018) *Bedminster's Tobacco Women*, Hampshire, Fiducia Press.

Hendrick, H. (1990) 'Constructions and Reconstructions of British Childhood: An Interpretative Survey, 1800 to the Present', in James, A. and Prout, A. (Eds.), *Constructing and Reconstructing Childhood: Contemporary Issues in the Sociological Study of Childhood*, London, Falmer Press, pp. 34–62.

Hendrick, H. (1997) *Children, Childhood and English Society, 1880–1990*, Cambridge, Cambridge University Press.

Hendrick, H. (2003) *Child Welfare: Historical Dimensions, Contemporary Debates*, London, Policy Press.

Hide, L. and Bourke, J. (2018) Cultures of Harm in Institutions of Care: Introduction, *Social History of Medicine*, vol. 31, No. 4, pp. 479–87.

Higginbotham, P. (2017) *Children's Homes: A History of Institutional Care for Britain's Young*, Great Britain, Pen and Sword History.

Higgs, E. (1983) Domestic Servants and Households in Victorian England, *Social History*, vol. 8, pp. 201–10

Hill, M. (2011) 'Methodological Complexities', in *Archival Strategies and Techniques*, Thousand Oaks, CA, Sage.

Hodgson, S. (2017) *Bristol's Pauper Children: Victorian Education and Emigration to Canada*, Bristol, Bristol Books.

Hollis, P. (1987) *Ladies Elect: Women in Local Government, 1865–1914*, Oxford, Oxford University Press.

Holmes, H. (2017) *In Bed with the Victorians: The life Cycle of Working-Class Marriage,* London, Palgrave MacMillan.

Holsinger, K. and Holsinger, A.M. (2005) Differential Pathways to Violence and Self-Injurious Behaviour: African American and White Girls in the Juvenile Justice System, *The Journal of Research in Crime and Delinquency*, vol. 42, No. 2, pp. 211–42. Available at: https://doi.org/10.1177/0022427804271938.

Horn, P. (1997) *The Victorian Town Child*, Stroud, Sutton Publishing.

The Howard League for Penal Reform (2020) *Reset: Rethinking Remand for Women.* Available at: Rethinking-remand-for-women.pdf (howardleague.org).

Howe, A. (1994) *Punish and Critique: Towards a Feminist Analysis of Penalty*, London, Routledge.

Howell, P. (2009) *Geographies of Regulation: Policing Prostitution in Nineteenth-Century Britain and the Empire,* Cambridge, Cambridge University Press.

Humphries, J. (1991) The Sexual Division of Labor and Social Control: An Interpretation, *The Review of Radical Political Economics*, vol. 23, No. 3–4, pp. 269–96. Available at: https://doi.org/10.1177/048661349102300315.

Humphries, S. (1981) *Hooligans and Rebels: An Oral History of Working-Class Childhood and Youth 1889–1939,* Oxford, Basil Blackwell.

Iacovetta, F. and Mitchinson. (1998) *On the Case: Explorations in Social History*, Toronto, University of Toronto Press.

Inciardi, J. A., Block, A. and Hallowell, L. (1977) *Historical Approaches to Crime: Research Strategies and Issues*, Cambridge, MA, MIT Press.

Jackson, L. (2000) *Child Sexual Abuse in Victorian England*, London, Routledge.

Jackson, L. (2000) The Children of the Streets: Rescue, Reform and the Family in Leeds, *1850–1914 Family and Community History*, vol. 3, No. 2, pp. 135–45.

Jamieson, J., McIvor, G. and Murray, C. (1999) *Understanding Offending amongst Young People*, Edinburgh, The Scottish Executive.

Jankiewicz, S. (2012) A Dangerous Class: The Street Sellers of Nineteenth-Century London, *Journal of Social History*, vol. 46, No. 2, Winter, pp. 391–415.

Johnston, H. (2015) *Crime in England 1815–1880: Experiencing the Criminal Justice System*, London, Routledge.

Johnston, H. (2019) Imprisoned Mothers in Victorian England, 1853–1900: Motherhood, Identity and the Convict Prison, *Criminology and Criminal Justice*, vol. 19, No. 2, pp. 215–31.

Johnston, H. and Turner, J. (2015) Female Prisoners, Aftercare and Release Residential Provision and the Support in the Late Nineteenth Century England, *British Journal of Community Justice*, vol. 13, No. 3, pp. 35–50.

Joyce, F. (2008) Prostitution and the Nineteenth Century: In Search of the 'Great Social Evil' Reinvention, *Journal of Undergraduate Research*, vol. 1, No. 1 https://warwick.ac.uk/fac/cross_fac/iatl/reinvention/archive/volume1issue1/joyce.

Kelly, K. (2016) Reforming Juvenile Justice in the Nineteenth-Century Scotland: The Subversion of the Scottish Day Industrial School Movement, *Crime, Histoire and Societies*, vol. 20, No. 2 https://journals.openedition.org/chs/1670.

Kerber, L. (1988) Separate Spheres, Female Worlds, Woman's Place: The Rhetoric of Women's History, *Journal of American History*, vol. 75, No. 1, pp. 9–39.

Kidd, A. (1993) *Manchester*, Keele, Ryburn Publishing.

King, A. (2004) The Prisoner of Gender: Foucault and the Disciplining of the Female Body, *Journal of International Women's Studies*, vol. 5, No. 2, March, pp. 29–39.

King, P. (1998) Rise of Juvenile Delinquency in England, 1870–1840, *Past and Present*, vol. 160, No. 1, pp. 116–66.

King, P. (2006) *Crime and the Law in England, 1750–1840*, Cambridge, Cambridge University Press.

Knupfer, A. (2000) 'To Become Good, Self-Supporting Women': The State Industrial School for Delinquent Girls at Geneva, Illinois, 1900–1935, *Journal of the History of Sexuality*, vol. 9, No. 4, October, pp. 420–46.

Kreager, D.A., Ross, L., Matsueda, R.L. and Erosheva, E.A. (2010) Motherhood and Criminal Desistance in Disadvantaged Neighbourhoods, *Criminology*, vol. 1, pp. 221–57.

Krieken, R. (1986) Social Theory and Child Welfare: Beyond Social Control, *Theory and Society*, vol. 15, No. 3, May, pp. 401–29.

Krueger, C. (1997) Literary Defences and Medical Prosecutions: Representing Infanticide in Nineteenth Century Britain, *Victorian Studies*, vol. 40, No. 2, 271.

Lacey, N. (1998) *Unspeakable Subjects: Feminist Essays in Legal and Social Theory*, Oxford, Hart Publishing.

Lammasniemi, L. (2020) 'Precocious Girls'': Age of Consent, Class and Family in Late Nineteenth Century England, *Law and History Review*, vol. 38, No. 1, pp. 241–66.

Lamont, R., Moss, E. and Wildman, C. (2020) Who Cares? Welfare and Consent to Child Emigration from England to Canada, 1870–1918, *The Liverpool Law Review*, vol. 41, No. 1, pp. 45–65.

Landman, M. (2006) Getting Quality in Qualitative Research: A Short Introduction to Feminist Methodology and Methods, *Proceedings of Nutrition Society*, vol. 65, pp. 429–33.

Laub, J.H. and Sampson, R.J. (1988) Unravelling Families and Delinquency: A Reanalysis of the Gluecks' Data, *Criminology* (Beverly Hills), vol. 26, No. 3, pp. 355–80. Available at: https://doi.org/10.1111/j.1745-9125.1988.tb00846.x.

Laub, J.H. and Sampson, R.J. (2003). *Shared Beginnings, Divergent Lives*, Harvard, Harvard University Press.

Lawrence, P. (2012) History, Criminology and the Use of the Past, *Theoretical Criminology*, vol. 16, No. 3, pp. 313–28.

Lawrence, P. (2019) Historical Criminology and the Explanatory Power of the Past, *Criminology and Criminal Justice, an International Journal*, vol. 19, No. 4, September, pp. 493–511.

Lawson, J. and Silver, H. (1973) *A Social History of Education in England*, London, Methuen & Co.

Lee, C. (2013) *Policing Prostitution, 1856–1886: Deviance, Surveillance and Morality* (1st edn.), London, Routledge.

Lerner, G. (1979) *The Majority Finds It's Past: Placing Women in History*, Oxford, Oxford University Press.

Lerner, G. (1986) *The Creation of Patriarchy Gerda Lerner*, New York, Oxford University Press.

Levine, P. (2007) 'Sovereignty and Sexuality: Transnational Perspectives on Colonial Age of Consent Legislation', in Grant, K., Levine, P. and Trentmann, F. (eds.), *Beyond Sovereignty – Britain, Empire and Transnationalism, 1880–1950*, London, Palgrave Macmillan, pp. 16–32.

Lewis, J. (1991) Separate Spheres: Threat or Promise? *Journal of British Studies*, vol. 30, No. 1, pp. 105–15.

Loader, I. and Sparks, R. (2004) For an Historical Sociological of Crime Policy in England and Wales since 1968, *Critical Review of International Social and Political Philosophy*, vol. 7, No. 2, pp. 5–32.

Lown, J. (1990) *Women and Industrialization: Gender at Work in Nineteenth-Century England*, Cambridge, Polity Press.

Lyman, J.L. (1964) The Metropolitan Police Act of 1829, *The Journal of Criminal Law, Criminology, and Police Science*, vol. 55, 141.

Macilwee, M. (2007) *The Gangs of Liverpool: From the Cornermen to the High Rip, the Mobs That Terrorised a City*, Ramsbottom, Milo Books.

Macilwee, M. (2011) *The Liverpool Underworld: Crime in the City, 1750–1900*, Liverpool, Liverpool University Press.

Mackinnon, C. (1987) *Feminism Unmodified; Discourses on Life and Law*, Harvard, Harvard University Press.

Mackinnon, C. (2005) *Women's Lives, Men's Law*, Harvard, The Belknap Press of Harvard University Press.

MacLaren, M.A. (2002) *Feminism, Foucault, and Embodied Subjectivity*, Albany, NY, State University of New York Press.

Magarey, S. (1978) The Invention of Juvenile Delinquency in Early Nineteenth Century England, *Labour History*, vol. 34, pp. 11–27.

Mahood, L. (1990) *The Magdalene; Prostitution in the Nineteenth Century*, London, Routledge.

Mahood, L. (1995) *Policing Gender, Class and Family, Britain 1850–1945*, London, UCL Press.

Mahood, L. and Littlewood, B. (1991) Prostitutes, Magdalenes and Wayward Girls: Dangerous Sexualities of Working-Class Women in Victorian Scotland, *Gender and History*, vol. 3, No. 2, pp. 160–75.

Mahood, L. and Littlewood, B. (1994) The 'Vicious' Girl and the 'Street-Corner' Boy: Sexuality and the Gendered Delinquent in the Scottish Child Saving Movement, 1850–1940, *Journal of the History of Sexuality*, vol. 4, No. 4, pp. 549–78.

Manton, J. (1976) *Mary Carpenter and the Children of the Streets*, London, Heinemann.

Margaret, M. (1973) Innocence and Experience: The Evolution of the Concept of Juvenile Delinquency in the Mid-Nineteenth Century, *Victorian Studies*, vol. 17, No. 1, pp. 7–29.

Marland, H. (2002) 'Getting Away with Murder? Puerperal Insanity, Infanticide and the Defence Plea', in Jackson, M. (ed.), *Infanticide: Historical Perspectives on Child Murder and Concealment, 1550–2000*, Aldershot, Ashgate, pp. 168–92.

Marshment, M. (1993) 'The Picture Is Political: Representation of Women in Contemporary Popular Culture', in Richardson, D. and Robinson, V. (eds.), *Introducing Women's Studies: Feminist Theory and Practice*, London, Macmillan, pp. 123–50.

Maruna, S. (2001) *Making Good: How Ex-Convicts Reform and Rebuild Their Lives*, Washington, DC, American Psychological Association Books.

Matza, D. (1964) *Delinquency and Drift*, New York, John Wiley and Sons.

Matza, D. and Sykes, G.M. (1957) Techniques of Neutralization: A Theory of Delinquency, *American Sociological Review*, vol. 22, No. 6, pp. 664–70.

May, M. (1973) Innocence and Experience: The Evolution of the Concept of Juvenile Delinquency in the Mid-Nineteenth Century, *Victorian Studies*, vol. 17, No. 1, pp. 7–29.

Mayhew, H. (1868) *London Labour and the London Poor*, New York, Dover Publications.

Mayhew, H. (1983) *London's Underworld*. London, Bracken Books.

McClintock, M. (1995) *Race, Gender and Sexuality in Colonial Context*, New York, Routledge.

McConville, S. (1981) *A History of Prison Administration, 1750–1887*, London, Routledge & Keegan Paul.

McDonald, L. (1982) Theory and Evidence of Rising Crime in the Nineteenth Century, *British Journal of Sociology*, vol. 33, No. 3, pp. 404–20.

McKee, A. (2003) *Textual Analysis: A Beginners Guide*, London, Sage.

McNay, L. (1992) *Foucault and Feminism: Power, Gender and the Self*, Cambridge, Polity Press.

McNay, L. (1994) *Foucault: A critical Introduction*, Cambridge, Polity Press.

McRobbie, A. (1991) *Feminism and Youth Culture: From 'Jackie' to Just Seventeen*, Basingstoke, Macmillan.

Menis, S. (2020) *A History of Women's Prisons in England: The Myth of Prisoner Reformation*, Cambridge, Cambridge Scholars Publishing.

Messerschmidt, J.W. (1993) *Masculinities and Crime: Critique and Reconceptualization of Theory*, Lanham, MD, Rowman & Littlefield.

Messinger, G. (1985) *Manchester in the Victorian Age: The Half-Known City*, Manchester, Manchester Polity Press.

Miller, J. (2001) *One of the Guys: Girls, Gangs and Gender*, New York, Oxford University Press.

Moffitt, T. (1993) Adolescent-Limited and Life-Course-Persistent Antisocial Behaviour: A Developmental Taxonomy, *Psychological Review*, vol. 100, pp. 674–701.

Moore, M. (2008) Social Control or Protection of the Child? The Debates on the Industrial Schools Acts 1857–1894, *Journal of Family History: Studies in Family, Kinship, Gender, and Demography*, vol. 33, No. 4, pp. 359–87.

Mort, F. (2000) *Dangerous Sexualities: Medico-Moral Politics in England since 1830,* London, Routledge and Kegan Paul.

Morton, P. (1970) A Woman's Work Is Never Done, *Leviathan,* vol. 2, No. 1, p. 32.

Muncie, J. (1999) *Youth and Crime,* London, Sage.

Muncie, J., Hughes, G. and McLaughlin, E. (2002) *Youth Justice; Critical Readings,* London, Sage.

Murdoch, L. (2001) 'From Barrack Schools to Family Cottages: Creating Domestic Space for Late Victorian Poor Children', in Lawrence, J. and Starkey, P. (eds.), *Child Welfare and Social Action in the Nineteenth and Twentieth Centuries: International Perspectives,* Liverpool, Liverpool University Press, pp. 147–73.

Murdoch, L. (2006) *Imagined Orphans: Poor Families, Child Welfare and Contested Citizenship in London,* New Brunswick, Rutgers University Press.

Naffine, N. (1997) *Feminism and Criminology,* Cambridge, Polity Press.

Nead, L. (1988) *Myths of Sexuality: Representations of Women in Victorian Britain,* Oxford, Basil Blackwell.

Neal, F. (1991) A Criminal Profile of the Liverpool Irish, *Transactions of the Historic Society of Lancashire and Cheshire,* vol. 140, pp. 161–99.

Nevell, M. (2017) Manchester: Making the Modern City, *The International Journal for the History of Engineering & Technology. Taylor & Francis,* vol. 87, No. 1, pp. 143–44. Available at: https://doi.org/10.1080/17581206.2017.1324084.

Newburn, T. and Stanko, E.A. (eds.) (1994) *Just Boys Doing Business? Men, Masculinities and Crime* (1st edn.), London, Routledge. Available at: https://doi-org.liverpool.idm.oclc.org/10.4324/9781315003566.

Noakes, L. (2007) Demobilising the Military Woman: Constructions of Class and Gender in Britain after the First World War, *Gender & History,* vol. 19, No. 1, pp. 143–62. Available at: https://doi.org/10.1111/j.1468-0424.2007.00468.x.

Odem, M. (1995) *Delinquent Daughters: Protecting and Policing Adolescent Female Sexuality in the United States, 1885–1920,* Chapel Hill, NC, The University of North Carolina Press.

Ogborn, M. (2010) 'Finding Historical Data', in Clifford, N., French, S. and Valentine, G. (eds.), *Key Methods in Geography,* London, Sage, pp. 89–102.

O'Malley, P. (2010) *Crime and Risk Pat O'Malley,* Los Angeles, Sage.

Padfield, N. and Maruna, S. (2006) The Revolving Door at the Prison Gate: Exploring The Dramatic Increase in Recalls to Prison, *Criminology and Criminal Justice,* vol. 6, No. 3, pp. 329–52.

Palk, D. (2006) *Crime and Judicial Discretion, 1780–1830,* Woodbridge, Boydell Press.

Parker, R. (2010) *Uprooted: The Shipment of Poor Children to Canada, 1867–1917,* Bristol, Polity Press.

Parr, J. (1994) *Labouring Children: British Immigrant Apprentices to Canada 1869–1924,* Toronto, University of Toronto Press.

Pasko, L. (2008) The Wayward Girl Revisited: Understanding the Gendered Nature of Juvenile Justice and Delinquency, *Sociology Compass,* vol. 2, No. 3, pp. 821–36. Available at: https://doi.org/10.1111/j.1751-9020.2008.00093.x.

Pasko, L. (2010) Damaged Daughters: The History of Girls' Sexuality and the Juvenile System, *The Journal of Law and Criminology*, vol. 100, No. 3, pp. 1099–130.

Pearson, G. (1983) *Hooligan: A History of Respectable Fears*, London, Macmillan.

Pembroke, S. (2013) The Role of Industrial Schools and Control over Child Welfare in Ireland in the Twentieth Century, *Irish Journal of Sociology: IJS*, vol. 21, No. 1, pp. 52–67. Available at: https://doi.org/10.7227/IJS.21.1.5.

Pinchbeck, I. and Hewitt, M. (1969) *Children in English Society – Volume 1: From Tudor Times to the Eighteenth Century,* London, Routledge and Kegan Paul.

Pinchbeck, I. and Hewitt, M. (1973) *Children in English Society Volume II: From the Eighteenth Century to the Children Act 1948*, London, Routledge and Kegan Paul.

Piper, A. and Nagy, V. (Autumn, 2017) Versatile Offending: Criminal Careers of Female Prisoners in Australia, 1860–1920, *Journal of Interdisciplinary History*, vol. 48, No. 2, pp. 187–210.

Piper, A. and Nagy, V. (2018) Risk Factors and Pathways to Imprisonment among Incarcerated Women in Victoria, 1860–1920, *Journal of Australian Studies*, vol. 42, No. 3, pp. 268–84.

Piquero, A.R., Farrington, D.P. and Blumstein, A. (2007) *Key Issues in Criminal Career Research: New Analyses of the Cambridge Study in Delinquent Development*, Cambridge, Cambridge University Press. Available at: https://doi.org/10.1017/CBO9780511499494.

Platt, A. (1969) *The Child Savers: The invention of Delinquency*, Chicago, University of Chicago Press.

Ploszajska, T. (1994) Moral Landscapes and Manipulated Spaces: Gender, Class and Space in Victorian Reformatory School, *Journal of Historical Geography*, vol. 20, pp. 413–29.

Plumb, J.H. (1975) The New World of Children in Eighteenth-Century England, *Past & Present*, vol. 67, No. 1, May, pp. 64–95.

Pollak, O. (1950) *The Criminality of Women*, Philadelphia, University of Pennsylvania Press.

Pollert, A. (1981) *Girls, Wives, Factory Lives*, Basingstoke, Macmillan.

Poovey, M. (1995) *Making a Social Body: British Cultural Formation, 1830–1864*, Chicago, University of Chicago Press.

Prochaska, F. K. (1980) *Women and Philanthropy in Nineteenth Century England*, Oxford, Clarendon Press.

Purvis, J. (1989) *Hard Lessons: The Lives and Education of Working-Class Women in Nineteenth-Century England*, Cambridge, Polity Press.

Purvis, J. (1995) *Women's History, 1850–1945*, London, UCL Press.

Radzinowicz, L. and Hood, R. (1986) *The Emergence of Penal Policy in Victorian and Edwardian England: A History of English Criminal Law*, London, Steven and Sons.

Radzinowicz, L. and Hood, R. (1990) *A History of English Criminal Law and Its Administration from 1750, Volume 5: The Emergence of Penal Policy in Victorian and Edwardian England*, Oxford, Clarendon Press.

Rafter, N. (1985a) Gender, Prisons and Prison History, *Social Science History,* vol. 9, No. 3, pp. 233–47.

Rafter, N. (1985b) *Partial Justice: Women in State Prisons, 1800–1935*, Boston, Northeastern University Press.

Rafter, N. (1990) *Partial Justice: Women, Prisons and Social Control* (2nd edn.), New Brunswick, Transaction Publishers.

Rafter, N.H. and Heidensohn, F. (1995) *International Feminist Perspectives in Criminology: Engendering a Discipline*, Buckingham, Open University Press.

Ramazanoglu, C. (2002) *Feminist Methodology: Challenges and Choices*, London, Thousand Oaks, CA, Sage.

Repo, J. (2014) Herculine Barbin and the Omission of Biopolitics from Judith Butler's Gender Genealogy, *Feminist Theory*, vol. 15, No. 1, pp. 73–88.

Repo, J. (2016) *The Biopolitics of Gender*, New York, Oxford University Press.

Rimmer, J. (1986) *Yesterday's Naughty Children*, Manchester, Richardson.

Ritter, L. (1999) Inventing Juvenile Delinquency and Determining Its Cure (or How Many Discourses Can You Disguise as One Construct?) Paper presented at the History of Crime. Policing and Punishment Conference, 9–10 December.

Roberts, E. (1977) Working-Class Women in the North-West, *Women's History Issue*, vol. 5, No. 2, pp. 7–30.

Roberts, E. (1993) *Motherhood and Crime*, Penn Law, Legal Scholarship Repository University of Pennsylvania Law School.

Roberts, E. (1984) *A Woman's Place: An Oral History of Working-Class Women 1890–1940*, New York, Basil Blackwell.

Roberts, R. (2014). 'Is Lady Justice Blind or Just Blinkered', in Mills, H., Roberts, R. and Townhead, L. (eds.), *Empower, Resist, Transform: A Collection of Essays*, London, Centre for Crime and Justice Studies. https://www.crimeandjustice.org.uk/resources/ladyjustice.

Rodgers, H. (2006) 'Women and Liberty', in Peter Mandler, ed., *Liberty and Authority in Victorian Britain,* Oxford, Oxford Press.

Rogers, H. (2017) 'Making Their Mark: Young Offenders' Life Histories and Social Networks', in Kilday, A.M. and Nash, D. (eds.), *Law, Crime and Deviance Since 1700*, London, Bloomsbury, pp. 227–50.

Rose, L. (1986) *Massacre of the Innocents: Infanticide in Britain 1800–1939*, London, Routledge, Kegan and Paul.

Rose, S. (1993) *Limited Livelihoods: Gender and Class in the Nineteenth-Century England*, Berkeley, University of California Press.

Ross, E. (1993) *Love & Toil: Motherhood in Outcast London, 1870–1918*, Oxford, Oxford University Press.

Rowbotham, S. (1873) *Hidden from History: 300 years of Women's Oppression and the Fight against It*, London, Pluto Press.

Rowbotham, S. (2015) *Women's Consciousness, Man's World*, London, Verso.

Rowbotham, J. and Stevenson, K. (2005) *Criminal Conversations: Victorian Crimes, Social Panic, and Moral Outrage*, United States, Ohio State University Press.

Rowbotham, J., Stevenson, K. and Pegg, S. (2013) *Crime News in Modern Britain: Press Reporting and Responsibility, 1820–2010*, Basingstoke, Palgrave Macmillan

Rumgay, J. (2004). Scripts for Safer Survival: Pathways out of Female Crime, *The Howard Journal*, vol. 43, No. 4, pp. 405–19.

Rusche, G. and Kirchheimer, O. (1938) *Punishment and the Social Structure*, New York, Russell and Russell.

Rush, P. (1992) The Government of a Generation: The Subject of Juvenile Delinquency, *The Liverpool Law Review*, vol. 14, No. 1, pp. 3–41.

Sampson, R. J. and Laub, J. H. (1993) *Crime in the Making: Pathways and Turning Points through Life*, Cambridge, MA, Harvard University Press.

Sampson, R.J. and Laub, J.H. (2005) A Life-Course View of the Development of Crime, *The ANNALS of the American Academy of Political and Social Science*, vol. 602, No. 1, 12–45. https://doi.org/10.1177/0002716205280075.

Sawicki, J. (1991) *Disciplining Foucault: Feminism, Power and the Body*, London, Routledge.

Sawicki, J. (1998) 'Feminism, Foucault and "Subjects" of Power and Freedom', in Moss, J. (ed.), *The Later Foucault: Politics and Philosophy*, London, Thousand Oaks, CA, Sage, pp. 93–107.

Saywell, R. J. (1964) *Mary Carpenter of Bristol*, issued by the Bristol Branch of the Historical Association, Bristol, The University of Bristol.

Schaffner, L. (2006) *Girls in Trouble with the Law*, New Jersey, Rutgers University Press.

Schlossman, S. and Wallach, S. (1978) The Crime of Precocious Sexuality: Female Delinquency in the Progressive Era, *Harvard Educational Review*, vol. 48, No. 1, pp. 82–5.

Schur, E. (1984) *Labeling Woman Deviant: Gender, Stigma and Social Control*, New York, Random House.

Schwan, A. (2001) 'Disciplining Female Bodies: Foucault and the Imprisonment of Women', in Dorfler, T. and Globisch, C. (eds.), *Postmodern Practices,* Germany, University of Erlangen.

Schwan, A. (2010) Dreadful beyond Description, *European Journal of English Studies*, vol. 14, No. 2, pp. 107–20.

Schwan, A. (2014) *Convict Voices: Women, Class, and Writing about Prison in the Nineteenth-Century England*, New Hampshire, University of New Hampshire.

Schwartz, L. (2019) *Feminism and the Servant Problem: Class and Domestic Labour in the Women's Suffrage Movement*, Cambridge, Cambridge University Press.

Scott, J.W. (1988) *Gender and the Politics of History*, New York Chichester, West Sussex, Columbia University Press. Available at: https://doi-org.liverpool.idm.oclc.org/10.7312/scot91266.

Scott, J. W. (1996) Gender: A Useful Category of Historical Analysis, *The American Historical Review*, vol. 91, No. 5, pp. 1053–75.

Selleck, R. (1985) Mary Carpenter: A Confident and Contradictory Reformer, *History of Education*, vol. 14, No. 2, pp. 101–15.

Sharpe, G. (2009) The Trouble with Girls Today: Professional Perspectives on Young Women's Offending, *Youth Justice*, vol. 9, No. 3, pp. 254–69.

Sharpe, G. (2011) *Offending Girls: Young Women and Youth Justice*, Routledge, London.

Sharpe, G.H. (2016) Re-imagining Justice for Girls: A New Agenda for Research, *Youth Justice*, vol. 16, No. 1, pp. 3–17. Available at: https://doi.org/10.1177/1473225415570358.

Sharpe, P. (1998) *Women's Work: The English Experience 1650–1914*, New York, Oxford University Press.

Shore, H. (2002a) *Artful Dodgers: Youth and Crime in Early Nineteenth-Century London*, Woodbridge, Boydell Press.

Shore, H. (2002b) 'Reforming the Juvenile: Gender, Justice and the Child Criminal in the Nineteenth Century', in Muncie, J., Hughes, G. and McLaughlin, E. (eds.), *Youth Justice; Critical Readings*, London, Sage, pp. 159–72.

Shore, H. (2011) Inventing and Re-Inventing the Juvenile Delinquent in British History, *Memoria Y Civilization*, vol. 14, pp. 105–32.

Showalter, E. (1985) *The Female Malady: Women, Madness and English Culture 1830–1980*, New York, Pantheon Books.

Siegel, J. and Williams, L. (2003) The Relationship between Child Sex Abuse and Female Delinquency and Crime: A Prospective Study, *Journal of Research in Crime and Delinquency*, vol. 40, pp. 71–94.

Silvestri, M. and Crowther-Dowey, C. (2016) *Gender and Crime: A Human Rights Approach*, London, Sage.

Simon, B. (1965) *Education and the Labour Movement 1870–1920*, London, Lawrence and Wishart.

Sindall, R. (1990) *Street Violence in the Nineteenth Century: Media Panic or Real Danger?* Leicester, Leicester University Press.

Skeggs, B. (1997) *Formations of Class and Gender: Becoming Respectable*, London, Sage.

Skeggs, B. (2004) *Class, Self and Culture*, London, Routledge.

Smaal, Y. (2013) Historical Perspectives on Child Sexual Abuse, Part 1, *History Compass*, vol. 11, No. 9, pp. 702–14.

Smart, C. (1977) *Women, Crime and Criminology: A Feminist Critique*, London, Routledge and Keegan Paul.

Smart, C. (1990) 'Feminist Approaches to Criminology or Post-modern Women Meets Atavistic Man', in Gelsthorpe, L. and Morris, A. (eds.), *Feminist Perspectives in Criminology*, Philadelphia, Open University Press, pp. 70–84.

Smart, C. (1992). *Regulating Womanhood: Historical Essays on Marriage, Motherhood and Sexuality*, London, Routledge.

Smith, D.J. and Ecob, R. (2007) An Investigation into Causal Links between Victimization and Offending in Adolescents, *The British Journal of Sociology*, vol. 58, No. 4, August, pp. 633–59. Available at: https://doi.org/10.1111/j.1468-4446.2007.00169.x.

Soares, C. (2023) *A Home from Home? Children and Social Care in Victorian and Edwardian Britain, 1870–1920*, Oxford, Oxford University Press

Sommers, I. and Baskin, D.R. (1994) Factors Related to Female Adolescent Initiation into Violent Street Crime, *Youth Society*, vol. 25, pp. 468–89.

Stack, J. (1979) The Provision of Reformatory Schools, the Landed Class, and the Myth of the Superiority of Rural Life in Mid-Victorian England, *History of Education*, vol. 8, No. 1, pp. 33–43.

Stack, J. (1982) Interests and Ideas in Nineteenth Century Social Policy, the Mid-Victorian Reformatory School, *Journal of Educational Administration & History*, vol. XIV, No. 1, pp. 36–45.

Stack, J. (1994) Reformatory and Industrial Schools and the Decline of Child Imprisonment in Mid-Victorian England and Wales, *History of Education*, vol. 23, No. 1, pp. 59–73.

Stafford, C. (2017) Exploring Sentencing Patterns for Female Drunkenness and Crimes of Violence in Mid-Victorian Lancashire, *Transactions of the Historic Society of Lancashire and Cheshire*, vol. 166, pp. 117–14.

Stanko, E.A. (1997) Safety Talk: Conceptualizing Women's Risk Assessment as a 'Technology of the Soul', *Theoretical Criminology*, vol. 1, No. 4, pp. 479–99. Available at: https://doi.org/10.1177/1362480697001004004.

Stanley, L. and Wise, S. (1993) *Breaking out Again: Feminist Ontology and Epistemology*. London, Routledge.

Stansell, C. (1987) Revisiting the Angel in the House: Revisions of Victorian Womanhood [Review of *Disorderly Conduct: Visions of Gender in Victorian America; Independent Women: Work and Community for Single Women, 1850–1920*, by C. Smith-Rosenberg & M. Vicinus], *The New England Quarterly*, vol. 60, No. 3, pp. 466–83. Available at: https://doi.org/10.2307/365026.

Stead, W. (2007) *The Maiden Tribute of Babylon: The Report of the Secret Commission*, Simpson, A.E. (ed.), Lamberville, NJ, The True Bill Press.

Steffensmeier, D. and Allan, E. (1996) Gender and Crime: Toward a Gendered Theory of Female Offending, *Annual Review Sociology*, vol. 22, No. 1, pp. 459–87. Available at: https://doi.org/10.1146/annurev.soc.22.1.459.

Steinbach, S.L. (2011) *Understanding the Victorians: Politics, Culture and Society in Nineteenth-Century Britain* (1st edn.), London, Routledge.

Sturma, M. (1978) The Eye of the Beholder: The Stereotype of Women Convicts, 1788–1852, *Labour History*, No. 34, May, pp. 3–10.

Summerfield, A. (2011) *Children and Young People in Custody 2010–11*. An Analysis of the Experiences of 15–18-Year Olds in Prisons, HM Inspectorate of Prisons Youth Justice Board.

Swift, R. (1997) Heroes or Villains? The Irish, Crime, and Disorder in Victorian England, *Albion: A Quarterly Journal Concerned with British Studies*, vol. 29, No. 3, Autumn, pp. 399–421.

Taylor, D. and Vintges, K. (2004) *Feminism and the Final Foucault*, Urbana, Chicago, University of Illinois Press.

Taylor, S. (2019) 'Conceptualising the "Perfect" Family in Late Nineteenth-Century Philanthropic Institutions', in Beardmore, C., Dobbing, C. and King, S. (eds.), *Family Life in Britain 1650–1910*. UK, Milton Keynes, pp. 155–77.

Tebbutt, M. (1983) Making Ends Meet: Pawnbroking and Working-Class Credit, New York, St. Martin's Press.

Thompson, E.P. (1963) *The Making of the English Working Class*, Toronto, Penguin Books.

Tilly, L.A. (1994) Women, Women's History, and the Industrial Revolution, *Social Research*, vol. 61, No. 1, pp. 115–37. Available at: http://www.jstor.org/stable/40971024.

Tobias, J. (1972) *Crime and Industrial Society in the Nineteenth Century*, New York, Penguin.

Todd, S. (2014) Class, Experience and Britain's Twentieth Century, *Social History (London)*, vol. 39, No. 4, pp. 489–508. Available at: https://doi.org/10.1080/03071022 .2014.983680.

Tomes, N. (1978) A 'Torrent of Abuse': Crimes of Violence between Working-Class Men and Women in London 1840–1875, *Journal of Social History*, vol. 11, No. 3, pp. 328–45. Available at: https://doi.org/10.1353/jsh/11.3.328.

Tosh, J. (1999) *A Man's Place: Masculinity and the Middle-Class Home in Victorian England*, New Haven, Yale University Press.

Tosh, J. (2005) Masculinities in an Industrializing Society Britain, 1800–1914, *Journal of British Studies*, vol. 44, No. 2, pp. 330–42.

Uggen, C. and Kruttschnit, C. (1998) Crime in the Breaking: Gender Differences in Desistance, *Law & Society Review*, vol. 32, pp. 339–66.

Vickery, A. (1993) Historiographical Review. Golden Age to Separate Spheres? A Review of the Categories and Chronology of English Women's History, *Historical Journal*, vol. 36, pp. 383–414.

Wade, L. (2017) *Beyond the Control of His parents, Juvenile Crime and Reform: Yorkshire 1856–1914*, Paper presented in The Digital Panopticon Conference 13–15th September.

Walby, S. (1990) *Theorizing Patriarchy*, Basil, Blackwell, Oxford.

Walklate, S. (1995) *Gender and Crime: An Introduction*, London, Prentice Hall, Harvester Wheatsheaf.

Walklate, S. (1997) Risk and Criminal Victimization: A Modernist Dilemma? *British Journal of Criminology*, vol. 37, No. 1, pp. 35–45. Available at: https://doi. org/10.1093/oxfordjournals.bjc.a014148.

Walklate, S. (2001) *Gender, Crime and Criminal Justice*, Cullompton, Willan.

Walklate, S. (2007). *Handbook of Victims and Victimology*, London, Routledge.

Walkowitz, J. (1980) *Prostitution and Victorian Society: Women, Class and the State*, Cambridge, Cambridge University Press.

Walkowitz, J. (1992) *City of Dreadful Delight: Narratives of Sexual Danger in Late-Victorian London*, Chicago, University of Chicago Press.

Warr, M. (1998) Life–Course Transitions and Desistance from Crime, *Criminology* (Beverly Hills), vol. 36, No. 2, pp. 183–216. Available at: https://doi.org/10.1111/j.1745-9125.1998. tb01246.x.

Warr, M. (2002) *Companions in Crime*, Cambridge, Cambridge University Press.

Watkins, E. (2020) *Life Courses of Young Convicts Transported to Van Diemen's Land*, London, Bloomsbury.

Watkins, E. and Godfrey, B. (2018) *Criminal Children: Researching Juvenile Offenders 1820–1920,* Yorkshire, Pen and Sword.

Watts, R. (2000) 'Mary Carpenter: Education of the Children of the "Perishing and Dangerous Classes"', in Hilton, M. and Hirsch, P. (eds.), *Practical Visionaries, Women Education and Social Progress 1790–1930*, Harlow, Pearson Education, pp. 39–51.

Weeks, J. (2012) *Sex, Politics and Society: The Regulation of Sexuality since 1800*, London, Longman.

Weeks, J. (2018) *Sex, Politics and Society: The Regulation of Sexuality since 1800* (4th edn.), London, Routledge, Taylor & Francis Group.

West, C. and Zimmerman, D.H. (1991) 'Doing Gender', in Lorber, J. and Farrell, S. (eds.), *The Social Construction of Gender*, Newbury Park, CA, Sage, pp. 13–37.

Wiener, M. (1990) *Reconstructing the Criminal: Culture, Law, and Policy in England, 1830–1914*, Cambridge, Cambridge University Press.

Wiener, M. (2004) *Men of Blood; Violence, Manliness and Criminal Justice in Victorian England*, Cambridge, Cambridge University Press.

Wilcock, A. (2011) *Living in Liverpool: A Collection of Sources for Family, Local and Social Historians*, Newcastle upon Tyne, Cambridge Scholars Publishing.

Williams, L. (2016) *Wayward Women, Female Offending in Victorian England*, South Yorkshire, Pen and Sword History.

Williams, L. and Godfrey, B. (2014) Intergenerational Offending in Liverpool and the North-West of England, 1850–1914, *The History of the Family*, vol. 2, No. 20, pp. 189–203.

Williams, L. and Godfrey, B. (2018) *Criminal Women, 1850–1920 Researching the Lives of Female Offenders,* South Yorkshire, Pen and Sword History.

Williams, L. and Walklate, S. (2020) Policy Responses to Domestic Violence, the Criminalisation Thesis and 'Learning from History', *The Howard Journal of Crime and Justice*, vol. 59, No. 3, pp. 305–16.

Wimhurst, K. (1983) Child Saving and Urban School Reform in South Australia at the Turn of the Century, *Critical Studies in Education*, vol. 25, pp. 203–21.

Windschuttle, E. (1980) Discipline, Domestic Training and Social Control: The Female School of Industry, Sydney, 1826–1847, *Labour History*, vol. 39, pp. 1–4.

Wohl, A. (2016) *The Victorian Family: Structure and Stresses*, London, Routledge.

Woollacott, A. (1994) *On Her Their Lives Depend: Munitions Workers in the Great War*, Berkeley, University of California Press.

Worrall, A. (1990) *Offending Women: Female Lawbreakers and the CJS*, London, Routledge.

Worrall, A. (1999) 'Troubled or Troublesome? Justice for Girls and Young Women', in Goldson, B. (ed.), *Youth Justice: Contemporary Policy and Practise*, London, Routledge, pp. 28–50.

Zedner, L. (1991a) *Women, Crime, and Custody in Victorian England*, Oxford, Clarendon Press.

Zedner, L. (1991b) Crime and Penal Responses: A Historical Account, *Crime and Justice*, vol. 14, pp. 307–62.

Unpublished theses

Alker, Z. (2014) *Street Violence in Mid-Victorian Liverpool*, Liverpool John Moores University.

Barr, U. (2017) *Voicing Desistance; Female Perspectives on Giving up on Crime*, University of Lancaster.

Cale, M. (1993) *Saved from a Life of Vice and Crime: Reformatory and Industrial Schools for Girls, 1854–1901*, Balliol, M.Phil.

Gear, G. (1999) Industrial Schools in England, 1857–1933: 'Moral Hospitals' or 'Oppressive Institutions'? Unpublished PhD thesis, University of London Institute for Education.

Giller, H.J. (1982) *Community Homes with Education on the Premises: A Study of the Policy and Practice of Residential Treatment for Juvenile Offenders*. University of Cambridge. Available at: https://doi.org/10.17863/CAM.19220.

Hartley, E. (1986) The Institutional Treatment of Juvenile Delinquency: Aspects of the English Reformatory and Industrial School Movement in the Nineteenth Century, Unpublished thesis, University of Leicester.

Howells, C. (2014) Wales' Hidden Industry: Domestic Service in South Wales, 1871–1921, Unpublished thesis, Swansea University.

Lori, A. (1996) *Illicit Sex and Legitimate Subjects: Victorian Constructions of Prostitution and the Working-Class Family*, University of Florida.

Sheldon, N. (2008) *School Attendance 1880–1939: A Study of Policy and Practice in Response to the Problem of Truancy*, University of Oxford.

Stafford, C. (2018) *'The Worst of Drunkards': Female Drunkenness in Mid-Victorian Lancashire*, University of Liverpool.

Williams, L. (2014) *'At Large': Women's Lives and Offending in Victorian Liverpool and London*, University of Liverpool.

Reports

The All-Party Parliamentary Group (APPG) (2012). *Inquiry on Girls: From Courts to Custody*, The Howard League.

The All-Party Parliamentary Group (APPG) (2012). *Women in the Penal System*.

Brennan, T., Breitenbach, M. and Dieterich, W. (2010) *Unraveling Women's Pathways to Serious Crime: New Findings and Links to Prior Feminist Pathways, American Probation and Parole Association*.

Bridge, M., Southgate, J., Goodfellow, P. and Antanaviciute, M. (2022) *'We've Not Given up' Young Women Surviving the Criminal Justice System*, Alliance for Youth Justice, Agenda.

Corston, J. (2007) *The Corston Report: A Report by Baroness Jean Corston of a Review of Women with Particular Vulnerabilities in the CJS*, London, Home Office.

Fitzpatrick, C., Hunter, K., Shaw, J. and Staines, J. (2022) *Disrupting the Routes between Care and Custody for Girls and Women*, United Kingdom, Nuffield Foundation

Goodfellow, P. (2019) *Outnumbered, Locked up and Overlooked? The Use of Penal Custody for Girls in England and Wales*, The Griffins Society, Research Paper 2017/02.

Guardian (24 May 2000) https://www.google.com/amp/s/amp.theguardian.com/society/2000/may/24/childrensservices.guardiansocietysupplement.

Lammy, D. (2017) *The Lammy Review: An Independent Review into the Treatment of, and Outcomes for, Black, Asian and Minority Ethnic Individuals in the Criminal Justice System*, London, Lammy Review. National Audit Office (2016) Transforming Rehabilitation.

Molina, J. and Levell, J. (2020) *Children's Experience of Domestic Abuse and Criminality: A literature Review*, Victims Commissioner, England and Wales.

Prison Reform Trust (2017) *Why Focus on Reducing Women's Imprisonment?* Prison Reform Trust Briefing.

The Report of the Commission to Inquire into Child Abuse (The Ryan Report) (2009). Available at: www. gov.ie.

Report of the Inter-Departmental Committee to Establish Facts of State Involvement with Magdalen Laundries. Available at: www.gov.ie.

Youth Justice Statistics 2020/21, England and Wales, Ministry of Justice (2022).

Databases and websites

A Virtual Archive – Children in Care
www.hiddenlives.org.uk

British Industrial Guide
www.graceguide.co.uk

British Home Children
www.britishhomechildren.com

Find my past
www.findmypast.co.uk

Ancestry
www.ancestry.com

Online Historical Population Reports
www.histpop.org.uk

Chrystal, P. *The Quakers and the English Chocolate Industry*.
https://paulchrystal.com/the-quakers-and-the-english-chocolate-industry/

Index

Milton Keynes UK
Ingram Content Group UK Ltd.
UKHW020746250424
441434UK00003BA/41